PETER & DAN SNOW'S

———

TREASURES OF
BRITISH
HISTORY

———

This is an André Deutsch book

This edition published in 2018
First published in 2016 by André Deutsch Limited
A division of the Carlton Publishing Group
20 Mortimer Street
London W1T 3JW

Text © Peter and Dan Snow, 2016
Design © André Deutsch Limited, 2016, 2018

A catalogue record for this book is available from the British Library.

ISBN: 978 0 233 00562 1

10 9 8 7 6 5 4 3 2 1

Printed in Dubai

Publishing credits:
Researcher: Philip Parker
Editorial Manager: Alison Moss
Design: Russell Knowles, Anna Matos Melgaco
Picture Manager: Steve Behan
Production: Emily Noto

PETER & DAN SNOW'S

TREASURES OF
BRITISH
HISTORY

THE NATION'S STORY TOLD THROUGH ITS
50 MOST IMPORTANT DOCUMENTS

ANDRE
DEUTSCH

Contents

Introduction

Paper is so fragile, yet, oddly it often survives the ravages of history. Stone buildings have been blasted, demolished, weathered and scavenged. Metals have been recycled, left to rust or melted down. Human flesh melts away. Yet, for over a thousand years some of our most important documents have survived. We are blessed in Britain to have such a rich and ancient collection of treasures – written records, maps, sketches and manuscripts from our past. Collectively they tell us who we are. Where we are. How we got here.

Nothing compares to handling a document that was touched by men and women who made history decades or centuries ago. Pious medieval pilgrims travelled great distances to see relics of saints. Today that same impulse sends crowds of us into museums and galleries to marvel at Magna Carta. We have both been privileged to handle documents which are literally national treasures. We were driven to write this book in order to bring together 50 documents that we think are critical to understanding how modern Britain came into being. We were spoilt for choice, working particularly closely with The National Archives, one of the world's greatest collections of documents from our past. They are part of a tradition of preserving our records that is more than a thousand years old, providing us with a vast reservoir of memory. Just as our past experiences as individuals have shaped all of us, so modern Britain has been crafted by the decisions, traumas, successes and failures of our governments and ancestors. That history is the foundation on which our society today is built.

There are so many documents that we have left out. We set ourselves a limit of 50. It was often excruciating to choose and led to many heated discussions! We wanted a blend. We ended up with state documents, personal letters, diagrams, a theatrical folio and much else.

There are many political documents here, as you would expect. Treaties like that which defined the borders of England between Alfred the Great and the Vikings, or the agreement between Henry VII and King James of Scotland which attempted to achieve a lasting peace between the two fractious neighbours and inadvertently established the royal dynasty that endures to this day. But there are also wonderful snapshots of the past. Maps and diagrams and letters, often scribbled out in haste, which have survived, bear witness to important moments in our history. The letter from one Roman settler to another, found at Vindolanda Fort near Hadrian's Wall is one of the earliest examples of handwriting ever found in Britain. It dates from a time when Britain was the colonised not the coloniser and imperial masters arrived from all over the Roman Empire, the Mediterranean, North Africa, the Middle East, to rule over us troublesome natives. We are fascinated by Ada Lovelace's letter to Charles Babbage in which she formulated the world's first computer program. We realise that she didn't, that this was the start of a journey that would take mankind to the stars. Our interest in military history is reflected in several documents that we selected. Drake, Marlborough, Nelson, Wellington, Haig and Montgomery are all featured. Their battles against King Philip's Spanish Armada, Louis XIV, Napoleon, the Kaiser and Hitler shaped the course of history. Our world would look very different today if any of those commanders had lost their battles.

For a small island Britain has had an enormous impact on human history. This book reflects that. From the millions of Africans transported as slaves across the Atlantic to the invention of mass production during the Industrial Revolution what has happened here has altered the lives of billions of people. These documents encompass Shakespeare, the invention of the World Wide Web, the development of professional sport and Beatlemania. Our history has given us a remarkable legacy. We believe that these documents take you as close as you can get to the moments that have made us what we are.

PETER & DAN SNOW, 2018

Map of the British Isles, 1883.

Vindolanda Tablet

It is a document from before the dawn of Britain, which overturns our idea of what it means to be British. The thin wooden wafer contains a letter written during the military occupation of Britain by a foreign power (the Romans). More surprising still, one of the earliest handwritten documents ever found in Britain is an invitation to a birthday party. It is a message from a woman named Claudia Severa to her friend Sulpicia Lepidina, wife of a Roman army commander.

Claudia is asking her friend to come to her party on 11 September (the precise year is unknown). "I give you a warm invitation … to make the day more enjoyable for me by your arrival," she dictates to the professional scribe who wrote most of the letter. But then she adds in her own hand "I shall expect you, sister. Farewell sister, my dearest soul."

After Julius Caesar's abortive – but showy – attempt to conquer Britain in 55 BC, the Romans came to stay a century later under the Emperor Claudius. By AD 83 they had reached the Highlands of Scotland. The defeated Caledonian war leader Calgacus pronounced – in a sentiment many colonized peoples might agree with – "they make a desert and they call it peace".

The demands of other wars soon caused Roman units to be pulled out of Britain. Scotland was evacuated, leaving a frontier line along the narrowest neck of England, from modern Newcastle to Carlisle. Here the Roman army did what it knew best: it fortified. A line of forts was built, first in wood and then in stone, which preceded the later and slightly more northerly line of Hadrian's Wall by several decades.

In these military encampments, a frontier life grew up, attracting farmers, merchants, hucksters and mistresses (for the ordinary soldiers, who were not allowed to marry during their 25 years of service). Many of the troopers were not Roman citizens. Just as much more recently the British army had a large number of Indians, Australians, Canadians or New Zealanders in its ranks, the Romans relied on troops from Gaul, the Rhineland and the Balkans. More exotically, Syrian archers and North African camel troops could be seen patrolling the Roman frontier.

At Vindolanda, a fort in northeastern England built around AD 85, the garrison was generally made up of a cohort of Batavians and Tungrians (from the modern Netherlands). We know more about Vindolanda than any other British fort of the time because of a discovery made by archaeologists in 1973. An unpromising mass of soggy wooden slivers turned out to be a hitherto undiscovered form of Roman record keeping. The millimetre-thick pieces of birch and oak, folded in two to form a kind of envelope, were letters. Piled in the command centre of the cohort, they had been discarded

OPPOSITE Excavations at Vindolanda yielded this coin of the emperor Trajan, Hadrian's predecessor, who ruled AD 98–117. He was the emperor at the time this tablet was written.

ABOVE The excavated site of the Vindolanda fort as it appears today. It is a Snow family favourite. It is one of the first Roman northern frontier forts, and became an important garrison base for the later Hadrian's Wall. After the Wall was abandoned, the fort remained in use for more than 400 years.

during a clear-out. Attempts to burn them failed and they fell into a waterlogged ditch where the lack of oxygen preserved them from decay.

The Vindolanda tablets, written in a cursive handwriting very different from monumental inscriptions, contain a treasure trove of insights into daily garrison life. Some are military documents: one from around AD 90 contains a record of the daily strength of the Tungrian cohort. Of the notional strength of 752, only 296 were actually present, and of those 40 were sick (10 with eye infections). If only the Britons across the frontier − whom another tablet refers to disparagingly as *Brittunculi* ("filthy little Britons") − had known how thinly their occupiers were stretched! Another is a letter back home, pleading for fresh underwear and socks to be sent (presumably to guard against the bitter winters that made Britain an unpopular posting).

Other documents contain requisitions, for pork, venison, beef and wheat, or contracts. The merchants who serviced the garrison were a cosmopolitan lot. A grave at Arbeia, a Roman fort near South Shields, was built by Barates, a merchant from Palmyra in Syria for his wife, Regina, a native Briton from Kent. Arbeia's garrison included Iraqi boatmen and a cavalry unit from Spain.

The woman this message is addressed to, Sulpicia Lepidina, was the wife of Flavius

Cerialis. He commanded the 9th cohort of Batavians who garrisoned Vindolanda around AD 100. He was probably a Batavian nobleman and no doubt he and his family were glad of the chance to make the best of this far-flung posting, far from home. Claudia Severa who sent the invitation was married to Aelius Brocchus, commander of another nearby fort. As was true for the British in India, theirs was a tiny ruling class, and opportunities for socializing were restricted.

So this is a very heartfelt appeal that Claudia makes to Sulpicia Lepidina to come to her celebration. It is the oldest piece of Latin known to have been written by a woman – both a precious insight into domestic life two thousand years ago and a testament to the ties of trade, friendship and conquest that bound Roman Britain tightly to Europe.

ABOVE Vindolanda tablet 291 is, like the other tablets, written in a distinctive cursive handwriting on a sliver of wood around 2mm thick. The greeting – "*Cl[audia] Severa Lepidinae*" – "Claudia Severa to her Lepidina" – can be made out at the top left. The writing at the bottom right is probably in the hand of the sender, Claudia Severa, who refers to her friend as "*soror, anima mea karissima*" - "sister, my dear soul".

The Treaty of Alfred and Guthrum

This is one of the very foundation stones of England's identity. The treaty between King Alfred of Wessex and Guthrum, the Danish Viking whom he had defeated in a decisive battle just eight years before, recognized the borders between their two territories. It also marked the moment that Wessex (the core of future England) won its fight for life. Despite several scares over the coming two centuries, England would not be an appendage of Scandinavia and Alfred would be one of its earliest heroes.

The Vikings had descended on an unsuspecting England at the end of the eighth century, beginning with an attack on the monastery of Lindisfarne in 793. Their raiding bands extended the range of their targets until no coastline and no city reachable within a day's horse-ride of a waterway was free of the terror of their onslaught. Contemporaries – and especially impressionable clerics – regarded the pagan pirates' pillaging as the judgement of God on a people who had sinned against his law.

Prayers achieved little as the Vikings, attracted in increasing numbers by the easy prey they found in England, began to overwinter in the 840s. Emboldened, they defeated and dismantled the Anglo-Saxon kingdoms. Northumbria, East Anglia and then Mercia fell one-by-one to the warbands of the "Great Army" that landed in England in 865.

Only Wessex in the south remained, wavering between defiance and appeasement. In autumn 870 the Danish army crossed the border, intent on conquest. The advantage swung between the men of Wessex – who won an engagement at Ashdown – and the Vikings, who transformed a rout to victory at Wilton, where they cut down their Anglo-Saxon pursuers in huge numbers.

At the end of it Wessex had an unlikely new ruler. King Aethelred had died of his wounds, and the royal council turned to his younger brother (the fourth sibling in a row to rule the kingdom). Alfred, though heir-apparent, was an unpromising choice. Pious, sickly and inexperienced, he was far more comfortable with book-learning than he was with the sword.

The worst fears of the doubters seemed to be confirmed in 875, when Alfred let the new Danish warlord Guthrum escape a siege at Wareham. Guthrum swore an oath, which the Viking broke the moment he was free. Then a worse disaster struck. On 6 January 878, as the royal court at Chippenham was feasting for Twelfth Night, a Viking army appeared at the gates. Alfred fled with a few followers and was reduced to skulking in the marshes at Athelney in the Somerset Levels, a pitiful and apparently friendless exile.

Alfred's legend was already being carefully cultivated, for he did have friends. Several Anglo-Saxon armies were still in the field and he summoned them and any other armed supporters to a great muster at Egbert's stone. From there, with three or four thousand men, Alfred made for Chippenham. His way was blocked by Guthrum, who had occupied an old hill fort near Edington. With the boldness of a man who knew that a rapid victory was all that could now secure his throne, Alfred seems to have launched a headlong assault on the Danes. As shield-wall clashed with shield-wall, the unexpected happened: the Vikings gave way and fled.

After besieging Guthrum in Chippenham for a few weeks, Alfred let him go again, but this time he insisted the Danish king accept baptism first. Reasoning that as a Christian Guthrum would not attack his co-religionists, Alfred set to restoring his kingdom. By 886 he had occupied London and then felt strong enough to make a final treaty with the Danes. Its terms set the boundary between "the men who are in East Anglia" (euphemistically avoiding any mention of foreigners) at the Thames and then in a northwesterly stripe up the Midlands, following the Ouse and the old

Roman road at Watling Street. Alfred was left with the south and the west Midlands. The Vikings got the rest.

Guthrum's lands would become the nucleus of the "Danelaw", a separate realm with its own laws, ruled over by a Viking elite from Denmark and Norway. It would endure until its last ruler, Erik Bloodaxe, was chased from York in 954. In some sense the notion of a separate northern identity can claim its roots from that century of Viking rule. Wessex, meanwhile, survived. Alfred reformed its defences, gave it a fleet and a sense of pride. His children and grandchildren took the offensive and reconquered the rest of England (or, strictly speaking, conquered, as it had never been Wessex land). Alfred's victory and his prudence in then making a treaty with the Danes had given Wessex the security it needed to start building the Kingdom of England. For his achievement he is the only English king to have been given the nickname "Great" and his treaty with Guthrum is the clearest piece of evidence that he merits the title.

OPPOSITE Portrait of Alfred the Great after a painting in the Bodleian Library. As well as a successful war leader, Alfred promoted the revival of learning in Wessex. He initiated the translation of important Latin texts into Old English. This and other innovations in sea power and fortress construction created the conditions that allowed Alfred's successors to conquer the whole of modern England.

RIGHT The treaty between Alfred and Guthrum survives in an early thirteenth-century collection of Anglo-Saxon laws preserved at Corpus Christi College, Cambridge. It is written in Old English – the first three lines read "*ðis is ðaet frið, ðaet Aelfred cyninc & Gyðrum cyning & ealles Angelcynnes witan & eal seo ðeod ðe on Eastaenglum beoð ealle gecweden habbað*" or "This is the treaty that King Alfred and King Guthrum, and the witan [royal council] of all the English nation, and all the people that are in East Anglia, have decreed."

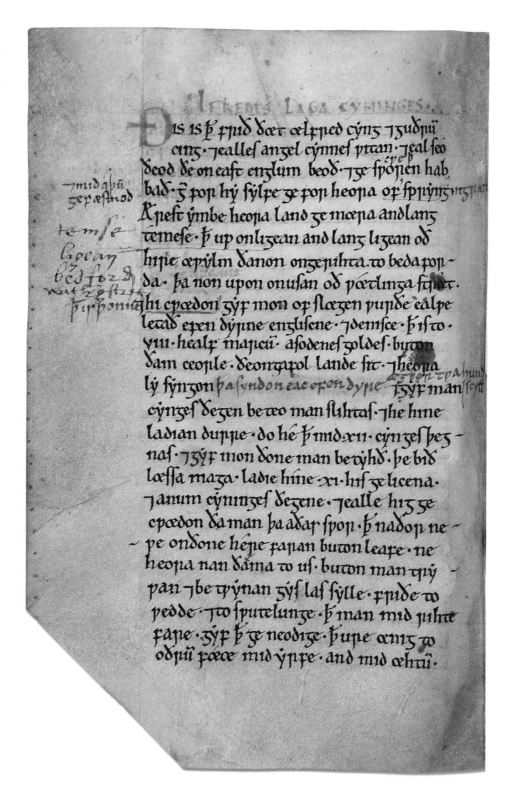

The Domesday Book

It is the most sophisticated English administrative document of its time and also a record of the largest land-grab in British history. The Domesday Book, compiled on the orders of William the Conqueror, records those who held land under Edward the Confessor (who died in 1066) and then those who held it in 1087. The names of the chief landowners at the later date are almost entirely Norman-French; those two decades earlier are all Anglo-Saxon. Rarely has the death of a ruling class been documented in such detail. Subsequent generations thought the scale of the project comparable to God's judgement at the end of the world and gave it the nickname which stuck.

William had ruled England for almost two decades since his victory at Hastings in 1066 had won him the English crown. His need to reward the retainers who had fought with him led to a first wave of confiscation of estates to add to the royal domain and the lands of the defeated King Harold's family. Serious uprisings in 1069 and 1075 had also led to the seizure of the rebels' lands and the devastation of a larger area, particularly in the north of England.

Even in 1085 William could not feel totally secure. Word had reached England that a fleet was gathering under King Cnut IV of Denmark, intent on completing what Harald Hardrada of Norway had failed to do in 1066. In the event a rebellion against Cnut ended in his death and the planned invasion was aborted. Yet William needed to know the resources he could command in the event of an invasion. If resort was needed to the age-old tactic of a geld, a tax raised to pay off the Scandinavian invaders (as it had been used to bribe their Viking forbears), then the king needed to be sure how much he could afford.

William also recognized that two decades since the Norman conquest of England had led to a chaotic and largely undocumented change of land ownership, which had muddied the question of who had legal title to the estates they held. In December 1085 he sent out orders that information was to be gathered on who had held land under his predecessors, who held it now and what its rental value was. Initially, tenants-in-chief, those who held land directly from the king, made preliminary returns, but then commissioners were sent out, three or four covering each of seven circuits, to check their statements and to compile more detailed information.

This was then assembled into summaries for each county, and these were eventually bound together, making what we now know as the Domesday Book (although it acquired that name only around 1180). By the time William died in 1087, the returns for Essex, Norfolk and Suffolk were still incomplete and these were gathered together separately into the Little Domesday Book.

The commissioners did their work well. As the Anglo-Saxon Chronicler remarked, "There was not one single hide nor a yard of land, nor indeed one ox nor one cow nor one pig which was there left out." In the page shown opposite, which details manors on the Isle of Wight, it is reported under the manor of Haselie (Heasley) that there is woodland for two pigs. Heasley had been worth £8 in rental in King Edward's time and only £5 by 1087, a devaluation in land values about which William cannot have been pleased.

The manor had been held by King Harold, who is referred to in almost all cases in the Domesday Book as "Earl Harold". William always claimed that he was the rightful heir to King Edward, and that Harold Earl of Wessex had stolen the crown. Clearly, even decades later, William was determined not to acknowledge that Harold was anything but a usurper. Harold's lands fell directly to William, as did those of other members of Harold's family. His mother

HIC: WILLELM DVX: IVSSIT NAVES: EDI FICARE:

Countess Gytha's estate at Wroxall (the entry that precedes Heasley) yielded £20 and this, too, filled William's coffers. The land at Nonoelle (Nunwell) had previously belonged to Earl Tostig, Harold's rebellious brother. He had joined Harald Hardrada's invasion in 1066 and fell at the Battle of Stamford Bridge; as a rebel his estates would in any case have been forfeit and they, too, were taken by William.

Across England as a whole William held 17 per cent of the land in 1087, another quarter was under the control of bishops and abbots, while around 190 lay tenants-in-chief held just over half between them.

Only a single member of the old nobility, Thorkill of Arden, whose family had collaborated with the Normans, had any substantial holdings.

England in 1087 was a land transformed. Within a generation its old elites had been utterly swept away and for the next two centuries it was tied by bonds of blood and power to northern France. The Domesday Book gave its ruler a greater knowledge of his resources than any other monarch in Europe and was the closest that England would get to a census until the nineteenth century.

ABOVE The 230-foot (70-metre) long Bayeux Tapestry, commissioned in the 1070s, is embroidered with scenes commemorating William of Normandy's conquest of England. Here Duke William (as he then was) orders the construction of a fleet to carry his army across the English Channel.

FOLLOWING PAGES These pages come from the section of the Domesday Book listing land holdings in Hampshire and the Isle of Wight before and after the Norman conquest in 1066. The third entry in the right-hand column (above) gives the ownership of the manor of Nonoelle (Nunwell) which Wulflaed *tenuit de Tosti* (held from Tostig). The former owner of Lacherne (Kern) in the entry below it is listed as "comes Herald" (Earl Harold).

REX ten' BACUBE. Lang tenuit de rege .E. T se defd' p̃ .xiiii. hid'.
Modo p̃ .xiii. T̃ra .ē. .xii. car'. In dnĩo .ē. .ii. car'. 7 .iii. serui. 7 .xxi. uilt'.
7 .xii. bord' cu̅ .x. car'. Ibi molin' de .xx. solid'. 7 .xiiii. ac' p̃ra. 7 pascua .l.i. den'.
In Wincon'. vi. dom.
hr̃ .i. ac' Silua .iiii.
por̃. Valuit 7 ual'
.xiii. lib. 7 tam̃
ad firmã p̃ .xvi. lib.
Rog' p̃ ea̅ bt e̅ m̃.

REX ten' in dnĩo SUBURNE. IN SUBURNE HUND.
Regale m̃ fuit. sed n̄ fuit p̃ hidas distributu̅. T̃ra .ē.
.x. car'. In dnĩo sunt .ii. car'. 7 .v. uilt' 7 .xi. bord'
cu̅ .viii. car'. Ibi .ii. serui. 7 .iii. molini de .xv. solid'. Ibi
.vii. colibti 7 .xx. ac' p̃a. pascua de .xvii. sol'. 7 .x. denar'
de herbag'. Huic m̃ p̃tin' soca duoȝ hund'. Ibi .ii. eccte
quibȝ p̃tin' dim̃ hida in elemosina.

Prefec̃ct' callian̄t' ad op̃ huĩ m̃ una̅ ṽ irg̃ 7 pascua̅ qu̅
uocan̄t dun̄a. que redd'. xv. solid'. Comes Mortõn' tenet.
Sed hund' testat̃ qd' in dnĩca firma regis iacere debet.
Ibi fuit T.R.E. 7 p̃ti in eod'.

HE TERRE INFRA SCRIPTE IACENT IN INSULA DE WIT.

REX ten' in dnĩo CHENISTONE a dom̃ .vi. ct' ibi h̃oes tenuer'
in alodiu̅ de rege .E. T̃ e geldau̅ p̃ .ii. hid'. modo p̃ nichilo.
Oda cu̅ .ii. ubĩ h̃oĩt' habuit dimid' hid'. 7 quartã parte̅
uni' ṽ. Aluuold' .i. uirg'. Heraldi .i. uirg'. Goduin' .i. uirg'.
Alric una̅ ṽ. Bricric dim̃ hid'. Vn̄quisqȝ hoȝ parte̅
molini. quel̃ parĩ. .xxii. denar'. hoȝ ṽ cairo̅ t̃ra̅
ten' rex in firma sua. 7 h̃o .ii. car' in dnĩo. 7 appeciat̃
c. sol'. 7 tam̃ redd'. viii. lib' de firma.   v. solid'.

Ra Oda tenuit .xi. sol'. Ra Aluuold' .v. sol'. Ra Heraldi.

LADONE 7 BEDINGEBORNE ten' rex in dnĩo. Oda
tenuit in alodiu̅ de rege .E. T̃ e geldau̅ p̃ .iiii. hid'. 7 m̃
p̃ dim̃ hida. T̃ra .ē. .iii. car'. Rex ten' in firma sua. Oda
habet .iiii. lib. de firma.

SANDFORD cu̅ WICA ten' rex in dnĩo. Rex .E. tenuit.
T̃ e .ii. hide. X̃do .vi. recep'. ii. hide 7 una ṽ.
T̃ra .ē. .xii. car'. In dnĩo sunt .iii. car'. 7 .x. uilt' 7 .ix. bord'
cu̅ .vi. car'. Ibi .x. serui. 7 ii. molini de .lxx. denar'.
7 .vi. ac' p̃a. De herbagio .xx. sol'. Silua sine pasnagio.
T.R.E. .xxv. lib' ad pensu̅ 7 arsura̅. X̃do rex recep'. xx.
lib. simili modo 7 n̄c .xx. lib' ad pensu̅. 7 tam̃ redd' de
firma'. xx.vi. lib' ad pensu̅ 7 c. denar'.

ADRITTONE ten' rex in dnĩo. Rex .E. tenuit. Ibi .iiii. hide.
T̃ra .ē. .v. car'. In dnĩo sunt .iii. car'. 7 .x. uilt' 7 .xii. bord'
cu̅ .x. car'. Ibi .vii. serui. 7 un̄ molin' de .xv. solid'.
huic m̃ ecctam ten' abb' de l̃ra. cu̅ una ṽ irg̃ 7 una ac'
p̃a. om̃ decima m̃. 7 appciat̃ .xx. solid'.
Totu̅ m̃ T.R.E. .x. lib. 7 post m̃. vii. lib. 7 tam̃
redd'. xii. lib. blancas. de .xx. in op̃a.

EVERELAI ten' rex in dnĩo. Rex .E. tenuit. Non fuit
hidata. T̃ra .ē. .v. car'. Ibi sunt .xii. uilt' cu̅ .v. car'.
T.R.E. ual'. c. sol'. 7 post m̃. iiii. lib'. Tam̃ redd'. c. solid'.

ABEDESTONE ten' rex in dnĩo. Tres ubĩ h̃oes tenuer'
in alodiu̅ de rege .E. T̃ e 7 m̃ geldau̅ p̃ una hida. T̃ra .ē.
iii. car'. Ibi sunt .xi. uilt' cu̅ .iiii. car'. Val' 7 ualu' .xl.
solid'. Tam̃ redd'. lx. sol'. albas.
In insula b̃t rex un̄ frustu̅ t̃re. unde exeu̅t .vi. uomeres.

SCALDEFORD ten' rex in dnĩo. Sauuord tenuit in alodiu̅

de rege .E. T̃ e m̃ n̄ geldau̅ p̃ dim̃ hida. T̃ra .ē. .i. car'. Ibi sunt .iii. uilt'
leu̅ .i. car' 7 .i. dim'. Val' 7 ualu' .xiii. sol'. Tam̃ redd'. xvi. sol' 7 vii. den'
LISCELANDE ten' rex in dnĩo. Ruinq' ubĩ h̃oes tenuer' in alodiu̅
p̃ .v. maner' de rege .E. T̃ e geldau̅ p̃ una hida 7 dimidia uirg'.
Modo p̃ dim̃ hida 7 dim̃ uirg'. Almar habuit dim̃ hid'. Vlnod'
dim̃ uirg'. Suaran dim̃ ṽ. Odeman. dim̃ ṽ. Godman. una̅ ṽ.
T̃ra .ē. .ii. car'. Ibi sunt .iii. uilt'. h̃nt in dnĩo. iii. car' 7 dim'. 7 v. ac'
p̃a. Val' 7 ualu' .xx. solid'.

LOVECUBE ten' rex. Sauuin tenuit in alodiu̅ de rege .E. T̃ e
geldau̅ p̃ una hida. m̃ p̃ .ii. parab'. uni' ṽ. T̃ra .ē. .i. car'. 7 ibi .ē.
in dnĩo. cu̅ .vi. bord' 7 .ii. seruis'. T.R.E. ualb'. iiii. lib'. 7 post m̃.
iii. lib. Tam̃ redd' de firma. iiii. lib.

NONOELLE ten' rex. Vlsiet tenuit de Tosti. sed n̄ fuit alodiu̅. T̃ c
geldau̅ p̃ .ii. hid'. modo p̃ una ṽ. T̃ra .ē. .i. car' 7 dim'. In dnĩo .ē. car'.
7 i. uilt' 7 .ii. bord' cu̅ dim̃ car'. 7 ii. seruis'. T.R.E. ualb'. ix. sol'. 7 post
7 modo. xl. sol'. 7 tam̃ redd' de firma alba.

LACHERNE ten' rex. Herald' tenuit. T̃ c geldau̅ p̃ una hida. m̃ p̃ro
nichilo. T̃ra .ē. .i. car'. 7 ibi .ē. in dnĩo. cu̅ .ii. bord' 7 .v. seruis'.
T.R.E. ualb'. xxv. solid'. 7 post 7 modo. xx. solid'.

VLWARTONE ten' rex. Eds eus tenuit de Goduino. T̃ c geldau̅ p̃ di
miã hida. m̃ p̃ nichilo. T̃ra .ē. .i. car'. 7 ibi .ē. in dnĩo. cu̅ .iiii. bord'
7 uno seruo. Val' 7 ualu'. x. sol'.

SANDE ten' rex. Vlnod tenuit de rege .E. in alodiu̅. T̃ c geldau̅
p̃ .ii. hid'. modo p̃ dim̃ 7 dim̃ ṽ. T̃ra .ē. .iii. car'. In dnĩo .ē. una car'.
7 vii. uilt' 7 uno bord'. cu̅ .iii. car'. 7 vi. ac' p̃a. Valuit .xl. sol' m̃ .xxx.

VAROCHESSETTE ten' rex. Gueda comissa tenuit de Goduino
in alodiu̅. T̃ c geldau̅ p̃ .v. hid'. Modo p̃ .ii. hid'. 7 dim̃ hid'. T̃ra .ē. .x. car'.
In dnĩo sunt .iiii. car'. 7 .x. uilt' 7 bord' cu̅ vii. car'. Ibi .xvii.
seruis'. 7 ii. molini de .xx. solid'. 7 ii. ac' p̃a. Silua de uno porc'.
T.R.E. ualb'. xx.vii. lib'. 7 post m̃. xx. lib'. Tam̃ redd'. xvii. lib'.

HASELIE ten' rex. Herald' tenuit. T̃ c geldau̅ p̃ .iii. hid'. modo
p̃ una ṽ 7 dim'. T̃ra .ē. .iiii. car'. In dnĩo sunt .ii. 7 .iii. uilt' 7 .iii. bord'
cu̅ .ii. car'. Ibi .xx. seruis'. 7 x. ac' p̃a. Silua de .ii. porc'. de .xx. in op̃a
T.R.E. ualb'. viii. lib'. 7 post 7 m̃. c. sol'. Tam̃ redd' viii. lib' de firma.

BENVERDESLEI ten' rex. Goduin' tenuit de rege .E. in alodiu̅. T̃ c geldau̅
p̃ una hida. m̃ p̃ dim̃ hida 7 dim̃ ṽ. T̃ra .ē. .ii. car'. Ibi sunt .iii. uilt'
cu̅ una car'. Silua. de uno porc'. Valuit. xl. sol' m̃ .xx. solid'.

CHOCHEPON & BIHARIN ten' rex. Duo ibi h̃oes tenuer' p̃ .ii.
maner' in alodiu̅ de rege .E. T̃ c geldau̅ p̃ una hida. m̃ p̃ .ii. uirg'
T̃ra .ē. .ii. car'. 7 ibi .ē. cu̅ .ii. uilt's. Valuit .xxx. sol'. Modo. xx. sol'.

HORELESTON ten' rex. Vlnod tenuit Tam̃ redd'. xxx. sol'.
de rege .E. in alodiu̅. T̃ c geldau̅ p̃ tciã parte̅ hide. modo p̃ dim̃
uirg'. T̃ra .ē. dim̃ car'. 7 ibi .ē. cu̅ .iii. bord'. Valuit .x. sol'. n̄ .xx. sol'.

STANEBERIE 7 WIPINGEHA ten' rex. Cheping tenuit in
alodiu̅ de rege .E. p̃ .ii. maner'. T̃ c geldau̅ p̃ .iii. hid'. m̃ p̃ .ii. hid'.
T̃ra .ē. .xii. car'. In dnĩo sunt .ii. 7 vii. uilt' 7 .x. bord'. cu̅ .vi. car'.
Ibi .xii. seruis'. 7 vi. ac' p̃a. Val' 7 ualu' sep̃ .xii. lib.

VENECHETONE ten' rex. Duo ibi h̃oes tenuer' in alodiu̅ de
rege .E. p̃ duob' m̃. T̃ c geldau̅ p̃ una hida. m̃ p̃ nichilo. T̃ra .ē.
ii. car'. 7 ibi sunt cu̅ .ii. uilt's. Valuit 7 ual'. iiii. lib.

De his tam̃ duob' m̃ exeu̅t de firma .xviii. lib'. de .xx. in op̃a.

EDEVA ten̄ de rege MINGEHĀ. Duo lib̄ hōes tenuer̄
de rege .E. in alodiũ. Tc̄ 7 m̄ geld̄ p̄ hida 7 dimid. T̄ra .ē.
unā car̄. Ibi sunt .iiii. bord. Valuit .xx. sol. m̄ .xiii. sol.
picot ten̄ de Edeva.

PICOT ten̄ de rege in BORGATE una v̄. Uluric
7 Collere tenuer̄ in alod de rege .E. Tc̄ 7 m̄ geld̄ p̄ una
v̄nḡ. T̄ra .ē. dim̄ car̄. 7 ibi .ē. cũ .ii. bord. 7 molinū
de .viii. solid 7 .viii. den. 7 .vii. ac̄ de p̄a. Silua sine pasnag.
T.R.E. ualb̄ .x. sol. 7 post .v. sol. modo .xii. solid.

ULVIET uenator ten̄ de rege RIPLE. IN SIRLEI HD.
Ipse met tenuit in alod de rege .E. Tc̄ geld̄ p̄ .v. hid.
Modo p̄ .ii. hid. T̄ra .ē. ii. car̄. In dn̄io .ē. una. 7 .vii.
bord 7 .iiii. serui. cũ .ii. car̄. 7 .xl. ac̄ de p̄a.
De isto m̄ sunt .iii. hide in foresta regis 7 uasti nem̄.
T.R.E. ualb̄ .viii. lib. modo .l. sol. 7 id in foresta .c. sol.

ASGARUS ten̄ de rege dim̄ hid in Tc̄. IN ROBBRIGE HD.
TINTONE. Ipse tenuit T.R.E. 7 m̄ p̄ dim̄ hida se defd.
7 tra .ē. i. car̄ 7 dim̄. Ibi sunt .ii. bord 7 .ii. uilli cũ car̄ 7 dim̄.
Ibi .v. ac̄ p̄a. 7 qnta pars molini de .v. sol. Valuit .xii. sol.

ALRIC ten̄ dimid hida. Hanc t̄c l̄m xv. sol.
nuit pat̄ .ē. de rege .E. Sed hic rex n̄ reisiuit p̄ morte
Godric sui auunculi. qui eā custodieb. 7 tra .ē. i. car̄ 7 dim̄.
Tc̄ 7 m̄ se defd. p̄ dimid hida. ibi sunt .ii. uilli 7 v. bord.
cũ .i. car̄ 7 dim̄. 7 .iii. ac̄ p̄a. 7 qnta pars molini de .v. sol.
T.R.E. 7 post uale .xii. sold. Modo .xx. sol.

FILIII Godrici ten̄ HANORE. pat̄ eoz̄ tenuit de rege .E.
Tc̄ 7 m̄ se defd. pro una hida 7 tra .ē. i. car̄. ibi sunt .ii. uilli
7 v. bord. cũ .i. car̄. 7 una ac̄ p̄a. Silua de .i. porc̄.
Valuit .xx. sol. Modo .x. sol. IN CLERE HD.

ALWIN ten̄ .ii. hid. Ipse tenuit T.R.E. Tc̄ se defd.
p̄ .ii. hid. m̄ p̄ dim̄ hida. Tra .ē. car̄ 7 dim̄. Ibi .ē. car̄ 7 ii. seru.
un uillꝰ 7 un bord cũ dim̄ car̄. Valuit .xl. sol. m̄ .xx. sol.
Hic Aluuin tenuit hanc t̄ra T.R.E. sub Wigoto p̄ manone.
m̄ ten̄ eand sub Milone. 7 fuit deliba p̄ hunfrid uicecō
lupo Wigoto in excābio de Bradewate sic ipse dic.
Sed hund inde nichil scit.

GODWIN ten̄ de firma regis .ii. hid. Rex .E. ded ei.
Tc̄ 7 m̄ se defd. p̄ una v̄. 7 tra .ē. ii. car̄. In dn̄io .ē. una. car̄.
7 ii. uilli 7 v. bord cũ .i. car̄. ibi .i. seru. 7 .ii. ac̄ p̄a. Val.

RAVELIN ten̄ de rege CLERE. Ipse met 7 ualuit .xxiii. sol.
tenuit T.R.E. 7 m̄ se defd. p̄ .iii. hid 7 dim̄ v̄. Modo p̄ .ii.
hid. 7 tra .ē. v. car̄. In dn̄io sunt .ii. 7 .iiii. uilli 7 xxiii. bord
cũ .iii. car̄. Ibi .iiii. serui. 7 molin de .l. den. 7 .ii. ac̄ de p̄a.
Ipberbagio .vi. sol 7 .ii. den. Val 7 ualuit .lxv. sol.

LEWIN ten̄ in CLERE una v̄ de rege. Ipse tenuit
T.R.E. 7 m̄ p̄ tanto se defd. 7 tra .ē. dim̄ car̄. 7 ibi .ē. cũ
uno seruo. 7 ii. ac̄ p̄a. 7 silua de ii. clausura. Val. v. sol.
Isd Leuuin ten̄ in HANTUNE. una hida. E. tam tenuit
in paragio de rege .E. Tc̄ 7 m̄ se defd. p̄ hida. Tra .ē. i. car̄.
Ibi .ē. un uillꝰ 7 ii. bord. iii. serui cũ dim̄ car̄. Val 7 ualuit
xxx. solid.

ELDRED fr̄ odonis ten̄ dim̄ hid de rege. Ipse tenuit de rege .E.
7 tc̄ se defd. p̄ dim̄ hida. m̄ p̄ una v̄. Tra .ē. i. car̄. In dn̄io dim̄ car̄.
cũ uno uillo 7 i. bord 7 dim̄ car̄. 7 ii. ac̄ p̄a. Val 7 ualuit .vi. sol.

ALVER ten̄ de rege dim̄ hid. Aluuin tenuit de rege .E. Tc̄
se defd. p̄ dim̄ hida. 7 m̄ p̄ una v̄. Tra .ē. i. car̄. Ibi sunt .ii. bord
7 una ac̄ p̄a. Val 7 ualuit .v. sol.

ULGRIC ten̄ de rege un cō. pat̄ ē tenuit de rege .E. Tc̄ se
defd. p̄ una hida. m̄ p̄ dim̄. Modo p̄ una hida. Tra .ē. ii. car̄.
In dn̄io .ē. una. 7 ii. uilli 7 ii. bord cũ .i. car̄. 7 ibi .xii. ac̄ p̄a.

ALSI ten̄ de rege SIDEPURNE. IN BASINGESTOC. Id 7 ualuit .xx. sol.
Elfelm tenuit de rege .E. ibi habebant .v. hide. sed tc̄ 7 m̄
se defd. p̄ .iii. hid. Tra .ē. v. car̄. In dn̄io sunt .ii. 7 v. uilli 7 m̄ bord
cũ .ii. car̄ 7 viii. serui. T.R.E. ualb̄ .c. sol. 7 post .lxx. sol. Modo .iiii. lib.

GODWIN accipitrari ten̄ de rege dim̄ hid. Ipse tenuit de rege .E.
Tc̄ 7 m̄ se defd. p̄ dim̄ hida. Val 7 ualuit .iiii. solid. IN ROSBRIGE HD.

ALWIN ten̄ de rege MERCODE. Uluiet pat̄ ē tenuit. Tc̄ 7 m̄ se
defd. p̄ dim̄ hida. Tra .ē. i. car̄. Ibi .ii. uilli 7 ii. bord brit. 7 iii. dim̄
7 m̄ ac̄ p̄a. Silua de .viii. den. Valuit .x. sol. Modo .xv. sol.

GODWIN ten̄ de rege 7 hugo de eo. unā v̄ in DERLEIE. Saulf
tenuit de rege .E. in paragio. Ibi .ii. uilli cũ .i. car̄. dim̄ac̄ p̄a.
Silua de .vi. porc̄. fuit sed m̄ .ē. Valuit .x. sol. Modo .iii. sol.

COLA uenator ten̄ dim̄ hid de Uluiet patre suo in LANGELIE.
Hanc tenuit de rege in paragio. Tc̄ se defd. p̄ dim̄ hida. m̄ p̄ quarta
parte uni v̄. Tra .ē. dim̄ car̄. 7 ibi .ē. in dn̄io cũ uno bord. 7 dim̄ ac̄ p̄a.
Silua de .v. porc̄. Val 7 ualuit .vi. solid.

ALURIC ten̄ una v̄ in FORESTA. Colebe tenuit in firma regis .m̄.
Aluric reclamat hunc m̄ de Saiuet. Tc̄ 7 m̄ se defd. p̄ una v̄.
Tra .ē. i. car̄. Valuit .vi. sol. modo .xii. sol.

GODWIN ten̄ SIENES de rege. Suuin 7 Elmar tenuer̄ in para-
gio. 7 qsq̄ habuit aula. Tc̄ 7 m̄ se defd. p̄ dim̄ hida. Tra .ē. ii. car̄. Ibi
.ē. un bord tant. T.R.E. ualb̄ .lx. sol. 7 post .x. sol. modo .v. sol.

HUGO de porth ten̄ in MIDELTONE un̄ hid 7 dim̄. 7 Willi de eo.
Aluuin tenuit in paragio. Tra .ē. iii. car̄. In dn̄io .ē. una. 7 v. uilli hnt
ibi .ii. car̄. Ibi un seruit. 7 m̄ ac̄ p̄a 7 dim̄. T.R.E. 7 post. ualb̄ .xl. sol.
Modo .xx. sol. T.R.E. se defd. p̄ hida 7 dim̄ Modo p̄ una hida.
Silua huiꝰ cō de .xx. porc̄ t̄c ꝓc in foresta. ualb̄ .xx. solid.

ISVO de s̄co amādo ten̄ LANGELIE p̄ Id IN ROBBRIGE HD.
baiocense ut dic̄. p̄ excābio uni molini qd̄ habet de uno hoe.
Quatuor aladiarii tenuer̄ in paragio. T.R.E. Tc̄ 7 m̄ p̄ una hida.
Tra .ē. ii. car̄. Ibi sunt .vi. uilli 7 m̄ bord cũ .ii. car̄.
T.R.E. 7 post. ualb̄ .xx. sol. modo .xxx. sol. IN ROSEDIC HD.

HUGO latinari ten̄ de rege .i. hid 7 una v̄ in ERNEAWDE.
Suuard tenuit de Tosti. Tc̄ se defd. p̄ una hida 7 una v̄. modo
p̄ nichilo. Tra .ē. ii. car̄. Ibi un uillꝰ 7 x. bord hnt .i. car̄. 7 v.
ac̄ p̄a. T.R.E. 7 post. 7 m̄ .iii. uilt. xx. sol. id .ē. in foret. .iiii. sol.

CANTORTUN ten̄ rex in foresta sua. Chenna tenuit de rege .E.
7 adhuc .ē. in ead. Tc̄ geld̄ui p̄ dim̄ v̄ modo p̄ una ferding. aliud ferding
iacet in foresta regis. In dn̄io .ē. dim̄ car̄. cũ .iiii. bord. Silua 7 p̄a
iacet in foresta T.R.E. ualb̄ .xx. sol. Modo Chenna .iii. sol. Rex .xvi. sol.
IN STETENE HD tenuit Goduin Wartha T.R.E. geld̄ui p̄ .i. hida
7 i. uirḡ. In eod HD tenuit de Goduin Indilborne. geld̄ui p̄ .i.
Tra .ē. ii. car̄. Preta ambaru terraru .xl. sol.

IN BURGO DE HANTUNE habet rex in dominio
quater xx hoes . iiii . min̄ . qui reddunt vii . lib de
gablo tre . 7 totid reddideř . T.R.E.
Hoȝ xx vii . reddt ꝗsꝗ . viii . denaꝝ . Duo ū . xii . den̄ .
7 alii .l. numero redd ꝗsꝗ . vi . den̄ .

Hii habuer̄ qʳqʳa tʳa in ipso burgo T.R.E. ab ipso rege .
Odo de Wincestre . Anschil pbr̄ . Cheteb fulghel . Tostall .
fili Elrici habuit . xcvi . aĉs tre . Bern̄ xviii . aĉs .
Cheping habuit . iii . domos ꝗ eas . 7 in Rad do morteny .
ten̄ eas . 7 Goduin . iii . domos . has ten̄ Bernard pancewold .
Posteaꝗ rex .W. uenit in anglia . sunt hospitati in
Hantone . lx v . francigene . 7 xxxi . anglig̃ .
hi uꝫ se oms̄ reddūt . iiii . lib 7 vi . den̄ de omib; esuetud .

Hii inscripta hn̄t in Hantone esuetud domoꝝ suaꝝ
eċssu .W. regis . G. eps̄ de una domo .
Abb cormeliensis . i . Abb de lira . i . Comes ebroicensis . ii .
Radulf de morteny . ii . Gislebť de breteuile . ii . Witts
filī Stur . ii . Rad de Todeni . i . Durand de blouecestre . ii .
hugo de port . i . hugo de Grentemaisnil . ii . Comes mo
ritonie . v . Aiulf camerari . v . hunfrid fr̄ ei . Osbn̄ . i .
Nigellus medic . iiii . Richeř de Andele . iiii . Ricardus . i .
Stefan̄ stirman . ii . Turstin̄ cameraꝝ . ii . Turstin̄ . ii .
Anschitl filī Osmundi . iii . Ramats . i .

Abbatissa de Waruuelle hř . i . piscariā 7 parū tre
ꞇe reddb . c . denaꝝ . modo . x . solid .

Rex Willelmus ten̄ in dn̄io Broc . Tosti tenuit
Ꞇe p . iiii . hid . modo p una hida . tʳa . e . xi . car̄ . In
dn̄io sunt . ii . car̄ . 7 in uitti 7 vii . bord cū . ii . car̄ . 7 dimid .
Ibi . ix . serui . 7 molin de . xv . den̄ 7 vi . ac tra .
T.R.E. ualb . viii . lib . 7 post . vi . lib . Modo . vii . lib . 7 tn̄
reddt . vii . lib plus .

Ipse rex ten̄ in dn̄io Cantune . com̄ . Tosti tenuit . Ꞇe se defd
p . iii . hid . modo p una hida . Ꞇʳa . e . iii . car̄ . In dn̄io . e una .
7 xiii . uitti 7 in bord cū . ii . car̄ . Ibi un̄ serui . vii . ac tra .
T.R.E. ualb . vi . lib . 7 post 7 m̄ . c . sot . tam redd . bc . sot plus .

Ipse rex ten̄ in dn̄io Atferne . Tosti tenuit . Ꞇe p . iii . hid
m̄ p . iii . hid una ū min̄ . Ꞇʳa . e . viii . car̄ . In dn̄io sunt . ii .
7 xiii . uitti 7 in bord cū . vi . car̄ . Ibi . xii . serui . 7 ii . ac tʳa .
T.R.E. ualb . x . lib . 7 post 7 modo . viii . lib . tam redd . x . lib .

Ipse Rex ten̄ in dn̄io Weltoe . Coolf tenuit in paragio
de rege . Ꞇe p . ii . hid . m̄ p . iii . uirg . Ꞇʳa . e . iiii . car̄ .
In dn̄io sunt . ii . 7 vi . uitti 7 in bord cū . ii . car̄ 7 dim . Ibi
iii . serui . 7 ii . ac tʳa . T.R.E. 7 post 7 m̄ . ualb . x . lib . tam . e̅ .

Ipse rex ten̄ in dn̄io Trescewate . Ad firmā de . xv . lib .
Tosti tenuit . Ꞇe se defd p . xv . hid . modo p . ii . hid .
Ꞇʳa . e . xv . car̄ . In dn̄io sunt . ii . car̄ . 7 xvii . uitti 7 x . bord
cū . viii . car̄ . Ibi . vii . serui . 7 vi . ac tʳa . T.R.E. ualb . xvi .
lib . 7 post . xx . lib . tam . e̅ . ad firmā de . xxx . lib .
De hii xv . hid . ten̄ abb de lira . iii . uirg .
7 Witts filī Azor una hid .

Ipse rex ten̄ in dn̄io Wilmingeha . Uluiet tenuit
in paragio . Ꞇe 7 m̄ p una hida . Ꞇʳa . e . ii . car̄ . Ibi . iii . uitti
cū . ii . car̄ . 7 dim ac tʳa . Val̄ 7 ualuit . xx . sot .
De hoc ꞇʳa regis ten̄ Raynab filī eps̄ una ū . 7 dicit
q̄ Rogeri com̄ ded eā patri suo . Valuit . v . sot . m̄ . e̅ . uastata .

Ipse Rex ten̄ in dn̄io Bovecome . De firma regis . e . fuit .
Ꞇe se defd p . iiii . hid . modo p nichilo . Ꞇʳa . e . xxv . car̄ .
In dn̄io sunt . iii . car̄ . 7 xxv . uitti 7 xv . bord cū . xxv . car̄ .
Ibi . x . serui . 7 vi . ac tʳa . 7 molin de . xl . den̄ . De theu
neo . xxx . sot . 7 salina sine censu . Silua de . v . porc .
De tʳa hui ço ten̄ Witts f . Stur dim ū . Ibi . e . i . car̄ cū
uno uitto . Val̄ . x . sot . Gozelin 7 Witts fr̄ ei ten̄ una ū .
que ante eos reddeb gablū . s; isti n̄ reddid q̄ .

Hui ço ecclam cū una ū tre ten̄ monachi de lire .
De hac ū tʳe ten̄ hunfrid tantū ubi hř . vii . hoes .
reddt . v . sot . 7 Witts f . Azor . ii . acs 7 dim . ubi hř . iiii .
dom . hi ten̄ absꞯ uolūtate pbr̄ . Ad hanc ecclam
adiacet . xx . masure bordarioꝝ . 7 redd . xiii . sot .
Ibi molin de . vi . solid . 7 oms̄ decime Bovecome su̅ eccle
Tot T.R.E. 7 post . 7 modo . ual̄ . xx . lib . 7 d̅ ꞇʳe abb . iiii . lib .

Ipse Rex ten̄ in dn̄io Heldeie . Cheping tenuit de
rege . E . Ꞇe se defd p . vi . uirg . modo p . ii . ū . vii ferding
min̄ . Ꞇʳa . e . iii . car̄ . In dn̄io . e una . 7 iii . uitti 7 un̄
bord hn̄t . ii . car̄ . Silua de . ii . porc . 7 v . serui . Val̄ . iii . lib .

De isto ᴍ ten' Liuol'. i. hiᵭ. 7 ibi hᵭ. ii. borᵭ cū dim̃ car'.
Tot̃ T.R.E. uatb. viii. lib. 7 post. vi. lib. Modo: vii. lib.

Isᵭ Gozelin' ten WERISTETONE. Tres libi hoēs tenuer'
in aloᵭ de rege. E. Tᵭ 7 m̃ geld̃ p. ii. hiᵭ 7 iii. uirg
7 tcia parte uni ᵿ. Tra. ē. iiii. car'. Hanc iᵭ m̃ tenet
iiii. hoēs de Gozelino. Willᵭ alt̃ Willᵭ. Goisfriᵭ 7 Doue
nolᵭ. Ibi ē in d̃nio una car'.
Tot̃ T.R.E. uatb. c. sot. 7 post 7 modo: L. soliᵭ. int oᵐs.

Ipse Gozelin' ten de rege SIDA. Ednoᵭ
renure de rege E. Tᵭ se defᵭ. p. ii. hiᵭ una ᵿ min'. Modo
p una hida 7 dim̃. Tra. ē. iiii. car'. In d̃nio ē una car'.
7 iii. utti 7 ii. borᵭ cū. i. car' 7 dim̃. Ibi. iii. seru. 7 ii.
molini de. v. soliᵭ. 7 ii. ac̃ pa.
T.R.E. 7 modo. uatb. L. sot. Cū recep̃. xL. sot.

Isᵭ Gozeliñ ten unā ᵿ in CELERTONE. 7 Goisfriᵭ ten
de Gozelino. Blacheman tenuit in paragio. Tᵭ 7 m̃
p una ᵿ. i. car'. Ibi ē in d̃nio. Vat̃ 7 ualuit. v. soliᵭ.

Isᵭ Goz̃ ten SORELLE. Vlnoᵭ tenuit in paragio.
Tᵭ p. ii. hiᵭ 7 una ᵿ. Modo p dim̃ hida. Tra. ē. ii. car'.
7 dim̃. In d̃nio ē una. 7 ii. utti 7 vi. borᵭ cū una car'
7 dim̃. Ibi. iii. seru. 7 molin de. xL. den'. 7 xiii. ac̃ pa.
T.R.E. 7 post. uatb. c. sot. Modo: iiii. lib.

Isᵭ Goz̃ ten SELBERLEI. Edricus tenuit. T.R.E. Tᵭ
se defᵭ. p. vi. hiᵭ. modo. p. iii. hiᵭ 7 dim̃ ᵿ. Tra. ē. xiii.
car'. In d̃nio sunt. ii. 7 xiii. utti 7 xiiii. borᵭ. cū. xx. car'.
7 ibi molin de. xL. den'. 7 iiii. ac̃ pa. Ibi eccta.
Silua de. xx. porc'.
De hac tra ten Goisfriᵭ. ii. uirg 7 dim̃. 7 ibi una car'
cū. ii. uittis 7 uno borᵭ. 7 Turgisus dim̃ hiᵭ. Liof'. i. hiᵭ.
hi hn̄t in d̃nio. ii. car'. 7 ii. uitts 7 ii. borᵭ cū una car'.
Totū T.R.E. 7 post. uatb. xx. lib. Modo. xv. lib int oᵐs.

Isᵭ Goz̃ ten HARESTEDE. Aluric tenuit in paragio.
Tᵭ 7 m̃. p dim̃ hiᵭ. Tra. ē. i. car'. Ibi. i. seru. 7 un uitt
cū dim̃ car'. Vat̃ 7 ualuit. xx. soliᵭ.

Isᵭ Goz̃ ten NUREDESTONE. Aluric tenuit in pa
ragio. Tᵭ 7 m̃ p una hida. Tra. ē. ii. car'. In d̃nio ē una
7 dim̃. 7 un uitts 7 iii. borᵭ cū. i. car'. Ibi. iiii. seru.
7 una ac̃ pa. Vat̃ 7 ualuit. Lx. soliᵭ. Turald ten de Goz̃.
Isᵭ Goz̃ hᵭ dim̃ hiᵭ in CELARTONE. Aluric tenuit
7 Tᵭ 7 m̃ p dim̃ hida se defᵭ. Tra. ē. i. car'. 7 ibi ē cū. ii.
uittis. 7 ii. ac̃ pa. Vat̃ 7 ualuit. x. soliᵭ.

Iterū Willᵭ filiuᵭ azor ten de rege MORRESTAN.
Quatuor taini tenuer' in paragio. Tᵭ p. ii. hiᵭ. modo
p. ii. uirg 7 dim̃. Tra. ē. ii. car'. In d̃nio. ē una car'.
7 ii. seru. 7 vii. borᵭ cū. i. car'. 7 xvi. ac̃ pa.
T.R.E. uatb. x. lib. 7 post 7 modo: vi. lib.

Isᵭ W. ten SEVRETONE. Leuing tenuit in paragio.
Tᵭ p una hida. m̃ p dim̃ ᵿ. Tra. ē. i. car'. Ibi sunt
ii. borᵭ. i. seru. 7 molin 7 ii. ac̃ pa. Vat̃. xL. soliᵭ.

Isᵭ W. ten HARESTEDE dim̃ hiᵭ. 7 Nigell̃ de eo.
Aluric tenuit in paragio. Tᵭ 7 m̃ p dim̃ hida. Tra. ē.
uni car'. 7 ibi ē cū. ii. uittis 7 ii. borᵭ. Vat̃ 7 ualuit. xx. sot.
Isᵭ W. ten dim̃ hiᵭ in CELARTONE. Willᵭ forsᵭ de eo.
Aluric tenuit in parig'. Tᵭ 7 m̃ se defᵭ p dim̃ hida.
Tra. ē. i. car'. Valuit. x. sot. modo: v. soliᵭ.

Isᵭ W. ten' in SIDA. unā hiᵭ 7 una ᵿ. Ednoᵭ tenuit
in paragio. Tᵭ p x. uirg'. m̃ p. iii. uirg'. Tra. ē. iii. car'.
In d̃nio nichil. sᵭ xv. borᵭ 7 iiii. seru. cū. ii. car' 7 dim̃.
Ibi molin de. x. soliᵭ 7 ii. ac̃ pa. Silua ad clausurā.
T.R.E. 7 post. uatb. xL. soliᵭ. Modo: Lx. soliᵭ.

Isᵭ W. 7 Roger' de eo ten in FRESCEWATRE. i. hiᵭ.
7 ᴘ tanto geld̃. hanc tenuit qᵭā ppostᵭ rosu in m̃
de fresceuuatre. Tra. ē. i. car'. 7 ibi ē in d̃nio. cū. i. borᵭ.
T.R.E. 7 modo. uatb. xL. sot. cū recep̃. xx. sot.
Isᵭ W. 7 Goisfriᵭ de eo ten in CELERTONE. unā ᵿ.
7 ᴘ tanto se defᵭ. Blacheman tenuit in paragio.
Tra. ē. i. car'. 7 ibi ē in d̃nio cū. ii. borᵭ 7 uno seruo.
Valuit. xx. sot. modo: xxx. soliᵭ.

TERRE TAINOꝛ REGIS.

Godric pbr ten de rege MELEUSFORD. Ipse tenuit
in paragio de rege. E. Tᵭ 7 m̃. p una hida 7 dim̃ ᵿ.
Tra. ē dim̃ car'. In d̃nio tam̃. ē una car'. cū uno borᵭ.
7 molin sine censu. 7 pa. i. ac̃ 7 dim̃. Vat̃ 7 ualuit. x. sot.

Alsi fili Bryxi ten TORLEI. Tosti tenuit.
Tᵭ se defᵭ p. iii. hiᵭ. modo p. iii. hiᵭ. Tra. ē. vii. car'.
In d̃nio sunt. ii. 7 x. utti 7 xi. borᵭ cū. iii. car'. Ibi. vii.
seru. 7 vi. ac̃ pa. T.R.E. 7 post. ualuit. viii. lib. m̃. xii. lib.

Alere ten 7 tenuit in ESSEVELE. i. hiᵭ. 7 ᴘ tanto
se defᵭ. Tra. ē. dim̃ car'. In d̃nio ē una. 7 i. seru.
7 un borᵭ. 7 molin sine censu. Valuit. x. sot. modo: xv. sot.

Vlnoᵭ ten 7 tenuit ALALEI. T.R.E. 7 m̃ geld̃ p una ᵿ.
In d̃nio. ē dim̃ car'. Vat̃. v. sot. Valuit. vii. sot.

Herbrand ten de rege LEPENE. Godric tenuit
de rege. E. Tᵭ 7 m̃ geld̃ p una hida. Tra. ē. iiii. car'.
In d̃nio. ē una car'. 7 iii. utti cū. ii. car'. Ibi. ii. ac̃ pa.
Silua sine pasnag'. Vat̃. iiii. lib. Modo: iii. lib.

Edric ten AVICESTONE. Ipsemet tenuit de rege. E.
Tᵭ 7 m̃ geld̃ p dim̃ ᵿ. Tra. ē dim̃ car'. Ibi. ē in d̃nio
cū. ii. borᵭ 7 ii. seruiᵭ. Vat̃ 7 ualuit. v. soliᵭ.

Oirant' ten CELVECROFT. pat' ei' ten de rege. E.
Tᵭ 7 m̃ geld̃ p dim̃ ᵿ. In d̃nio. ē dimiᵭ car'. cū uno
borᵭ. Vat̃ 7 ualuit. v. soliᵭ.

Alsi ten de rege ABAGINGE. Ipsemet tenuit de
rege. E. in aloᵭ. Tᵭ 7 m̃ geld̃ p una ᵿ. Tra. ē dim̃ car'.
Ibi dimiᵭ ac̃ pa. Valuit. v. soliᵭ. modo: iii. soliᵭ.

Viuard ten de rege WIRINCEHA. Ipse tenuit de
rege. E. in aloᵭ. Tᵭ 7 m̃ geld̃ p dim̃ hida. In d̃nio. ē dim̃ car'.
cū iiii. borᵭ. Vat̃ 7 ualuit. x. soliᵭ.

Alric 7 nepos ei' ten de rege HORELESTONE. Ipsemet
tenuit in aloᵭ de rege. E. Tᵭ 7 m̃ geld̃ p tcia parte uni
hide. Tra. ē dim̃ car'. 7 ibi ē in d̃nio. Vat̃ 7 ualuit. v. sot.

Huntriᵭ ten de rege tcia parte uni hide in HORE
LESTONE. Godesa tenuit in aloᵭ de rege. E. Tᵭ 7 m̃
geld̃ p una hida. Tra. ē. iii. car'. In d̃nio. ē una car'.
7 ii. ac̃ pa. Valuit. Lx. sot. Modo: xx. soliᵭ.

Edwi ten APLEDEFORDE. Ipsemet tenuit de rege. E.
in aloᵭ. Tᵭ 7 m̃ geld̃ p dimiᵭ hida. Tra. ē. i. car'.
In d̃nio. ē dimiᵭ car'. cū uno borᵭ 7 ii. ac̃ pa 7 dim̃.
Valuit. xx. sot. modo: x. soliᵭ.

Magna Carta

Magna Carta, "The Great Charter", has come to be regarded as the cornerstone of liberty and is one of the most important documents in British constitutional history. It was reissued several times – this version comes from 1225, during the reign of Henry III. But collectively the various versions have come to symbolize the placing of legal constraints on arbitrary, despotic government. It has been invoked on countless occasions in the centuries since by defenders of the rights of individuals against the crown or state. And yet this agreement extorted from King John by his barons in June 1215 was a fundamentally conservative document, intended to protect the rights of a narrow feudal aristocracy.

Medieval English kings regularly ran out of money. They lacked a consistent source of revenue, and had long resorted to stratagems such as "scutage", a taxation levied on landholders in lieu of providing fighting-men for royal campaigns, as their feudal dues obliged them. King John's ruinously expensive French wars – which resulted in the loss of Normandy and the mocking nickname "Lackland" – brought a remorseless increase in these demands. These included a tightening of the screw on estates where the holder died with no heir, or left a widow and small children (and which fell to the crown to administer).

Discontent among the barons, the king' s leading subjects, rose dangerously. In 1209 the King fell out with the Church. He was excommunicated, and this gave the nobility a suitable pretext for their opposition: how could they be loyal to a king rejected by the Church? Attempts at diplomacy failed and in May 1215 the barons seized London. This forced John to negotiate. At Runneymede, by the banks of the Thames, Archbishop Langton brokered an agreement between the two sides. Opposing drafts of the charter were exchanged and finally on 15 June, a compromise text was agreed.

It would not be known as Magna Carta until later – to distinguish it from a charter covering royal forests issued in 1217 – but its import was clear. Or at least it seemed so at the time. The major royal abuses in imposing excess scutage, denying access to royal courts and confiscating intestate estates were to be curbed. The barons even forced through a committee of 25 of their number who could seize the king's lands if he broke the terms of the 63-point charter.

Within months, though, John had abrogated the agreement and succeeded in having his excommunication lifted, and the country descended into civil war. The barons were helped by an army from France. In 1216 John made the only smart move of his reign: he died. His son, Henry,

was 9. Henry's advisors offered the barons a version of Magna Carta to end the war and send the French invaders home. The barons preferred a young weak king to a French one and accepted. The clause on the baronial committee was dropped but, crucially, Clause 39 was retained. This protected all free men from extra-judicial actions by the crown, granting them "lawful judgement" according to the "law of the land".

Over the centuries, as scutage became an antiquarian curiosity and feudal "reliefs" levied on estates an all-but-forgotten anachronism, this clause formed the central element of the myth of Magna Carta. For the first time the king had made an agreement with his people as a whole, recognizing the nation's existence as a corporation separate from the body of the king. The great Elizabethan jurist Edward Coke invoked it, and opponents of Charles I pointed to his arbitrary taxation as a breach of Magna Carta's time-hallowed principles. In 1689 the Bill of Rights, passed after the deposition of James II, once more enshrined the principles of the Magna Carta in law and ensured its continuing reputation as the guardian of fundamental freedoms.

In the eighteenth century Magna Carta became a rallying cry for the American colonists chafing under British colonial rule. The feeling that the British government was betraying the principles of the charter,

helped fuel the revolutionaries' fervour. The seal chosen by the colony of Massachusetts showed a militiaman holding both a sword and the Magna Carta. Once independence was won, more than a dozen states incorporated the charter into their state statute books. Needless to say it was the right to due process of law, rather than rights of baronial inheritance, that prompted them to do so.

Over the centuries since King John affixed his seal, the clauses of Magna Carta have fallen away one by one, superseded by other laws, or fading into irrelevance. Only a handful remain in force. Tellingly, the key one of these is Clause 39. What began as a list of barons' concerns in 1215 was seized on by jurists and rebels as they battled royal tyranny. By the twentieth century it came to be seen as the ultimate source of human rights legislation. King John at Runneymede could never have imagined its impact, but given that in the end it undermined the power of feudal nobility as much as his own, he might have been forgiven a wry smile.

OPPOSITE The Great Seal of King John used to authenticate royal charters. The text around the edge reads: *Johannes Dei Gracia Rex Anglie Dominvs Hibernie* (John, by the grace of God King of England and Lord of Ireland). Magna Carta is a towering epitaph to one of England's worst kings.

LEFT This is the 1225 version of the Magna Carta, the third to be issued by Henry III and the first to bear his own seal. The previous two had been issued while he was still a boy. Clause 29 (which was Clause 39 in the original, 1215 version) is five lines up from the second hole in the manuscript. It guarantees that "no free man shall be taken or imprisoned … except by the lawful judgment of his peers or by the law of the land" (*"nullus liber homo capiatur, vel imprisonetur…nisi per legale judicium parium suorum vel per legem terrae"*).

William Caxton's Printed Indulgence

Appended with the magnificent seal of the Abbot of Abingdon this indulgence, a form of remission of sins granted on papal or episcopal authority, was produced by William Caxton in 1476 and may be the earliest printed document in Britain. It represents the start of an information revolution.

WILLIAM CAXTON
Who first practiced the Art of Printing in England in 1471.

For Caxton printing was a business opportunity. He had spent nearly 30 years as a trader in the Low Countries, latterly as governor of the community of English Merchant Adventurers. But his position as a supporter of the House of York during the Wars of the Roses led to his removal in 1470 during a brief Lancastrian upsurgence. He decamped to Cologne, where he was introduced to the new technology of printing with movable type, which had been employed for the first time in Europe some 20 years earlier by Johannes Gutenberg in Mainz.

Caxton had already displayed literary ambitions by translating a popular courtly romance, the *Recuyell of the Historyes of Troye*, into English. In Cologne he collaborated with a German printer to produce a compendium by Bartholomaeus Anglicus, a thirteenth-century encyclopaedist. In 1473, when it was safe for him to return to Bruges, he set up his own printing press, and his first production was a printed edition of his translation of the *Recuyell*. Two years later, Caxton went back to England and established a printing shop in Westminster.

Caxton's inclination was to print crowd-pleasing books such as *The History of Jason* (by Lefèvre, the author of the *Recuyell*) and, most notably, Chaucer's *Canterbury Tales* (which he published in 1477), but like any businessman he needed to ensure a solid cash flow. With his printing press just a stone's throw from Westminster Abbey, this could best be achieved by producing works of popular piety and, even more lucratively, by printing indulgences.

Indulgences lifted sin from the shoulders of the guilty – for a price. The Catholic Church had a monopoly on granting absolution for sin. In return for a payment (in prayers or cash) the Pope and certain bishops could forgive penitents. There was a tariff of indulgences, which varied from a standard 40 days to – in the most extreme

The manuscript at the top of the page shows Latin text in medieval script, with a wax seal suspended below on cords.

cases – the remission of 137,000 years of torment in purgatory. The purchase of the indulgence still had to take some form of practical action, such as the saying of prayers or a pilgrimage, which would unlock the benefits, but they came to be seen by both the Church and later critics such as Martin Luther as a revenue-raising exercise, which could pay for projects such as church building and mounting crusades.

By the late fourteenth century the practice of Jubilee Years had become established; a 12-month period of general absolution in which by visiting Rome or specific churches in their home countries – and by purchasing an indulgence to fund expeditions to the Holy Land – pilgrims could receive a "plenary" indulgence (absolving all their sins). Caxton's first printed version was granted to Henry Langley and his wife Katherine on 13 December 1476, as part of an extension of the fund-raising activities of the 1475 Jubilee Year.

The Langleys' names are carefully inserted by hand in red ink in blank sections on the pre-printed document, which is authorized by Johannes (John) Sant, the Abbot of Abingdon, appointed Papal collector of revenues from the indulgence earlier in the

OPPOSITE Portrait of William Caxton. Among his other works were a 1490 edition of the parliamentary statutes of Henry VII, the first time England's laws were printed in English rather than French.

ABOVE Authenticated with the seal of John, Abbot of Abingdon, Caxton's first printed Indulgence promises "the grace of the Jubilee" to the bearer and releases them from any vows they have made except for those to make a pilgrimage to Compostela, or to enter a religious order. The space for the purchasers of the indulgence (in the third line) was left blank. Their names, Henry Langley and his wife Katherine, were filled in later using different-coloured ink.

year. The procedure offered benefits to all parties. Henry Langley did not have to wait until a monastic scribe laboriously wrote out the whole indulgence by hand; the printer could produce thousands of copies in the time; and the church authorities could raise more revenue more quickly – the Papacy received some 8,000 florins from one particular indulgence to fund an expedition against the Turks, who were beginning to raid the coastline of Italy just 20 years after their conquest of Constantinople.

Caxton, continued to produce more populist works, such as *The Golden Legend* (1489) and a new edition of *The Canterbury Tales* in 1484, but he was too much of a businessman to turn down other, more lucrative, work and in 1480 accepted a contract for a further indulgence. Printing would change the world, spreading literacy and ideas. It would slowly erode the elite's monopoly on information and education. But in the early years, rather than acting as an agent for the spread of knowledge, printing was in far more common use for spreading cheap novels and easy promises of the remission of sins.

OPPOSITE William Caxton presents a copy of his English translation of *Recueil of the Histories of Troyes* to Margaret of York. She was Richard III's sister. This was the first book printed in English. Printing was such a novelty that at the end of the book, Caxton wrote that it "is not written with pen and ink as other books have been, to the end that every man may have them at once".

ABOVE The first illustration of a printing press appeared in the *Dance of Death*, or *Danse macabre*, published in Lyon by Mathias Huss in 1499.

06

Letters Patent to John Cabot

A single entry on a parchment roll indicating a royal grant to an Italian merchant adventurer in 1496 marks the first faltering beginnings of the British empire. Europe was in the grip of a revolution. Ships were sailing thousands of miles into uncharted oceans to exploit the riches of the world.

Eight years earlier, Portuguese mariner Bartholomew Dias had rounded the Cape of Good Hope into the Indian Ocean. Four years later, Christopher Columbus had stumbled upon the Americas. Now Henry, King of England, wanted to get involved. It was in some ways an act of remorse on the king's part: he had rejected Columbus, who had come to him looking for royal investors for his project to find a quick route to the spice islands of Eastern Asia.

Henry VII was not about to make the same mistake. His letters patent to John (or Giovanni) Cabot empowered him to "find, discover and investigate whatsoever islands, countries, regions or provinces of heathens and infidels, in whatsoever part of the world placed, which before this time were unknown to all Christians". He was determined that the Spanish and Portuguese would not monopolize the new discoveries across the Atlantic. News of

Christopher Columbus's voyage to a "New World" had reached England in the summer of 1493 and excited great interest in the merchant community of Bristol.

The chosen instrument of England's nascent imperialism was a foreigner. John Cabot had settled in Bristol in 1495 after an apprenticeship in the Mediterranean trade, which had allegedly taken him as far as Mecca and left him with a distinct taste for adventure. Cabot soon began lobbying for funds to mount an English-sponsored expedition to investigate the lands that Columbus had claimed to find. The Italian secured an interview with Henry to outline his plans, and afterwards the king had the letters patent drawn up, a form of legal document granting rights to a private individual to act on behalf of the crown.

The initial expedition was not a lavish one. A single ship, the *Matthew*, set out from Bristol in the spring of 1497 carrying 18 sailors, including John Cabot and possibly his son Sebastian. The first part of the voyage, to the west coast of Ireland and then north to Iceland, was through waters familiar to English mariners. The rest of the tiny vessel's route, due west across the Atlantic, was a calculated gamble on Cabot's part.

His crew members spent 52 nervous days at sea, before sighting land. The coast along which they found themselves sailing seemed fertile and the seas were filled with vast shoals of cod. Cabot ordered a single landing to take on fresh supplies and, though the crew encountered no natives, they found signs that the area was inhabited; there were the remains of a fire, nets and needles. His landfall, on 24 June 1497, had most likely been in Newfoundland in roughly the same area where the Vikings, the first Europeans to visit North America

five centuries before, had established a short-lived colony. Having claimed the new land for England and raised flags, Cabot turned back across the Atlantic to bring back news of his discovery.

Henry VII was busy seeing off threats to his crown, and in any case the results of the expedition – certainly in terms of the trove of gold which a successful voyage to East Asia might have been expected to garner – were paltry. Cabot was rewarded with a meagre £10 and, no doubt after further lobbying, an annual pension of £20. As a further gesture to his pretensions, he was allowed to refer to himself as "Grand Admiral", exactly the same title that Columbus had assumed after his discoveries.

Finally, in early 1498 Cabot got what he had really wanted, a grant allowing him to mount a further expedition, this time on a larger scale. In May, five ships left Bristol, some of them carrying goods such as lace, suggesting that Cabot hoped this time to encounter and trade with natives. The fate of the expedition is unknown; although one ship got into difficulties around Ireland and turned back, there is no further record of the other four. John Cabot was lost to history, but whatever his fate he had made a vital start. The letters patent he received in 1496 and his subsequent voyage are the foundations of English (and consequently British) imperialism. North America would endure centuries of warfare as Europeans battled each other for supremacy, but in the end the English-speaking peoples triumphed, ensuring that this mighty continent would be dominated by nations of English and British descent, rather than Spanish or French. The consequences for subsequent world history are almost incalculable.

OPPOSITE Like many medieval English administrative texts, the letters patent issued by Henry VII to John Cabot were recorded on a roll that included other documents. The text at the top left-hand corner specifies that the grant is for John Cabot and his sons. The main part of the letters patent empowers them "*super Terra Incognita investiganda*" – to investigate unknown lands. Optimistically they are given the right to set up Henry's banner in any "town, city or castle" they might come across.

ABOVE Born Giovanni Caboto in Italy, John Cabot moved to Bristol in around 1495. There are no records of him after 1498, giving rise to the belief that he perished on his last voyage.

FOLLOWING PAGES Map of the Old and New Worlds, c.1500 by Juan de la Cosa. It is the earliest undisputed plan of the Americas, and shows the lands discovered up to the end of the fifteen century by expeditions to the Americas led by the Spanish, Portuguese and English (Cabot's).

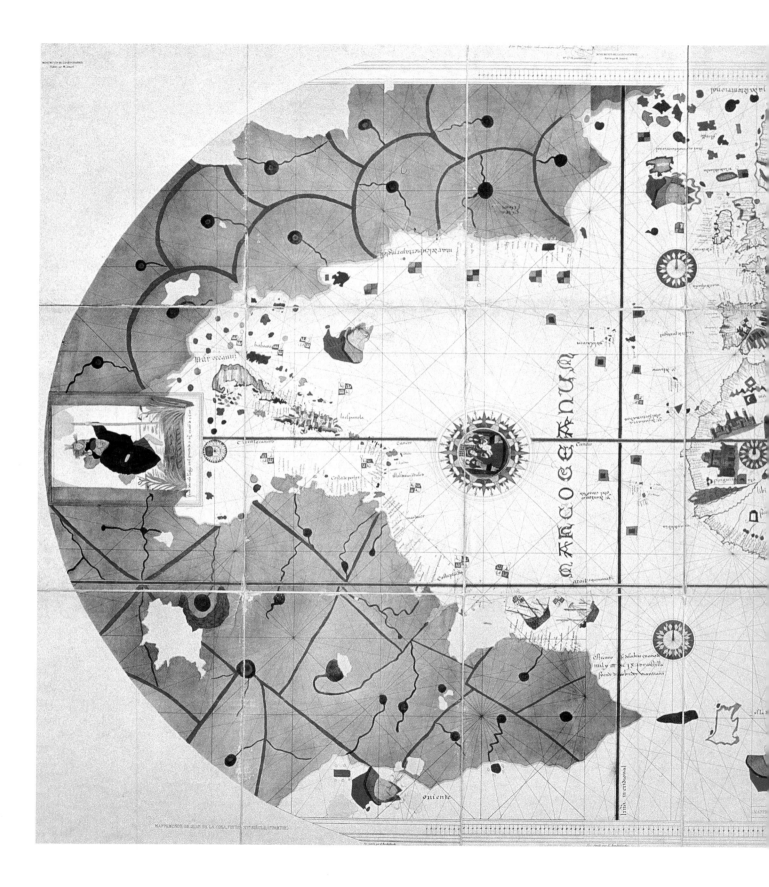

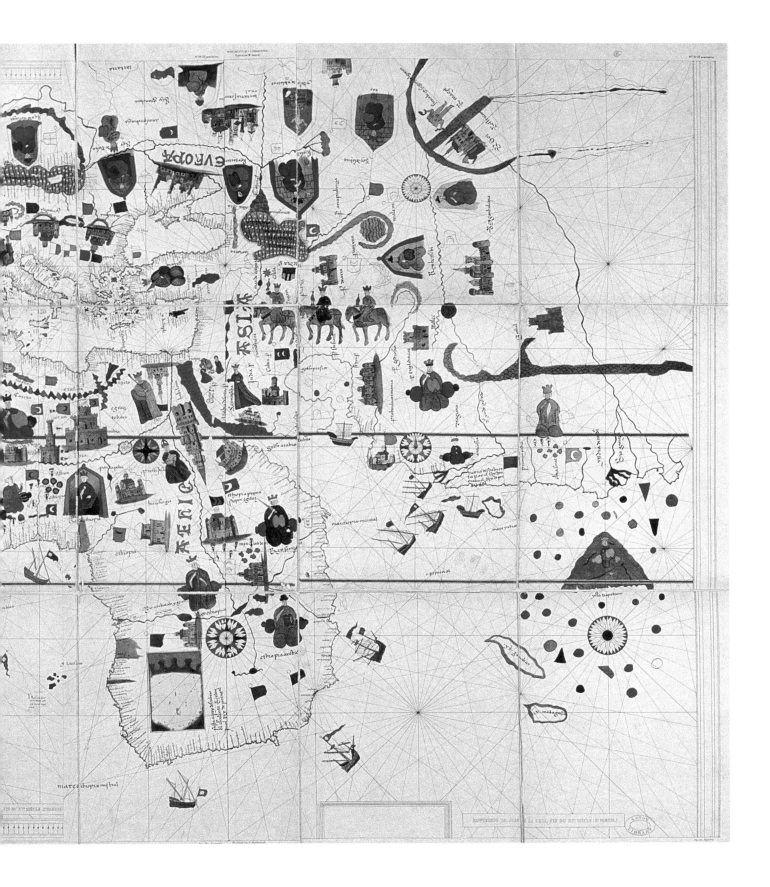

07

The Treaty of Perpetual Peace

Gorgeously illuminated with thistles representing Scotland and Tudor roses for England, the 1502 treaty between the two countries promised to be a "Perpetual Peace". The agreement between James IV of Scotland and his English counterpart Henry VII, far from lasting "from this day forth in all times to come" survived just 11 years before a shift in European alliances caused the Scots to break it. Yet the effect of the treaty was far more momentous than a decade's pause in the centuries-long conflict between the two countries. Included in its terms was a marriage between Henry's daughter Margaret and James's son, which ultimately led to the union of the crowns of Scotland and England in 1603.

Relations between Scotland and her southern neighbour had veered between violence and watchful calm since Edward I of England invaded in 1296. Scottish independence was secured by Robert Bruce's victory at Bannockburn in 1314 and recognized by the Treaty of Berwick in 1357. But the border country was still plagued by chronic raiding and the ever-present threat of open warfare. The Scots sought protection in an alliance with France. First signed in 1295 by John Balliol, it was renewed by almost every subsequent Scottish monarch and was affectionately known as the "Auld Alliance".

In 1496, James IV took advantage of Henry VII's troubles with the rebel Perkin Warbeck (who was masquerading as Richard, Duke of York, one of the "princes in the tower" murdered in 1483) to launch an invasion of England. James penetrated just 4 miles (6 kilometres) before turning back, and the pause in hostilities led to a new peace initiative. The Spanish had just negotiated a marriage alliance between Catherine of Aragon and Arthur, Henry's eldest son (whose untimely death in 1502 meant that she subsequently married Henry VIII). They now sought to isolate France further by detaching the Scots from the Auld Alliance.

James IV could see the benefits of peace with his southern neighbour. It would leave him free to concentrate on pacifying the western Highlands and Isles, where royal authority was weak. So, after months of negotiation, a peace was agreed, signed by Henry VII on 31 October 1502 and by James seven weeks later. It was to be a "true, sincere, whole and unbroken peace, friendship, league and alliance", which forbade either side giving shelter to rebels against the other (Henry did not want any repeat of the Warbeck incident). The penalty of excommunication was imposed on whichever of the two monarchs broke the treaty, which meant it had to go to Rome for ratification by Pope Alexander VI.

Henry's 13-year-old daughter Margaret married James, 17 years her senior, at

Holyrood on 8 August 1503. Neither the dowry of 30,000 gold nobles she brought with her nor the threat of papal wrath was sufficient to make the treaty last. In 1511, the Spanish forged a new alliance against France. Before the year was out, the new king, Henry VIII, had been persuaded to join this "Holy League". In response, Louis XII of France invoked the Auld Alliance, leaving James with a dilemma. Should he honour the Perpetual Peace and listen to the pleadings of his English Tudor wife, or stay true to Scotland's traditional French allies?

James judged that if France were crushed, then England would be free to

resume her northern adventures. He sent an ultimatum to Henry, calling on him to desist from the invasion of France he was engaged in. To this the English king rather tactlessly replied, "I am the very holder of Scotland – he holds it of me by homage!" Angered, James raised a large army and on 22 August 1513 crossed the River Tweed into England. An English host under the Earl of Surrey awaited him. On 9 September, the Scottish pikes proved ineffective against the English halberds on the slippery, hilly terrain at Flodden Field in Northumberland. The battle became a massacre. As many as 10,000 Scots died, including 9 earls, 14 lords and the King.

OPPOSITE Margaret Tudor was 13 when she married James IV of Scotland in 1503. She endured a period of exile in England after James's death at Flodden.

ABOVE Scottish knights advance, the banner of Scotland flying, in this depiction of the Battle of Flodden by John Gilbert.

Scotland was riven by successive minorities. James IV's son was a baby when he became king. His daughter Mary Queen of Scots was just a week old when he died and her son James VI was in turn only a year old when she abdicated in June 1567. The country was further destabilized by the arrival of the Reformation in Scotland and the vicious struggles between pro-French and pro-English factions at court. Only in 1560 did the Peace of Edinburgh bring calm to Anglo-Scottish relations.

The Perpetual Peace had a far more lasting consequence. Elizabeth I never married – despite the hopes of various English aristocrats and European princes. On her deathbed in March 1603 she nominated James VI as her heir. He was, as the great-grandson of Margaret Tudor, Elizabeth's second cousin once removed and had the closest blood claim to the throne. In April, James set out for London and a new reign as James I of England. The British royal family today are his direct descendants. The 1502 treaty may not have brought lasting peace, but it did bring lasting union.

RIGHT This version of the Treaty of Perpetual Peace, signed by Henry VII, is decorated with red Tudor roses. The one signed by James IV was adorned with thistles to represent Scotland. William Dunbar, the Scottish court poet, composed "The Thrissil and the Rois", a poem in celebration of the treaty.

08

Indictment of Anne Boleyn

The salacious testimony in this 1536 indictment of Anne Boleyn seems more worthy of a tabloid newspaper than of court proceedings against a Tudor queen. Having fallen out of favour with Henry VIII for her failure to produce a male heir, she is accused of all manner of vile crimes, including incest with her brother, adultery with several members of her retinue and plotting to murder her husband. This sensational document led to the first execution of a queen in British history, just three years after Henry VIII's first marital scandal had led to England's break with the Roman Catholic church.

Henry's need for an heir was the root cause of his difficulties. No amount of success in war or awards from the Pope of the title of "Defender of the Faith" could compensate for the dynastic woes that would follow if there were no son to succeed him. His first wife, the Spanish princess Catherine of Aragon, underwent six pregnancies. The only child to survive more than a few months was a girl, Mary, born in 1516. A vain bully who was vulnerable to flattering suggestions from his advisers, Henry resolved to get rid of Catherine. He had also fallen for Anne Boleyn, one of the queen's maids of honour, who was young enough to provide an heir and clever enough not to settle for being his mistress.

Henry at first tried a conventional route, asking Cardinal Wolsey to seek an annulment from Pope Clement VII. The grounds were that Catherine had – though she denied it – consummated her brief marriage with Henry's older brother Arthur, who had died prematurely. Canon law forbade Henry's marriage to his brother's wife, and so the marriage was null and void. Or it would have been if the Pope had accepted this arguement. Instead, several years of wrangling broke out over the "King's Great Matter", which ended in Henry establishing himself as head of the English Church in 1532, backed by his new Archbishop of Canterbury, Thomas Cranmer. This done, Cranmer granted the King a divorce.

Anne and Henry were married on 25 January 1533. Catherine was stripped of her title as queen and Anne crowned as queen consort on 1 June 1533 (an act which finally drove Pope Clement to excommunicate Henry). Anne was already pregnant and all might have been well had the child who was born in September not been a girl – the future Elizabeth I. Anne then suffered two successive miscarriages, in December 1534 and January 1536. Henry, by now 45 years old, found himself in the same situation as before. He had no male heir, and the woman for whom he had torn apart the unity of Christendom looked like she was not going to provide him with one.

Anne's growing faction at court, notably her brother Lord Rochford, threatened the position of Henry's chief minister, Thomas Cromwell, who had been instrumental in Anne's rise. The very characteristics of the

ANNA · BOLEYN · REGINA ANGLIÆ · 1534

queen which had first caught Henry's eye – her vivacious manner and craving for attention – proved her downfall. Cromwell's spies overheard a flirtatious conversation with Mark Smeaton, a musician, and then gathered enough circumstantial evidence to implicate Sir Henry Norris, Sir Francis Weston and her brother Lord George Rochford.

Smeaton was arrested on 1 May and by the following day Anne was in the Tower. The indictments drawn up against her pulled no punches. She was said to have allowed her "natural brother" Lord Rochford "to violate her, alluring him with her tongue in the said George's mouth, and the said George's tongue in hers" and to have committed similar acts with Smeaton, Norris and Weston. Worse, she was said to have "conspired the death and destruction of the King ... often saying she would marry one of them as soon as the King died."

The trial, on 15 May, was a summary affair, as all such treason trials of the time were. Anne had no lawyer, could not present her own witnesses, or cross-examine those of the crown. The spirited defence she made did her no good, for her fate was predetermined once Henry had made up his mind. The death sentence was passed and Anne agreed to the annulment of her marriage to the king, possibly in a vain bid to save her life. Henry

at least granted Anne the right to death by decapitation rather than by hanging, drawing and quartering. The Calais executioner was summoned, who had skill in beheading with the sword – a much cleaner death than hacking away with the traditional axe.

When Anne walked to the scaffold on 19 May, a mantle of ermine protecting her from the chill, Henry was already involved with his next queen, Anne's former lady-in-waiting Jane Seymour. He became betrothed to her just three days later. Anne refused to speak ill of Henry, asking God to "save my sovereign and master the King", only seconds before she died. But the two biggest marital scandals in British royal history, which centred around her rise and fall from grace, refused to die.

OPPOSITE This version of the Indictment of Anne Boleyn was sworn before a jury in Middlesex on 10 May 1536. It covers crimes the queen was said to have committed at Whitehall and Hampton Court Palace. Other alleged adulterous encounters, at Greenwich and Eltham, fell within the jurisdiction of the Kent courts and were the subject of a separate indictment sworn at Deptford.

ABOVE LEFT Anne needed to produce a male heir and her first child, born in 1533, had been a girl. She was pregnant at the time this portrait was painted in 1534, but the child was still-born.

ABOVE RIGHT In this engraving of Anne Boleyn's execution, she is depicted wearing a crown, stressing her regal status. In fact, she wore a cap into which she tucked her long hair as she knelt upright on a bed of straw to await the executioner's blow.

09

Princess Elizabeth's Tide Letter

On one level this letter is a touching declaration of loyalty from one sister to another, as the future Elizabeth I assures her half-sister Queen Mary that "I never practised, counselled or consented to anything that might be prejudicial to your person in any way". On another, it is a desperate attempt to avoid the fate which had befallen her own mother Anne Boleyn eighteen years beforehand. It is also a reminder that Elizabeth, destined to be one of England's most celebrated monarchs, was once a frightened princess, begging for her life in troubled times.

The letter was written on 17 March 1554 as Elizabeth was about to be escorted from Whitehall Palace to the Tower of London. The princess was stalling. The extreme slowness with which she wrote it – inserting slashed lines across the page above her signature to prevent any forged additions – bought her an extra day, as by the time it was finished the tide on the Thames had gone down and boats could not safely convey her and her household from Whitehall Palace to the Tower. This act of successful procrastination gave it the nickname "The Tide Letter".

Elizabeth was under suspicion for involvement in the rebellion of Sir Thomas Wyatt, crushed just two weeks previously. The uprising aimed at overthrowing Mary: the announcement of her marriage to the Catholic King Philip II of Spain in December 1553 had raised fears among English Protestants that Catholicism, and a foreign sovereign, was about to be foisted on the country. Elizabeth, still the heir to the throne, and a devout Protestant, was aware of the dangers of becoming ensnared by malcontents plotting to overthrow her sister, but she could do little to stop those who invoked her name in their schemes.

The queen herself was in a delicate position. She needed an heir, and she needed allies among the Catholic powers. A marriage to Philip of Spain was an ideal opportunity to secure both her dynastic succession and the re-establishment of Catholicism in England. Yet it was not a popular policy and the country was already wary of the first ruling queen in its history. Her ill-fated cousin, Lady Jane Grey, hardly counted: the ultra-Protestant party tried to place her on the throne after Edward VI's death in summer 1553, but her reign lasted just nine days.

Yet every move Mary took had the vexing result of boosting the popularity of her sister. They had both suffered the indignity of being declared illegitimate by their father in 1536, only to be restored to the line of

succession in 1543. But Mary's mother Catherine of Aragon had been divorced by Henry VIII in favour of Anne Boleyn, whose child Elizabeth was. This and their strong religious disagreements meant they could never really be close.

Mary did not hesitate long before ordering Elizabeth's arrest over the Wyatt plot. Her sister claimed she was too ill to move, but was carried in painful stages by litter from Ashridge House in Hertfordshire to Whitehall. There she would have heard of the execution of Lady Jane Grey and then, five weeks later, came her own summons to the Tower. No wonder she resisted.

Elizabeth bought herself just a day's grace and on 18 March, Palm Sunday, she was taken by boat to the Tower. As she entered, she despairingly cried out, "I come in as no traitor, but as true a woman to the Queen's Majesty as any is now living." She need not have feared. Although she was kept imprisoned two months, there was little concrete to connect Elizabeth to Wyatt's plot and Mary hesitated to have her popular sister executed. Besides, she had other things on her mind. The royal wedding took place on 25 July in Winchester Cathedral. Grave offence was caused to Philip's royal dignity by the dais on which he sat being lower than that of his bride, and over the next year his unique position as king consort failed to evolve into the position of real power that he had hoped.

The marriage resulted in little more than a phantom pregnancy in 1555 and an entanglement in a war in France leading to the loss of Calais, England's last possession there in 1558. As Mary became ever more ill – possibly with cancer of the womb – Elizabeth's star rose remorselessly. She had been released from the Tower after two months at the instigation of Philip, who believed Mary was about to give birth, which would have removed Elizabeth as heir to the throne. As she made her way to a kind of house arrest at Woodstock Palace in Oxfordshire, housewives lined the route to offer her cakes. Mary's power seeped away as her health failed and she died in November 1558 abandoned by her husband. Her councillors scrambled to make their peace with her sister, who was crowned as Queen Elizabeth I. It was a far cry from the day when the ebbing of the Thames tide had seemed a matter of life or death.

OPPOSITE This painting is considered to be the finest and most compelling portrait of Princess Elizabeth before she acceded to the throne, probably painted for her father Henry VIII, c.1546.

ABOVE Queen Mary with her husband, Philip II of Spain, painted in 1558 by Hans Eworth. Mary was 37 at the time of the marriage, and the production of an heir to the throne was becoming urgent. The queen is wearing a large pearl set in a pendant, given to her as a wedding present by Philip.

FOLLOWING PAGES Writing in her own hand, Princess Elizabeth (as she then was) reminds her sister Mary in the fourth line of a promise "that I not be condemned without answer". At the bottom left of the second page, a desperate Elizabeth signs off with a plea that "I humbly crave but one word of answer from yourself" and then scores across the second page to prevent any text being added.

If any euer did try this olde sayinge that a kinges worde was more tha
n another mans othe, I most humbly beseche your. M. to verefie it in
me and to remember your last promis and my last demaunde that I
be not condemned without answer and due profe, wiche it semes that now I am for
that without cause proued I am by your counsel frome you comanded
to go vnto the tower a place more wonted for a false traitor, tha a true
subiect wiche thogth I knowe I deserue it not, yet in the face of
al this realme aperes that it is proued wiche I pray god I may die the
shamefullist dethe that euer any died afore I may mene any suche
thinge and to this present hower I protest afor God (who shal iuge
my trueth) whatsoeuer malice shal deuis) that I neuer practisd
counciled nor cosented to any thinge that migth be preiudicial
to your parson any way or daungerous to the state by any
mene and therfor I humbly beseche your maiestie to let
me answer afore your selfe and not suffer me to trust your
counselors, yea and that afore I go to the tower (if it
be possible) if not afor I be further codemned: howbeit I
trust assuredly your highnes wyl giue me leue to do it afore
I go for that thus shamfully I may not be cried out on as now I shal
be yea and without cause let cosciens moue your highnes to
take some bettar way with me tha to make me be condemned
in al mens sigth afor my desert knowen. Also I most humbly
beseche your highnes to pardon this my boldnes wiche
innocecy procures me to do together with hope of your natural
kindnis wiche I trust wyl not se me cast away without desert
Wiche what it is I wold desier no more of God but that you
truly knewe. Wiche thinge I thinke and beleue you shal
neuer by report knowe vnles by your selfe you hire. I haue
harde in my time of many cast away for want of cominge
to the presence of ther prince and in late days I harde my
lorde of Somerset say that if his brother had bine suffered
to speke with him he had neuer suffered but the
perswasions wer made to him so gret that he was brogth
in belefe that he coulde not liue safely if the admiral liued
and that made him giue his consent to his dethe thogth
thes parsons ar not to be copared to your maiestie yet I
pray god the like euil perswatios perswade not one sistar agenst
the other and al for that the haue harne false report and
not harkene to the

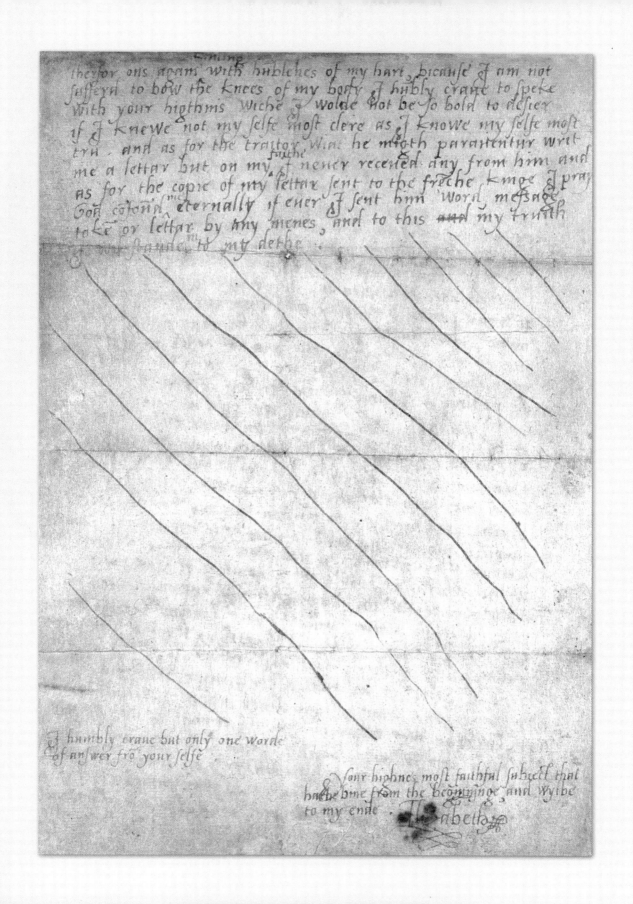

Endinge

therfor ons again with humbelnes of my hart, because I am not
suffernd to bow the knees of my body I humbly crave to speke
with your highnis Wiche I wolde not be so bold to desier
if I knewe not my selfe most clere as I knowe my selfe most
tru. and as for the traitor Wiat he micht parauentur writ
me a lettar but on my faithe I neuer receued any from him and
as for the copie of my lettar sent to the freche kinge I pray
God cofonnd me eternally if euer I sent him Word, message
toke or lettar by any menes, and to this and my truth
I will stande in my dethe.

I humbly crane but only one worde
of answer fro your selfe

Your highnes most faithful subiect that
hathe bine from the begninge and wylbe
to my ende. Elizabeth

39

10

Drake announces the English victory over the Spanish Armada

Scrawled in the flush of victory, this triumphant letter from Sir Francis Drake to his sovereign, Elizabeth I, announces the victory of the English fleet over the Spanish Armada in 1588, and marks a key moment in Britain's rise to global maritime dominance.

The nation was now safe, for the Spanish fleet had been driven "so farre to the northewards, as they could neither recover England nor Scotland". Drake's haste to get news of the victory to his queen was understandable. Elizabeth risked losing her life if the Spanish had won the battle and marched on London, and she must have been anxious indeed as she waited for letters which were days out of date by the time they arrived. Yet Drake's letter was also profoundly self-interested; he notes that "The absence of my Lord Admirall has

emboldened me to putt my penne to the paper." By ensuring that he was the one to deliver the welcome message, rather than the overall commander, Lord Howard, Drake was aiming to secure the rewards the messenger might receive.

Drake was a remarkable figure, a talented mariner and a daring adventurer with an eye for self-promotion. He was also a firm favourite with Elizabeth, not least for the amount she had earned from his adventures – during his successful circumnavigation of the globe in 1577–80 he had captured

OPPOSITE Portrait of Francis Drake, by Nicholas Hilliard, painted in 1581 after his successful circumnavigation.

RIGHT Drake made this water-stained copy of his letter to Queen Elizabeth and sent it to Sir Francis Walsingham. The first line, "The absence of my Lord Admirall, most gratious Soverayne hath enboldened me to putt my penne to the paper", suggests that Drake wants to be seen to be the first man to deliver the good news. Drake's sign-off at the end that he has written it "abord your Majestie's verie good ship the Reveng this 8th of August 1588", betrays the haste with which the letter was written and the script degenerates into a scrawl.

the treasure ship *Cacafuego* off Ecuador, complete with a cargo that included 80 pounds of gold and 25 tons of silver. That Drake had the formal permission of Elizabeth for his venture didn't mean a thing to the Spanish who considered him a savage pirate.

To the pious Philip II the very existence of Protestant England was an abomination he was determined to snuff out. His resolve was stiffened when Elizabeth made a treaty with the Dutch rebels in 1585, pledging them aid to throw off the Spanish yoke, and by the execution of her Catholic cousin, Mary "Queen of Scots". In 1587 she despatched Drake on a pre-emptive raid against the main Spanish naval base at Cádiz. This sank 28 Spanish vessels, sent large quantities of supplies up in smoke, and prompted an enraged Philip to push forward his preparations to take revenge against Drake – *El Draque* ("the dragon").

By April 1588 the 129-strong *Grande y Felicisima Armada* (Great and Most Fortunate Fleet) was assembled at Corunna on the northwest tip of Spain. Commanding it was the Duke of Medina Sidonia, more bureaucrat than sea dog, and a replacement for the more experienced Admiral Santa Cruz who had died of typhus two months earlier.

The plan was simple – to push through the English Channel and link up with an invasion force being assembled by the Duke of Parma in the Netherlands. The Armada, having bested the English fleet, would escort Parma's army, loaded on flat-bottomed barges, which would then disembark in Kent and march on London. The Armada suffered early losses in a storm but arrived off Plymouth, base of the English fleet, with Drake's ships apparently at their mercy. The English were trapped in harbour by wind and tide. This is why, when news of the Armada's sighting was said to have reached Drake during a game of bowls along the seafront,

he insisted on completing the game before boarding his ship. He knew it would be hours before he could get to sea.

Medina Sidonia thought about attacking the English in their port but decided that Philip's instructions must be obeyed to the letter. He set off up the Channel to rendezvous with the army. The English followed and attacked several times but could not defeat the Armada. After only a few losses, Medina Sidonia's fleet finally reached Calais on 5 August, but Parma could not load his troops onto their barges quickly enough to launch the invasion. The English commanders were almost out of options and so resorted to a desperate gamble. In the middle of the night of 7/8 August, eight vessels were packed with rags, old timber and tar, set alight and steered towards the Spanish fleet.

The fire ships were blown inexorably into the harbour and, amid chaotic scenes as the Spanish vessels manoeuvred to avoid the blazing hulks, Medina Sidonia's fleet surged out of the safety of harbour in a disordered mass. At dawn the English pounced on the scattered Armada, blasting the ships at close range. Only a few ships were captured or driven ashore, but the rest fled out into the North Sea, far away from the Duke of Parma's invasion force.

Retracing their course against the prevailing wind was impossible, so the Spanish Armada limped back home via a circuitous route around Scotland and Ireland, losing further ships to storm and shipwreck; of the 129 vessels which had left Corunna, at least 50 failed to return. English losses in contrast were minimal. Drake became the subject of adulation at home. His glorious defeat of the Armada – somehow Howard became forgotten in the popular mythology – established him as the saviour of England and his monarch as "Gloriana", the embodiment of English greatness.

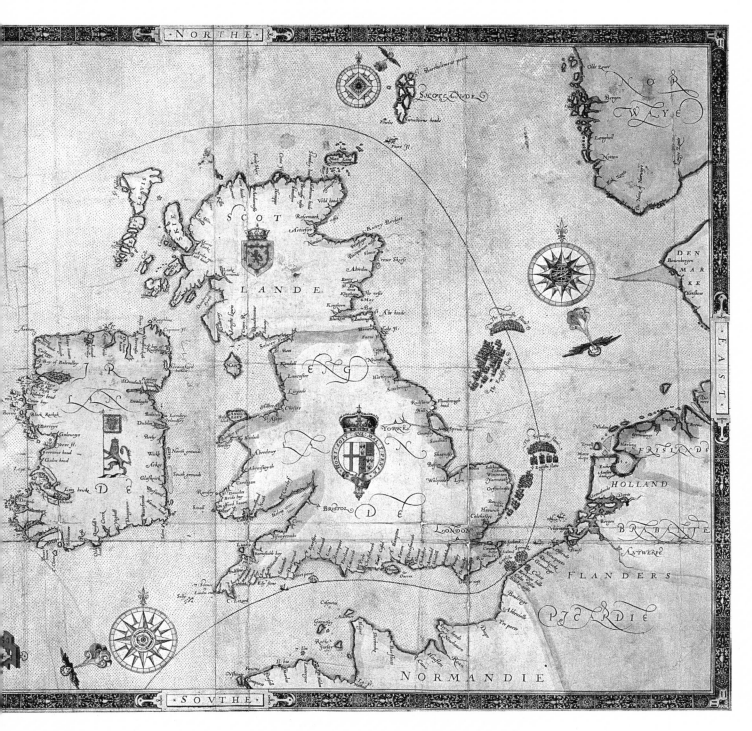

ABOVE Map showing the route of the Spanish Armada through the English Channel, and then, following its defeat, into the North Sea, around northern Scotland, and into the Atlantic Ocean.

FOLLOWING PAGES Theatrical interpretation of the English fire ship attack on the Spanish ships in the Calais Roads, which turned the course of the battle. Fire ships struck terror into the hearts of any enemy. Sailors were horrified by the threat these vessels presented, packed as they were with combustible materials.

11

Guy Fawkes' Confession

The signature at the bottom right – "Guido Fawkes" – is a poorly written scrawl. Fawkes's confession shows the physical and mental effects of days of torture, which forced him to spill out the names of the confederates with whom he had plotted to blow up King James I at the opening of Parliament on 5 November 1605. Fawkes confesses to two secret meetings with the other conspirators one in central London and one in Enfield Chase.

Uncovering the identity of the conspirators was a matter of the utmost urgency for a king who was well aware that sectarian divisions between Protestant and Catholic could tear his realm apart. So James signed a warrant allowing the use of the "the gentler tortours" and the agonizing caress of the rack soon elicited the desired intelligence.

The Gunpowder Plot was born out of the frustrations of English Catholics. They had hoped that Elizabeth I, who had failed to name an heir, might be succeeded by a monarch sympathetic to them. When the crown fell in the end to her cousin, the Protestant James VI of Scotland, Catholic hotheads launched a series of abortive plots. The result was a severe tightening of measures aimed at recusants – Catholics who refused to attend Church of England services. Malcontents began to plot once more, convinced that there was no hope of toleration from King James.

Although Fawkes played a central role in the plot, he was not its original instigator. In the swirl of radical Catholic discontent, the conspiracy crystallized around Robert Catesby, a young nobleman who had fallen out of grace for his participation in the Earl of Essex's rebellion against Elizabeth I in 1601. He met Fawkes in 1603, when both formed part of a mission that travelled to plead (in vain) with Philip III of Spain for assistance in launching an invasion to restore Catholicism to England.

In April the next year Catesby called Fawkes over from Flanders, where he had been serving with the Spanish army. Then, to a small party of conspirators gathered at the Duck and Drake tavern off the Strand, he announced his shocking plan. They would assassinate King James at the opening of Parliament by blowing up a large charge of gunpowder beneath the House of Lords and replace him with his 9-year-old daughter Elizabeth. The confession document refers to their designs on the princess with the

words: "we resolved to serve our turn with the Lady Elizabeth".

As the plot developed, more and more conspirators were let in on the secret. In March they managed to lease a cellar right beneath the House of Lords and the plot began to take its final shape. Fawkes, who was a soldier and familiar with explosives,

topher
it

John
Wright

Thomas
Percy

Guido
Fawkes

Robert
Catesby

Thomas
Winter

arranged for barrels of gunpowder to be deposited in the cellar concealed beneath piles of wood and iron bars.

The opening of Parliament had been put back to 5 November and this delay and the ever-widening circle who knew about the plot proved its undoing. On 26 October a letter was delivered to Lord Mounteagle, a Catholic peer, warning him to stay away from the opening. Six days later the letter had reached the court and royal spies began trying to decipher its meaning.

On the evening of 4 November, Fawkes was discovered by the Lord Chamberlain, the Earl of Suffolk, lurking in the cellar. He managed to bluff it out, but when another search party

ABOVE A 1606 engraving shows the Gunpowder Plot Conspirators. Guy (Guido) Fawkes is shown third from the right next to Robert Catesby, the ringleader.

Towne on the monday night following and Confesseth also that the said Percy, this Examinate, Robert Catesby, Thomas Wintour, John and Xpofer Wright mett at the fore named howse on the backside of St Clements Inn on sonday night last.

He further saith, that the widnesday before his apprehension he went forthe of the Towne to a howse in Enfield Chase on this side of Theobalds where Wally doth Ly, and thither came Robert Catesby, Graunt and Thomas Wintour, where he stayed untill sonday night following.

He Confesseth also that there was speech emongst them to drawe Sr Walter Raweley to take part wth them, being one that might stand them in good sted; us others of the sort were named

Taken before us and subscribed by the examinate before us

Edw Coke   J Waad
Edward Forsett

Guy Fawkes's signature is barely legible at the bottom right in this, his third confession of 9 November. He confessed after being subjected to considerable torture, which caused him to reveal the names of some of his fellow conspirators: in the fourth line of the second paragraph he names Catesby, Grant and Thomas Wintour. In the final section Fawkes implicates Sir Walter Raleigh, who was already held in the Tower and probably not involved in the Gunpowder plot at all.

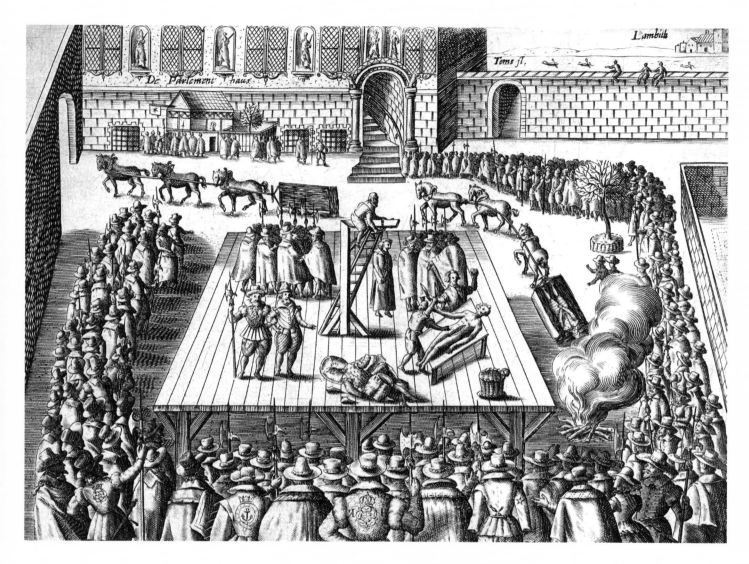

The following labels appear within the illustration:

De Parlement Thaus

Tems fl.

Lambith

returned just after midnight, they uncovered the barrels of gunpowder and found Fawkes still there in possession of a slow fuse to set off the explosion.

Fawkes resisted torture for several days, insisting his name was John Johnston. He admitted he had intended to kill the king, but claimed to have acted alone. It took torture to make him confess. Most of the Gunpowder plotters had by then fled to Holbech House in Staffordshire, where a posse led by the Sheriff of Worcester caught up with them. In the firefight that followed Catesby and several of the others died; the survivors were dragged back to London, tortured and then tried alongside Guy Fawkes in January 1606.

The result was never in doubt. Eight of the plotters suffered the agonizing death of hanging, drawing and quartering (though Fawkes broke his neck on the scaffold, and escaped the further pain of being dismembered whilst alive). Further severe penalties were announced against recusants, including the forced swearing of a strengthened Oath of Allegiance to the Crown. As he scrawled out his confession, his brutalized limbs burning with pain, Guy Fawkes must have known he was signing the death sentence of hopes for an early restoration of a Catholic monarchy.

ABOVE The public execution of Guy Fawkes and his associates on 31 January 1606. The illustration shows them being hanged, drawn and quartered. Even those who had died in the shoot-out at Holbech did not escape; the bodies of Thomas Percy and Robert Catesby were disinterred and their heads displayed on spikes outside Parliament.

Shakespeare's *King Lear* folio

It is a remarkable moment in the history of English literature: this 1608 edition of *King Lear* is the first time a play has been printed with a clear attribution by name to William Shakespeare, the nation's greatest dramatist. Having begun his illustrious career as a lowly provincial actor and aspirant playwright two decades earlier, Shakespeare wrote three dozen plays that propelled him to lasting worldwide fame. His work soon became Britain's most enduring cultural export.

Surprisingly little is known about Shakespeare's early life; even his date of birth is unknown. It is usually calculated by working back from his baptism three days later — to get to 23 April 1564. Married at 18, young William did not follow his father into the family glove business. Instead, by 1592 he was in London putting on plays that he had written. His first review was not a favourable one; the pamphleteer Robert Greene referred to Shakespeare as "an upstart crow".

Elizabethan London was a vibrant, rapidly changing city. Its population grew quickly from around 50,000 in 1500 to four times that number a century later. To meet the demand for entertainment, new pleasure gardens and theatres sprang up. Playwrights such as Christopher Marlowe transformed the predominantly religious drama of preceding centuries into works that were secular, nationalistic and exciting.

ABOVE Shakespeare's Globe Theatre, from Visscher's panoramic engraving of London made in 1616.

OPPOSITE The "Pide Bull" Quarto of *King Lear*, named after the location of Nathaniel Butter's bookshop near St Paul's, is the first printed attribution of a play to Shakespeare. The text has 285 lines that do not appear in the First Folio edition of 1623. It shows signs of being put together in haste and there are many misreadings.

M. William Shak-speare:

HIS
True Chronicle Historie of the life and
death of King L E A R and his three
Daughters.

With the vnfortunate life of Edgar, *sonne*
and heire to the Earle of Gloster, and his
sullen and assumed humor of
T O M of Bedlam :

As it was played before the Kings Maiestie at Whitehall vpon
S. Stephans *night in Christmas Hollidayes.*

By his Maiesties seruants playing vsually at the Gloabe
on the Bancke-side.

LONDON,
Printed for *Nathaniel Butter,* and are to be sold at his shop in *Pauls*
Church-yard at the signe of the Pide Bull neere
S^t. *Austins* Gate. 1608.

Marlowe in particular pioneered a new form of dramatic language, using blank verse to lend immediacy and flexibility to his dialogue. Groups of professional actors formed around the theatres, many of them owned or managed by the dramatists who wrote the plays they performed.

Shakespeare threw himself enthusiastically into this buzzing community. He served his apprenticeship by writing history plays. The genre had first appeared in the 1530s (with John Bale's *Kynge Johan*). It had obvious appeal in allowing writers to curry favour with the Queen. In his work Shakespeare flattered her royal ancestors such as Henry IV, Henry V, Henry VI and Richard II, but damned Richard III, the Yorkist, whose defeat by Elizabeth's grandfather Henry VII put her Tudor dynasty on the throne. Shakespeare's company, called the Lord Chamberlain's Men from 1594, became the most popular theatrical group in London.

As his stature increased, his style became more assured. He scoured classical writers and medieval chronicles for gripping stories. His refined blank verse and linguistic innovation reached a pitch of perfection. By coining hundreds of new words and offering his audiences a penetrating insight in to the human condition, he created drama of rare power.

In 1603 Shakespeare faced a potentially tricky political situation. Elizabeth I died and her Scottish cousin became King James I. Shakespeare thought it prudent to turn to fresh subjects, which he hoped would please the new monarch. *Macbeth* features a Scottish usurper who meets a grizzly end, a theme designed to appeal to King James. *King Lear*, written around 1605, looks back to the distant past, when Britain was ruled over by a single king, who tragically descends into madness after giving up his power. The play had its first performance before King James on 26 December 1606. It was a success and Shakespeare was soon a royal favourite. Shortly after James's accession, his acting company had been given the right to call themselves the "King's Men".

Shakespeare's artistic output tailed off in his later years, and his choice of subjects mellowed. Stark tragedies like *Hamlet* were replaced by tragicomedies such as *The Tempest* and the *The Winter's Tale*. His reputation as one of the greatest dramatists of all time was secured after his death in 1616 when his friends produced an edition of 36 of his plays. It is now known as the First Folio, and half of the works in it had never before appeared in print. Had they not been published, these masterpieces might have been lost forever.

As the centuries passed, Shakespeare's fame grew. His plays were studied, analyzed and canonized as the centrepiece of English literature. In the Victorian era in particular they were seen as proof of British superiority. In 1841 the critic Thomas Carlyle referred to Shakespeare as a "real, marketable, tangibly useful possession" in uniting Britain's English-speaking empire. Shakespeare's plays have been translated into dozens of languages, ranging from Russian and Urdu to the Klingon language of the science-fiction series *StarTrek*.

Those who read the 1608 printing of *King Lear*, or watched its first staging two years earlier, may have enjoyed the performance, but they cannot have dreamt its author's fame would last so long.

RIGHT Scottish artist William Dyce's 1851 painting powerfully portrays the scene in Act 3 of King Lear when the Fool and Lear, by now utterly mad, face the full fury of the storm. Lear rages: "Blow, winds, and crack your cheeks! Rage! Blow! You cataracts and hurricanoes, spout. 'Till you have drench'd our steeples, drown'd the cocks."

13

The Death Warrant of Charles I

The 59 signatures on the death warrant of King Charles I mark one of the most traumatic episodes in British history. This formal order to execute the king was drawn up on 27 January 1649 after the conclusion of a short trial that found him guilty of High Treason. "Whereas Charles Steuart Kinge of England is and standeth attaynted and condemned of High Treason", the warrant reads, he is ordered to be put to death "by the severinge of his head from his body". Three days later he was executed at Whitehall Palace. As the headsman's axe swung down, England's monarchy was terminated. It was the bloody baptism of a period of republican rule – the only one in British history – under Oliver Cromwell: his signature is the third one down the first column on the warrant.

Strongminded and with a strong belief in the supremacy of the royal will, Charles was in many ways the author of his own misfortunes. Chronically short of money, he twisted and turned in an effort to avoid seeking parliamentary sanction to raise taxation. He had to resort to devices such as Ship Money, a levy traditionally imposed only on coastal settlements in time of war. His extension of the tax inland and in peacetime in 1634 caused bitter resentment.

Finally, in 1640 Charles recalled Parliament, demanding that it vote him extra funds. Sensing his weakness, it refused. The two sides tussled, with radicals on Parliament's side becoming more strident and attracting new followers, until finally Civil War broke out in 1642. The advantage swung between the Royalists and the forces of Parliament. The latter eventually prevailed, aided by their holding of the more populated areas around London and the better quality of Parliament's troops (such as the New Model Army, established in early 1645).

Charles fell into Parliament's hands in January 1647, but he continued to manoeuvre. He signed a secret agreement with the Scots in December, agreeing to replace Anglicanism with a form of Presbyterianism favoured in Scotland, and this ignited a second Civil War. Royal hopes were dashed when a joint Royalist and Scottish force was defeated at Preston in August 1648. Moderates in Parliament still favoured continued negotiations with the captive King, but the army's patience, and in particular that of Cromwell, its commander, was exhausted. He ordered a purge of those MPs still inclined to treat with Charles and the "Rump Parliament" which remained duly voted on 6 January 1649 to put the King on trial.

The High Court of Justice which assembled two weeks later had a novel task. How could they legally try the king, the ultimate source of legal authority? Charles sought to exploit this weakness, questioning the court's jurisdiction and proclaiming that "a King cannot be tried by any superior jurisdiction

on earth". Parliament's legal commissioners dismissed his challenges, took evidence from a wide array of witnesses (including a ferryman and a shoemaker) to the effect that the King had fomented war against his subjects, and pronounced him guilty.

Twenty-eight signatures were initially appended to the document finding him guilty of "High Treason and other high Crymes" and condemning him to die. When the officers named to carry out the warrant refused to do so, their names were scratched out and others added. Parliament did not want any of the 28 to have second thoughts, so did not have a new warrant drawn up. For good measure, 31 more commissioners were prevailed upon to sign.

At around 2 p.m. on 30 January, Charles was led to a scaffold erected outside the Banqueting House at Whitehall Palace. He wore two heavy shirts against the winter's cold to avoid shivering, which might be mistaken for fear. He tried to make a speech to the crowd of notables, soldiers and foreign ambassadors, but few could hear his words of self-justification. Then he laid his head on the block, made a signal to the executioner and assuring himself: "I go from a corruptible to an incorruptible crown", he met his fate.

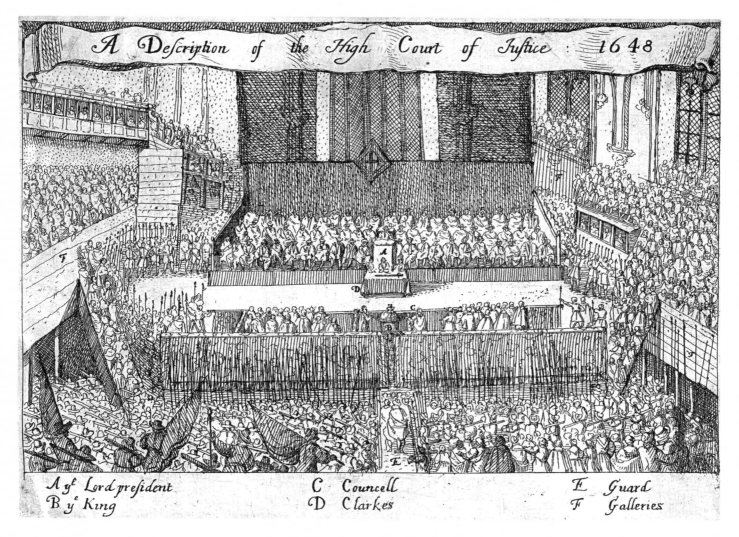

A Description of the High Court of Justice : 1648

A yᵉ Lord president   C Councell   E Guard
B yᵉ King   D Clarkes   F Galleries

The English Republic which assumed power after Charles's death was short-lived. It failed to bridge the gap between the increasing demands of radicals and those who wanted a return to the old ways of doing things. Even the device of appointing Oliver Cromwell as a quasi-monarchical Lord Protector failed when his son Richard proved unequal to the task after his father's death.

In 1660, the monarchy was restored, to almost universal relief. Charles II proved magnanimous, approving an amnesty for all those who had supported the Republic. His clemency, though, had limits. The pursuit of the regicides was merciless. Those not already in custody were hunted down and arrested, some smuggled back from European refuges. In the end nine suffered the agonizing death of hanging, drawing and quartering and most of the rest had their death sentences commuted to life imprisonment. Even the dead were not spared: Oliver Cromwell's corpse was exhumed, and its head hacked off and displayed on a pike, in a ghastly parody of the punishment inflicted on the king.

The death warrant served as a warning for the future; to Parliament that operating outside constitutionally accepted limits could end in bloodshed; and to future monarchs that taking the consent of the people for granted could cost them their head.

OPPOSITE The bronze-cast statue of Charles I which stands in Trafalgar Square looking down Whitehall has had a turbulent history. Cast in 1633 and commissioned by Richard Weston, 1st Earl of Portland, it was seized when England became a republic. Charles II eventually purchased it and commissioned the ornate pedestal on which it stands.

ABOVE An engraving of the trial of Charles I. The King was brought to trial in Westminster Hall. He sits in the centre opposite the Lord President. It was important that the trial was held in public, and the illustration shows the wooden partition that separated the court proceedings from the crowd.

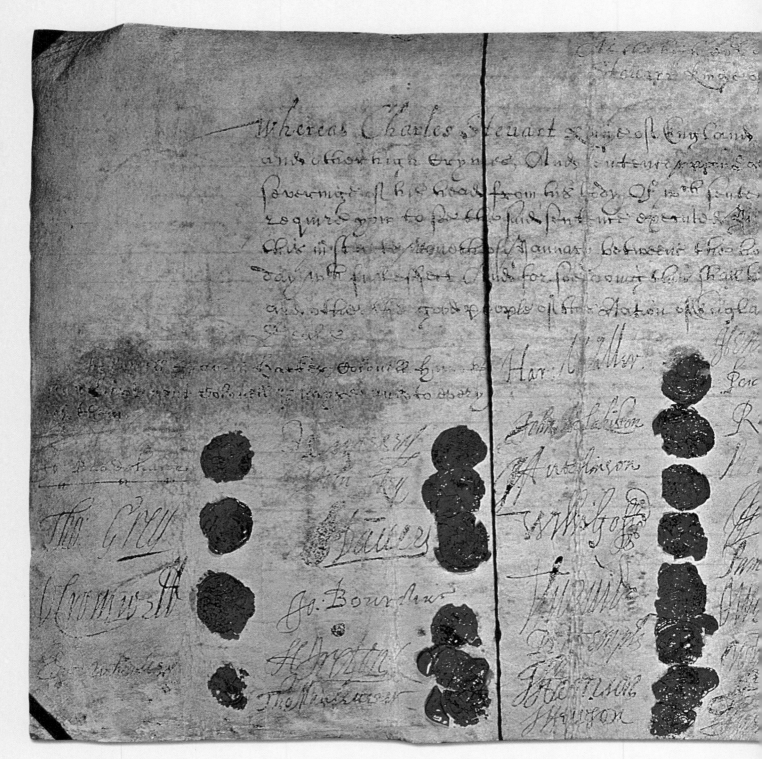

Charles I's Death Warrant is signed by 59 commissioners; the sixth column is more crowded, as it became clear more would sign than expected. In the third line the means of the king's execution is specified: he is to be beheaded. There are a number of erasures where the warrant had to be changed. Just above the first row of signatures, the names of Colonels Hacker and Phayre, the officers charged with carrying out the warrant, have been substituted for other names, presumably those of the officers who refused to implement it.

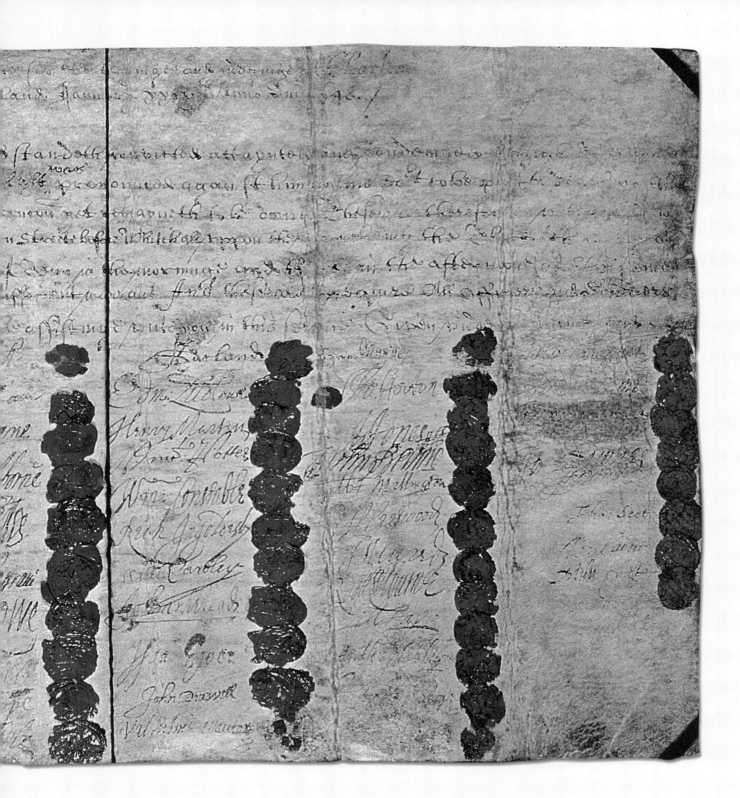

14

Wren's Blueprint for St Paul's Dome

It is a blueprint for a phoenix. Samuel Gribelin's 1702 engraving shows almost the final version of Christopher Wren's plan for a new dome for St Paul's. This is Wren's proposal for the crowning top half of London's magnificent new cathedral. The previous building had been reduced to ashes by London's Great Fire of 1666. Wren shows spectacular boldness with his soaring dome and cupola – unparalleled in British architectural history. He made only a few changes to this design before the cathedral was completed in 1715. No wonder it has become a national icon.

The journey from Wren's fertile mind to the breathtaking power of the final building was not an easy one. The son of a dean and the nephew of a bishop, he had strong connections to the Church. But the young Wren's quicksilver mind drew him in all sorts of directions – including the invention of a "diplograph", a pen that could write in duplicate – until he finally seemed to have settled on observing the heavens. He became Professor of Astronomy at Gresham College in 1657.

Even so, Wren continued to dabble; his fascination with mathematics drew him to the pleasing linearity of architecture. He was intrigued by the way it could manipulate weight to make stone masses seem elegant and light, and in 1663 he submitted a design for the new Sheldonian Theatre at Oxford. Soon after, he became involved in the discussions about the remodelling of Old St Paul's cathedral, a Gothic monolith which fashionable circles in London agreed did not suit the intellectual vigour of the age.

In August 1666, his proposal, which involved the superimposition of a dome on the existing structure, was accepted. Wren's delight was short-lived: just a month later St Paul's, in common with much of the city of London, perished in the Great Fire, and the project had to be deferred. Nonetheless, London's ruin presented Wren – and other would-be urban planners such as the diarist John Evelyn – with an extraordinary opportunity to remodel, not just St Paul's, but the entire city.

Within a week of the fire, Wren had presented his plans for a London reshaped, with spacious octagonal plazas and 90-foot//27-metre wide boulevards radiating like spokes. Wren's imagination, though, outran the more limited ambitions of those tasked with the reconstruction, and his vision of wide thoroughfares to replace the capital's squalid medieval slums never came to pass. But this disappointment brought his focus back to St Paul's, a task made immeasurably easier in March 1669, when he was appointed Surveyor General – in effect, the royal architect.

Soon after, Wren presented his first plan for a new church to a commission of Anglican divines. His drawings, based on the Temple of Peace in Rome, baffled the clerics, who thought his adaption of a pagan building deviated worryingly from the brooding Gothic certainties of the old St Paul's. Wren remained devoted to the classical style of the Renaissance, but his second try, a Greek cross design with equal arms, went down just as badly: it smacked too much of Catholicism for the Anglican grandees. It was turned down, as was a modified version with a long nave added. Then, in 1675, a new committee was set up, including privy councillors and London city officials, as well as clergy. Faced with all their competing views of how the new church should be, Wren presented the "Warrant Design". It passed muster by virtue of not being too strongly identified with any particular architectural style. One

OPPOSITE A 1711 portrait of Sir Christopher Wren by Godfrey Kneller. Wren was 79 at the time this portrait was made. He holds a pair of dividers and is positioned beside the plan of St Paul's Cathedral.

ABOVE LEFT *St Paul's Survives* by Herbert Mason. The Dome of St Paul's cathedral stands defiant amidst the searchlights and smoke during the raid on 29/30 December 1940 at the height of the London Blitz. This profoundly symbolic image of courage and resilience was published in the *Daily Mail* the following day.

ABOVE RIGHT An engraving of "Vision of the City of London, Constructed on the Plan Left by Sir Christopher Wren, drawn under the direction of Mr Godwin", which was published in *The Builder*, on 4 July 1875.

look at it and you'll agree with us: it was a dreadful mishmash.

Fortunately, Wren was granted permission by Charles II to make "some Variations ... as from Time to Time he should see proper", a licence he made full use of as the construction of the church – which finally began in 1673 – crawled on through the reign of four different monarchs. Financing the project proved hard – despite the concession of an additional tax on coal to fund it – and only in 1700 did the dome finally begin to rise. Wren had been fascinated by the dome of the Church of Hagia Sophia in Constantinople and was determined that his church would be just as awe-inspiring. He borrowed the trick of combining an internal and external dome to support the weight and spread it over the transepts that projected from the central nave.

Despite some unpleasantness in the last years of the project, as the commissioners took a closer interest and tried to rein back spending – calculated at a colossal £804,758 by its end – the church was declared complete on Christmas Day 1711. By then, the dome had had a cupola added to bring it to a height of 364 feet (111 metres), and a weight of 65,000 tons, dimensions only surpassed by St Peter's Basilica in Rome. Wren, who also rebuilt 50 other churches destroyed by the Great Fire, had earned his place as Britain's greatest architect by creating the country's most magnicient church. When he died, he was interred in the south aisle, where his grave bears an epitaph that perfectly suits his achievement: *Si Monumentum Requiris, Circumspice* ("If you need a monument, look around").

RIGHT This 1702 print by Samuel Gribelin shows almost the last stage of Wren's design for the cathedral's dome and its supporting structure. The double portico with two towers to either side was based on Italian designs by Bramante. In the end Wren modified these to something more whimsical and topped them all with golden pineapples.

...ndini ab Occidente Descriptio Orthographica.

15

Map of the Battle of Blenheim

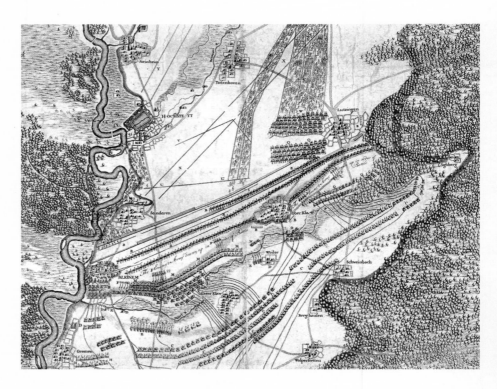

This magnificent map in all its elaborate detail displays the topography around the Bavarian village of Blenheim on the river Danube. The vast size of the canvas gives an appropriate scale to the Battle of Blenheim, one of the greatest victories of the English army. John Churchill, Duke of Marlborough shattered a numerically Franco-Bavarian force there on 13 August 1704. The victory secured not only his reputation as a military genius but identified the country that would soon be Great Britain – the unitary state of England, Wales and Scotland – as a land power to be reckoned with.

The battle had its origin in the death in 1700 of Charles II, the invalid king of Spain. His bequest of the Spanish throne and its land in the Netherlands to Philip, Duke of Anjou, the grandson of Louis XIV of France, ignited a European conflict. England, Austria and the Dutch Republic feared the vast increase in France's power represented by its acquisition of Spain's resources and colonial empire. And they could not accept the prospect of France and Spain being one day united under a single crown.

The Grand Alliance was formed in 1701 but had limited success in the first years of what became known as the Spanish War of Succession. But in John Churchill, the Earl (and later, Duke) of Marlborough, they found a general to match the best the French could field. Having gained experience in the Nine Years War against France in the 1690s, he was put in command of the English, Dutch and German armies. In the spring of 1704 he saw that a large Franco-Bavarian army despatched to Austria was close to knocking an important ally out of the war. Without informing his

Dutch allies – who worried about being left defenceless – he marched over 250 miles (400 kilometres) from the Netherlands down to the river Danube. His careful attention to logistics ensured that his 40,000 men arrived in considerably better shape than the French, whose extended supply lines had reduced them to locust-like plundering of local farmers.

OPPOSITE AND ABOVE The map is entitled "A plan of the Famous Victory at Bleinem, obtained by his Grace the Duke of Marlborough over the Elector of Bavaria, and the Marechals Tallard and Marcin, the 13th August, 1704" and shows the forests, towns and villages on which the battle of Blenheim was fought. The French and Bavarian forces are drawn at the top of the map, a dense cluster protecting the village of Blenheim. A series of lines labelled with letters describes the course of the battle. A marks the Allies' advance from their overnight camp, M and W their line after crossing the Nebel on pontoons, R the point the cavalry reached after pushing back the French, and U where the French briefly rallied before retreating from the battlefield.

For two months Marlborough and his ally Prince Eugene of Savoy manoeuvred to protect the Austrian capital Vienna. Finally, on 12 August the French under Marshals Tallard and Marsin and the Elector of Bavaria drew up their forces by the Danube at Blenheim. Their forces are near the top of the map – three lines snaking across from the hills on the right to Blenheim on the Danube at the left. Just below, Marlborough's army has moved up to face them. It has advanced from the bottom of the map. The image above shows an enlargement of the area where the battle took place. By midday the long lines of opposing infantry and cavalry

faced each other across the tiny River Nebel. It flows from right to left into the Danube with marshland (gently shaded) on either side of it.

The French commanders were confident. Their position was secure, they had superiority in numbers (56,000 against the Allied 52,000) and if Marlborough wanted to dislodge them he would have to attack across boggy terrain. The massed ranks of pikes and artillery at the top of the map show how strongly placed his enemy was.

Yet they had fatally underestimated Marlborough. He himself took a position with some of his best troops in the centre,

determined to split his enemy in two. He ordered his commanders to attack at both ends of the enemy's line while he held off. There was a fierce struggle for Blenheim village and the French poured in reinforcements from their centre. As a result, most of their elite troops were penned in there while units at the other end of the line were under pressure from Prince Eugene. Marlborough seized the moment to thrust through the weakened centre and put them all to flight.

In the flush of victory, Marlborough scribbled a hurried note to his wife, Sara: "I have no time to say more but to beg you will

give my duty to the Queen, and let her know her army has had a glorious victory." Yet success at Blenheim did not win the war. Nor did subsequent victories at Ramillies (1705), Oudenaarde (1708) or Malplaquet (1709). Each time he defeated his French adversaries, they raised fresh armies, hydra-like. In the end, weary of fighting, the English began secret talks aimed at securing a peace.

The 1712 Treaty of Utrecht saw little territory change hands: the Dutch received a few fortresses from the Spanish Netherlands to act as a barrier, the French ceded a few more to the Habsburgs.

England gained Minorca and Gibraltar from Spain. These were minor changes, but the conflict was a major stepping-stone on what would soon be Britain's journey to global domination.

England had won a war in Europe, and Marlborough's victory at Blenheim had made it possible. A grateful nation granted him land at Woodstock near Oxford on which he built a palace he named after his most glorious achievement. The landscape there is very different to that depicted on this battlefield map, but both are monuments to one of England's most celebrated military victories.

ABOVE LEFT The Great Court and north front of Blenheim Palace near Oxford. Work began on the Palace in 1705 and was completed in 1733, when the chapel was consecrated. Winston Churchill was born there on 30 November 1874.

ABOVE Marlborough grips his sword in one hand and his marshal's baton in the other in this portrait by Sir Godfrey Kneller.

FOLLOWING PAGES *The Battle of Blenheim, 13 August 1704,* oil on canvas by John Wootton, depicts the final phase of the battle. The Duke of Marlborough is shown bottom right with his sword in hand, surrounded by his staff. Behind him, the defeated French Marshal Tallard, is being driven off the battlefield in Marlborough's coach.

16

Arkwright's Spinning Frame Specification

The carefully drawn lines on Richard Arkwright's patent specification for his improved spinning frame mark an important stage in Britain's burgeoning cotton industry. It's not only a game-changing invention in itself, but is also a landmark in the development of the factory system that drove production to such a pitch that it was named "the Industrial Revolution".

Britain in the 1760s was a country alight with the spirit of discovery. Its coal-fired furnaces produced increasing quantities of iron; the textile industry consumed vast amounts of yarn to feed the improved weaving machines such as John Kay's flying shuttle, invented in 1733. The Revolution was gathering pace and with it the need for new means to transform raw materials into finished goods ever faster and in greater quantities.

More advanced weaving machines had created a new problem: a shortage of yarn to keep them operating. James Hargreaves devised an initial solution in 1764 with his spinning jenny, a frame with multiple spindles, which multiplied the output of the user eight-fold. Yet it was still operated by hand and the yarn it produced tended to be weak.

The unlikely saviour of the British textile industry was Richard Arkwright, the son of a Preston tailor. He began his career as a barber and even after he came into money following a second marriage, he initially spent this windfall on marketing a new method for dying wigs. But by the 1760s Arkwright, living at the centre of the Lancashire cotton industry, saw a chance in a machine that another John Kay, a clockmaker, had worked on with an inventor named Thomas Highs.

This machine, just like Hargreaves', used multiple spindles to pull the cotton fibres through and stretch them, and then give them a strengthening twist with a bobbin. Each roller rotated faster than the one before and they were spaced to do so at slightly different intervals to take account of the increasing speed with which the fibre went through the machine. Having secured investors, Arkwright began the tortuous process of gaining a patent.

Although he managed to do so, the protection granted was for a period of just 14 years. Arkwright did not make himself popular, ruthlessly seeking to exclude competitors from using his spinning frame: other textile magnates enviously craved after its efficiency, which was enhanced by the addition of a water wheel. He came to be seen as a tyrant stifling innovation and progress in industry with his patent. Thomas Carlyle caricatured him as the "bag-cheeked, potbellied, much-enduring, much-inventing barber".

OPPOSITE The mill at Cromford in Derbyshire was at the heart of Arkwright's spinning empire. Opened in 1771, it was the first successful water-power cotton mill and remained in use until 1840, when difficulties with the supply of water forced its closure. It became a bakery, print works and finally a museum.

RIGHT This drawing of Arkwright's spinning frame formed part of the specification for his 1769 patent application. Arkwright carefully labels all the parts, including the vital rollers (I) and the levers with lead weights (N), that differentiated his device from predecessors.

BELOW RIGHT Richard Arkwright seems every inch the self-assured and prosperous businessman in this 1790 portrait by Joseph Wright of Derby.

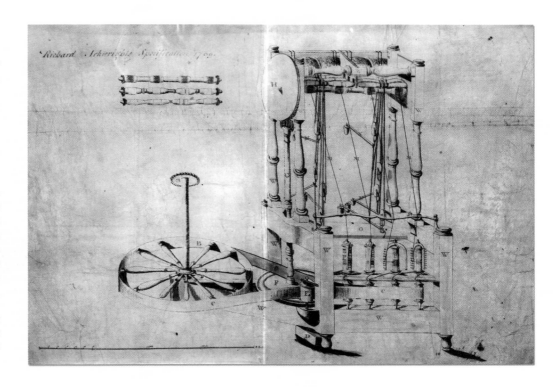

In 1785 a court struck down Arkwright's patents on the grounds the spinning machine was not sufficiently novel, being based on earlier inventions. The court added that its patent specification wasn't clear, and that it was "Not that fair, full, true discovery which the public had a right to demand". It mattered little, for the period during which Arkwright had enjoyed protection enabled him to establish an industrial empire that would be a blueprint for future entrepreneurs.

Arkwright was the Henry Ford of his era. Tight control of production meant his first factory at Cromford was extremely efficient, multiplying the effects of the new looms which it operated. The mill had two 12-hour shifts, with a one-hour overlap in between, and so was almost constantly running. In 1784, one observer remarked that it worked "Night and day or at least 23 of the 24 hours; one hour is allowed for oiling and cleaning." The Cromford Mill was a giant of its time; over seven storeys high and 120 feet (37 metres) long. Its sheer size and efficiency meant traditional operators could not

compete. It accelerated the rush to build rival factories, particularly after Arkwright's patents were overturned.

Remorselessly, Arkwright expanded his empire: in 1777 a new mill was built at Birkacre, near Chorley in Lancashire; in November that year he acquired more land at Lumford and Holme Bank in Derbyshire, near the River Wye; and in 1780 he installed a reciprocating engine at a new mill at Haarlam Mill on the Derwent. It was the first ever to be used in a cotton mill, compensating for inadequate water pressure to power the mill wheels and opening up new areas to Arkwright's enhanced techniques. Weavers flocked to the villages where his mills were situated, attracted by the promise of guaranteed work and a week's holiday a year.

By 1800 Arkwright had factories in Lancashire, Derbyshire, Staffordshire and Scotland. His network of mills employed between 1,800 and 1,900, making it the largest cotton empire of its day. Only Robert Owens' New Lanark (with 1,700 employees) and the mills controlled by the Strutt family

(with 1,600 workers) could approach it. Arkwright had set the course for the future. Although his spinning frame was not itself innovative (as the court found when it removed his patent), the setting in which he operated was. Factories were the future, and Arkwright was their prophet.

Cook's Chart of Botany Bay

This map marks the moment that Europeans first came ashore in eastern Australia and the beginning of the European colonization of the continent. The landfall at Botany Bay on 29 April 1770 also assured Captain James Cook, the commander of the expedition that discovered it, immortality as one of the most famous of all British explorers.

It had been a long voyage, and already full of incident. The *Endeavour*, originally a Whitby collier, had set out in July 1768 with the overt task of observing the Transit of Venus, a rare astronomical phenomenon when the planet crosses the face of the Sun. Cook's crew consisted of 73 officers and sailors, 12 marines, an astronomer, four artists and two naturalists (Joseph Banks and Daniel Solander). He had also brought extensive provisions, including 600 barrels of rum, a mound of sauerkraut to ward off scurvy and a goat to provide milk for the officers.

Having taken the observations at a specially built observatory on Tahiti, discovered just two years before, Cook revealed the true purpose of the voyage. He had been ordered by the Admiralty to sail south in search of the *Terra Australis Incognita* (Unknown Southern Land), a continent which was believed to lie somewhere in the ocean beyond Indonesia. It wasn't quite unknown, as Spanish sailors had grazed its northeast tip in 1606, and the Dutchman Abel Tasman had visited Van Diemen's Land (the future Tasmania) in 1642. Cook's mission, therefore, was to find land and claim it for Britain before any other European power could do so.

With the assistance of a Tahitian named Tupaia, Cook reached New Zealand in October 1769 and mapped virtually its entire coastline. Relations with the Maori whom they encountered soured rapidly after four were killed in a skirmish when the Europeans first came ashore. Enormously important discovery though it was, New Zealand was clearly not large enough to be the fabled southern continent (and Cook in any case had a shrewd idea where Van Diemen's Land lay).

So the *Endeavour* made an uncomfortable two-week crossing of the Tasman Sea, before the appearance of sheerwaters told Cook that land must be near. On 21 April 1770 they sighted Australia (or New Holland as it was then called, in deference to early Dutch explorers), but did not go ashore, instead sailing north in search of a good harbour.

Cook made landfall on 29 April at a sheltered cove with white sands fringed with woods. Several aboriginal men on the shore threw stones and darts to drive the newcomers off, and in return Cook's party shot at them with muskets. They stayed there a week, encountering the local people on several more occasions, but they were unable to communicate (unlike in New Zealand, Tupaia's Polynesian was of little use). Banks and Solander collected a large quantity of samples, after which Cook decided to call the place Botany Bay, and then the *Endeavour* sailed north. Just beyond Botany Bay they sighted Sydney Harbour, which Cook named Port Jackson, where the first British colony would be established in 1788.

The next months were spent surveying the entire east coast of Australia, enlivened by occasional trips ashore to take on fresh water

and other provisions. Disaster struck the expedition on 11 June, when the *Endeavour* ran aground on the Great Barrier Reef and was refloated only with great difficulty after the ship's cannons and tons of supplies were pitched overboard to give her buoyancy.

The ship limped ashore near modern Cooktown. It took almost five weeks for the carpenters to repair the gash in her underbelly, giving ample time for the naturalists to make new observations. These included the first European encounter with a kangaroo, which Cook described as "of a light mouse-colour and the full size of a grey hound". Finally, on 22 August the expedition rounded the northeast tip of Australia and at Possession Island, Cook laid formal claim to all the lands he had surveyed for the British crown.

Cook doubtless failed to mention that he had muscled in on what had previously been a Dutch sphere of influence when he put into Dutch-controlled Batavia in October to prepare for the long voyage home. The *Endeavour* reached Deal on 13 July 1771, after three years away. Although Banks and Solander initially received the lion's share of praise for the new discovery, the Admiralty was well pleased with Cook's work, and within a month promoted him from Lieutenant to Commander. His exploring days were not over. He returned to New Zealand in 1774 and on a third Pacific voyage in 1776–9 he attempted and failed to find the Northwest Passage. He turned south to Hawaii in 1779 and was murdered by native people there. It was a sad end to a spectacular career. But Cook will always be remembered for this landing in Botany Bay when he opened up a whole new continent to European exploration and British imperial ambition.

OPPOSITE John Webber was just 24 when he was selected to be the expedition artist on Cook's third and final voyage of exploration. His watercolours, sketches and subsequent oil paintings of the South Pacific caused a stir in British artistic circles, unused to such exotic imagery. Cook was murdered on Hawaii during the voyage, and in 1780 Webber presented this portrait of him to his widow.

ABOVE The solidly built 100-foot (30-metre) long bark the *Earl of Pembroke* was destined for obscurity as a Whitby coal-ship. But in 1768 the Admiralty bought her for around £2,800. With a shallow draft she was ideal for beaching on unknown shores without conventional harbours and Cook remarked, "a better ship for such service I could never wish for". She was rechristened *Endeavour* and is here shown leaving Whitby Harbour in 1768.

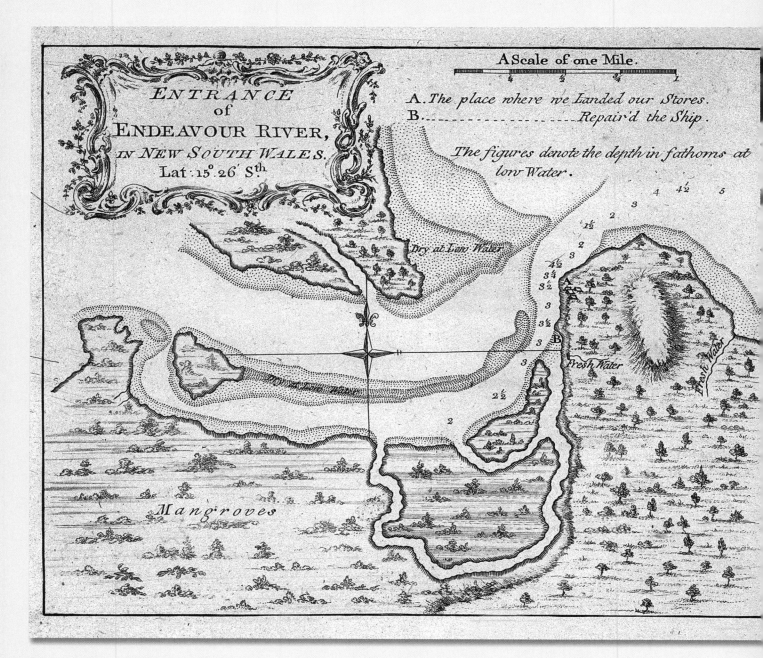

ENTRANCE
of
ENDEAVOUR RIVER,
IN NEW SOUTH WALES.
Lat: 15°. 26' Sth

Dry at Low Water

Fresh Water

Fresh Water

Mangroves

These maps, prepared during Cook's *Endeavour* voyage, were the first of the east coast of Australia. Cook named many topographical features, including some for the crew; the points to either side of the entrance of Botany Bay are named for Solander and Banks, the two expedition naturalists. On the map of Endeavour River, where the ship had to be repaired after hitting the Great Barrier Reef, Cook has marked with letters the place where the ship landed (A) and the spot they beached it (B). They are hard to read but just visible on the east side of the river entrance.

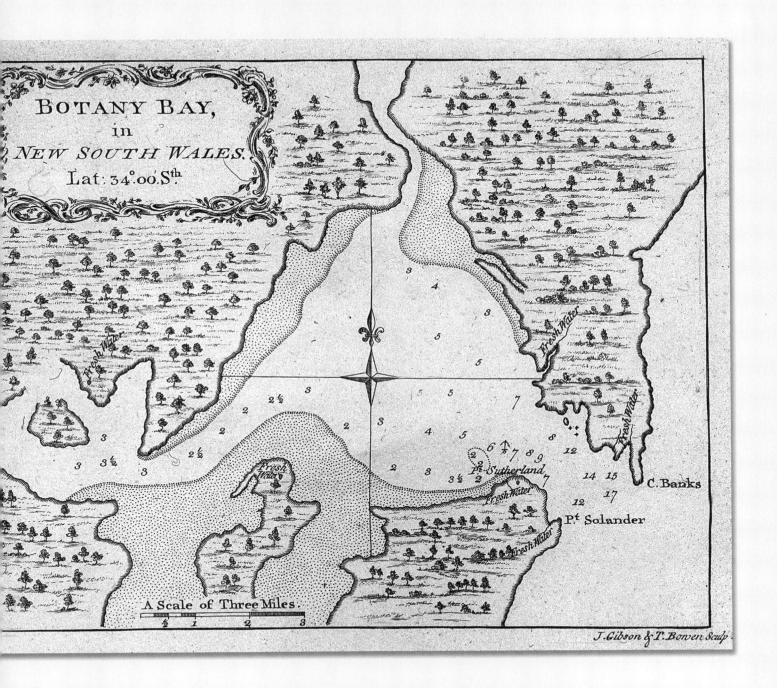

BOTANY BAY,
in
NEW SOUTH WALES.
Lat: 34°.00'.S.th

Fresh Water

Fresh Water

Fresh Water

Fresh Water

3

4

3

5

5

5

5

3

2½

2

2½

2

3

3

3½

2½

3

2

3

2

3

4

5

5

7

6

2

7

8

9

8

12

14   15

17

12

Pt. Sutherland

Fresh Water

Fresh Water

Fresh Water

Fresh Water

C. Banks

Pt. Solander

A Scale of Three Miles.
½   1   2   3

J. Gibson & T. Bowen Sculp.

18

The American Declaration of Independence

The Declaration of Independence is one of the most important documents in American history. And in Britain's too. For though it severed the Thirteen Colonies of British North America from the control of the British crown and set them on the path to independent nationhood, it was born out of the colonists' image of themselves as Britons and appealed to British historical rights and precedents. It also ensured that two entirely separate English-speaking powers would emerge on either side of the Atlantic.

As the thirteen colonies established by Britain in North America in the seventeenth and early eighteenth centuries grew in size and wealth, tensions inevitably arose with the mother country. These centred on issues of trade, taxation and the right to political representation. The colonists argued that, because they had no right to direct representation in the British Parliament, that body should have no right to levy taxes on them. An additional tax on tea in North America in 1767 caused particular outrage. In December 1773 a party of colonial protestors pitched a shipment of tea sent by the East India Company into Boston Harbour.

The Boston Tea Party, as it became known, provoked a severe reaction by the British authorities. The Intolerable Acts, passed to punish the colonists, closed Boston Harbour and placed severe restrictions on the government of the colony of Massachusetts. They led to a crisis in authority and polarized opinion. In September 1774 the anti-British colonists established a First Continental Congress at Philadelphia to direct their response. Matters were spiralling out of control and in April 1775 fighting broke out

between colonial militia and British troops at Lexington and Concord.

Even now there were relatively few who advocated open independence. But as the fighting continued and the British response grew harsher – including the closing of all colonial ports in February 1776 – it became clear that a compromise settlement was unlikely. The publication of Thomas Paine's *Common Sense* in January 1776 helped articulate feelings in favour of independence. He argued that the British government had breached its fundamental duty to protect the lives, freedom and property of American colonists and that dispensing with the British monarchy and establishing an independent democracy was the logical choice.

Individual colonies and districts made their own declaration of independence, and on 11 June the Congressional Congress appointed a committee to draft a general declaration. The five members, including Benjamin Franklin, John Adams and Thomas Jefferson, delegated the task to Jefferson and on 28 June an agreed version was laid before Congress. It took several redrafts and some serious arm-twisting to persuade all the

74

colonies to agree, but on 4 July the declaration came into effect – a date subsequently celebrated as the United States' birthday.

It was a decisive and shocking move. Overthrowing the legal authority of the crown and claiming justification for doing so was almost unprecedented. Yet the declaration of independence did have antecedents and these, ironically, drew from British constitutional history. The barons' imposition of the Magna Carta on King John in 1215, with its clauses defending the individual from arbitrary royal persecution, was cited by the colonists as a touchstone of liberty. And the removal of James II and his replacement by William III in the Glorious Revolution of 1688 offered a clear precedent. The English philosopher John Locke had argued in his *Second Treatise* that James had violated the fundamental compact that subjects make with their sovereign, namely to offer protection. It was not only right, but natural to overthrow him.

The drafters of the American Declaration of Independence drew on this deep-seated sense of a fundamental natural law, more important than the claims of monarchs. In their preamble to the Declaration they state this principle clearly: "We hold these truths to be self-evident, that all men are created equal, that they are endowed by their Creator with certain inalienable rights: that among these are Life, Liberty and the pursuit of Happiness", and that "whenever any Form of Government becomes destructive of these ends, it is the Right of the People to alter or abolish it."

The Declaration crystallized opposition to Britain, forcing moderates to choose sides. It also enabled the American colonists to seek international assistance, most notably an alliance with France. This was crucial in securing their ultimate victory and the recognition by Britain of their independence in 1783. Despite the hiccough of a war between them in 1812, Britain and the United States have generally been firm allies. Their shared

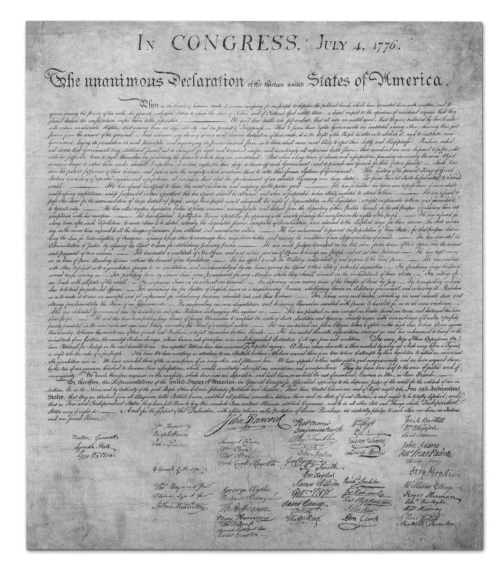

history, and common view of the rights of individuals which dates back over eight centuries, has brought them together far more than the act of rebellion that the Declaration represents has driven them apart.

OPPOSITE Jean Leon Gerome Ferris's 1921 painting *Writing the Declaration of Independence* shows Benjamin Franklin (seated, with spectacles), John Adams (centre) and Thomas Jefferson (right) at work on the first draft. Roger Sherman and Robert R. Livingston, the two other members of the Committee of Five appointed by Congress to draw up the documents, are not shown.

ABOVE The wording of the US Declaration of Independence, as passed by the Continental Congress on 4 July 1776, had been argued over for weeks in an effort to reach a consensus. Among the 56 signatures, the first and most flamboyant is that of John Hancock, a Massachusetts merchant who made his fortune in smuggled tea and was principal supporter of the Boston Tea Party.

FOLLOWING PAGES The Colonial patriots who boarded three British tea ships in Boston Harbour on 16 December 1773 were dressed as Mohawk Indians. Up to 150 men took part in the dumping of the tea, but they remained anonymous for fear of British reprisals.

19

Bligh's Report on the Mutiny on the *Bounty*

The language is terse, almost matter-of-fact, understating the drama of what became the most notorious mutiny in British naval history. No story appeals more to our sense of adventure than the ordeal of Captain William Bligh and the uprising on his ship the *Bounty*. In his report to the Admiralty he downplays his harrowing experience as simply "a voyage of the most extraordinary nature". Yet Bligh suffered a gruelling two-month voyage in the small boat in which he and the loyal members of his crew were cast adrift. His bitterness almost seeps through in the very precise list he includes of those who had betrayed him. Top of the list is the name "Fletcher Christian, Master's mate", the mutineers' ringleader, leaving no doubt as to whom Bligh thought should hang.

Raised in the naval port of Plymouth, Bligh was destined for the sea, and his selection as sailing master for the *Resolution* on Captain Cook's ill-fated third expedition seemed to set the seal on a promising career. But he was disappointed when, seven years later, he was made nursemaid to a cargo of tropical fruit. Even worse, command of his new ship the *Bounty* did not carry the rank of captain and, to cut costs, he would be the sole commissioned officer on board. Worse still, the vessel was to carry no marines, a decision with ultimately disastrous consequences. The *Bounty* was to carry breadfruit, a cheap food crop from Tahiti, to the West Indies where it would be fed to slaves. The vessel had two botanists assigned to its crew, but the space allocated for the 1,000 plants meant that conditions aboard for the other 44 seamen were more than usually cramped.

Bligh was a pretty ruthless disciplinarian. Although he tried to avoid flogging his crew, his rigid enforcement of rules on sanitation was the cause of persistent grumbling. When the *Bounty* finally reached Tahiti in October 1788 after a 10-month voyage, discipline collapsed. While Bligh persuaded the local ruler, Tynah, to donate him the required number of breadfruit trees, his crew slipped into a life of indolence, enjoying the easy pace of life on Tahiti, the abundant food and the local women.

When the men re-embarked on 5 April 1789 – minus the ship's surgeon Huggan, who had died in an alcoholic stupor – it proved impossible to mould them back into an efficient naval crew. Bligh began to lash out, targeting in particular Fletcher Christian, whom he accused of stealing coconuts, and cutting the entire crew's food rations in half. In the claustrophobic conditions on board, resentment turned to hatred. Christian, who had been about to desert aboard a makeshift raft, was instead persuaded by another malcontent to take control of the ship. The pair recruited several other allies and on the night of 28 April seized the *Bounty*'s muskets, arrested Bligh and invited the remainder of the crew to join them.

A dangerous mix of fear, confusion and loyalty ruled the day and half the crew refused to mutiny. Christian could not afford to keep sailors faithful to Bligh aboard, so 18 men, plus Bligh, were set adrift in the ship's launch, provided with five days' food and water and four cutlasses tossed in at the last moment. After a fight with natives on one island, Bligh directed his little boat towards Dutch-controlled Timor, 3,500

miles (5,630 kilometres) from where they had left the *Bounty*. Somehow they made it; Bligh's iron will and determination to get his revenge on Christian saw them through as they eked out their meagre rations through two months' sailing.

By the time Bligh landed back in England in March 1790, the mutineers had split up. Christian had realized it might be easy to track him down and while two-thirds of the mutineers opted to take their chances back on Tahiti, he and nine others went in search of an even more remote haven.

So, when the *Pandora*, despatched by the British Admiralty to track down the mutineers, arrived at Tahiti in March 1791, its crew arrested all the mutineers on the island, but found no trace of Christian. They

were incarcerated in a prison rigged on the ship's deck which became known jokingly as "Pandora's Box". Ironically, the *Pandora* sank off the Great Barrier Reef and crew and mutineers were all forced into the ship's launch to make the same arduous voyage that Bligh had undertaken two years before.

Bligh's report played a key role in the trial of the mutineers when they were court-martialled in 1792. In the end six men were convicted, three of whom were hanged. Christian avoided their fate by escaping with nine others to Pitcairn, an isolated volcanic speck far to the east of Tahiti. By the time two Royal Naval ships visited the island in 1814, only one of the mutineers was still alive. But their families lived on, and Christian is a common surname on Pitcairn today.

OPPOSITE Bligh gestures almost wistfully at a South Pacific island in this portrait of him in the second edition of *A Voyage to the South Sea*.

ABOVE The mutineers cast Bligh and 18 other officers adrift in the *Bounty*'s launch with only five days' food and water.

FOLLOWING PAGES In his report to the Admiralty Bligh reflects how lucky he has been that "thus happily ended through the assistance of divine providence without accident a Voyage of the most extraordinary nature that ever happened in the world". He has clearly been brooding on the mutineers; the names of the 25 rebels are carefully inscribed on page 6.

Cape of Good Hope 16: Dec. 1789

Sir

You will please to inform the Lords Comm.rs of the Admiralty that I have but just arrived at this place, where I found a French Ship ready to sail for Europe & Hope their Lordships will therefore excuse my not being so particular as might have been expected, as the only reason for it is that I feared of losing the opportunity altogether.

I am unhappily to inform their Lordships of the loss of his Maj.ts Armed Vessel Bounty under my Command which was taken from me by some of the inferior Officers & Seamen on the 28th. Apr.l 1789 in the following manner.

A little before Sun rise, Fletcher Christian, who was Mate of the Ship, and Officer of the Watch, with the Ships Corporal came into my Cabbin while I was asleep, and seizing me, tied my Hands with a Cord, assisted by others who were also in the Cabbin, all Armed with Musquets & Bayonets.

99

into the Boat — This being done I was told by Christian, Capt.n Bligh your Officers & Men are now in the Boat & you must go with them, and with the Guard they carried me across the Deck with their Bayonets presented on every side, when attempting to make another effort one Villain dared to the other, blow his Brains out. I was at last forced into the Boat & we were then veered astern in all nineteen Souls. I was at this time 10 Leagues to the S.W. of Tofoa, the North Westermost of the Friendly Islands, having left Otaheite the 4: April with 1015 fine Bread fruit Plants, and many other Fruit kind, in all 774 Pots, 39 Tubs and 24 Boxes. These Plants were now in a very flourishing Order — I anchored at Anamoka the 24 April and left it the 26th.

The Boatswain & Carpenter, with some others, while the Boat was alongside, collected several necessary things and Water, & with some difficulty a Compass & Quadrant were got, but Arms (a) of no kind or any Maps or Drawings, of which I had many very valuable ones. The Boat was very deep & much lumbered, & in this condition we

(a) To Ourselves after the Boat was veered astern.

* Size 23 Feet

were

I was now threatened with instant death if I spoke a word, I however called for assistance, and awakened every one, but the Officers who were in their Cabbins were secured by Centinels at their doors, so that no one could come to me. The Arms were all taken possession of, and I was forced on Deck in my Shirt with my Hands tied behind my back, and secured by a Guard abaft the Mizen Mast during which the Mutineers expressed much joy that they would soon again see Otaheite.—

    I now demanded of Christian the cause of such a violent act, but no other Answer was given, than hold your Tongue Sir or you are dead this instant, and holding me by the Cord which tied my hands, he often threatened to stab me in the Breast with a Bayonet he held in his right hand.— I however did my utmost to rally the disaffected Villains to a Sense of their duty, but to no effect.— The Boatswain was ordered to hoist the Launch out, and while I was kept under a Guard with Christian at their head abaft the Mizen Mast, the Officers & Men not concerned in the Mutiny were ordered out

were cast adrift with about 28 Gallons of Water, 150 lbs Bread, 30 lbs Pork, 6 Quarts Rum, & 6 Bottles Wine. The day was calm attended with light Breezes and I got to Tofoa by 7 oClock in the Evening, but found no place to land, the Shore being so steep and Rocky.— On the 30th I found landing in a Cove on the N.W. part of the Island, & here I remained in search of Supplies until the 2d May, when the Natives, discovering we had no fire Arms, they made an Attack on Us with Clubs & Stones, in the course of which I had the misfortune to lose a very worthy Man, John Norton, Quarter Master & most of Us hurt more or less.— Our getting into the Boat was no security, for they followed Us in Canoes loaded with Stones, which they threw with much force & exactness, happily Night saved the rest of Us.—

    I had determined to go to Amsterdam in search of Provisions, &c., but taking this transaction as a real Sample of their natural dispositions there was little hope to expect much from them, for I considered their good behaviour hitherto owing to a dread of our Fire Arms which now knowing Us to have none would not be the case, & that supposing our Lives were in safety, our Boat & every thing would be taken from Us, & thereby I should never be able to return. I invariably earnestly solicited by all hands to take their towards home & when I told them in no hopes of relief remained for us but what I might find at New Holland until I came to Timor a distance of 1200 Leagues they all agreed to live on one ounce of Bread a day & a Jill of Water; I therefore after recommending this promise for ever to their Memory bore away for New Holland & Timor across a Sea but little known, and in a small Boat deep loaded with 18 Souls without a single Map of any kind, & nothing but my own recollection and general knowledge of the Situation of places to direct us. — Unfortunately we lost part of our Provisions, our Stock therefore only consisted of 20 lb of Pork, 3 Bottles of Wine, 5 Quarts of Rum, 150 lbs Bread & 28 Gallons Water.

I steered to the W. & W.S.W. with Strong Gales and bad Weather, suffering every calamity and distress I discovered many Islands, and at last on the 28 May the Coast of New Holland, and entered a break of the Reef in Lat. about 12.50 S and Long. 145.00 E: I kept on the direction of this Coast to the Northward, touching at such places as I found convenient, refreshing my People by the best means in my power, these Refreshments consisted only of Oysters & a few Clams, we were however greatly benefited by them, and a few good Nights rest. On the 4th June I passed the North part of New Holland & steered for Timor, & made it on the 12th —

which was a happy sight to every one, particularly several who perhaps could not have existed a Week or a day longer I followed the direction of the South side of the Island, & on the 14 in the afternoon saw the Island of Rotty, & the west part of Timor, round which I got that Night and took a Malay on board to shew me Coupang where he described to me the Governor resided. On the next Morng before day I anchored under the Fort & about 11 oClock saw the Governor who received me with great humanity & friendship. Necessary directions were instantly given for our Support, & perhaps a more miserable set of Beings were never seen. Thus happily ended thro the assistance of Divine Providence without accident a Voyage of the most extraordinary nature that ever happened in the World, let it be taken in its extent, duration & so much want of the Necessarys of Life:

The People who came in the Boat were		The People who remained in the Ship were	
Jno. Fryer ... Master	Robt. Tinkler Ab.	Flet. Christian ... Masters Mate	Wm. McCoy ... Ab.
Wm. Cole ... Boatswn.	Jno. Smith Ab.	Geo. Stewart ... Actg. do	Wm. Millward ... Ab.
Wm. Peckover ... Gunner	Thos. Hall Ab.	Pet. Heywood ... do Midn.	Wm. Brown ... Ab.
Wm. Purcell ... Carpenter	D.P. Portrain ...	Edwd. Young ... do	Matt. Quintal ... Ab.
Thos. Dn. Ledward actg Surgeon	Robt. Lamb ... Ab.	Chas. Churchill ... Corporal	Mich. Byrne ... Ab.
Wm. Elphinston Masters Mate	Dad. Nelson (died D.D. Timor)	Jas. Morrison ... Boats.n Mate	Wm. Muspratt ... Ab.
Fr. Hayward ... Midshipn.		Jno. Mills ... Gunrs. Mate	Jno. Martin ... Ab.
Jno. Hallett ... do	Total 18.	Chs. Norman ... Carpr. do	Alex. Smith ... Ab.
Jno. Samuel ... Clerk		Thos. McIntosh ... do Crew	Wm. Muspratt ... Ab.
Peter Linkletter Quarter Master		Jno. Coleman ... Armourer	Wm. Brown ... Botanist
Jno. Norton Qr. Master Killed at Tofoa		Thos. Burkitt ... Ab.	
Geo. Simpson ... Qr. Mate		Jno. Sumner ... Ab.	Total 25.
Laur. Lebogue ... Sailmaker		Jno. Williams ... Ab.	
		Matt. Thompson ... Ab.	

The Secrecy of this Mutiny
was beyond all conception, so that
I cannot discover that any who were
with me had the least knowledge
of it, & the comparative Lists will
shew the strength of the Pirates.

I found three Vessels at Timor
bound for Batavia, but as their
sailing would be late, I considered it
to the advantage of His Majs service to
purchase a Vessel to take my People
to Batavia before the sailing of the Fleet
for Europe in October, as no one could be
hired but at a price equal to a purchase.
I therefore gave publick notice of my
intent, & assisted by the Governor
I got a Vessel for 1000 Rix Dollars and
called her the Resource.

I have had the misfortune to lose
Mr Nelson the Botanist who died at
Timor the 20th July, whose good Conduct
in the course of the whole Voyage and
manly fortitude in our late disastrous
circumstances deserves this tribute
to his Memory.

On

On the 19th Augt. I was ready for Sea
having finish'd all my business and
informed my Lords Commrs of the
Reality of my proceedings.

I beg leave to acquaint their
Lordships that the greatest kindness
& attention has been shewn to us
whilst at Timor by Mr Timotheus
Wanjon who seconded every friendly
wish of the Governor with real services
& will ever deserve our grateful thanks.

The Surgeon of the Town Mr Max
has also been ever attentive to my sick
People, & has daily & hourly attended
them with great care, for which I
could not get him to render me any
Account or other Answer, than that
he thought it his duty.

I find the situation of the Fort at
Coupang to be 10°.12 S. Longd 127.09 Et
by the Dutch 10.11 S. 125..51 Et of Greenwich.

On the 20th Augt. I sailed from Timor,
and on the 30th passed through Streights
Mangaryne, & after touching at several
places on the Coast of Java. Arrived at
Batavia in the 2 of Octr. And I landed

about

20

Battle Plan of Trafalgar

It is noon on 21 October 1805 and a legend is about to be born. The two lines of a British fleet commanded by Vice Admiral Lord Nelson (in red) are on the point of slicing through the disordered blue and yellow arc of the French and Spanish flotilla under Admiral Villeneuve. Within three hours the Franco-Spanish fleet will be utterly defeated. But, Nelson, the charismatic architect of victory will be dead, shot by a sharpshooter from the rigging of *Redoutable*. The crushing British triumph at Trafalgar lent Great Britain an aura of invincibility at sea that it retained for over a century and which established Nelson as the greatest of its maritime heroes.

The map was drawn by Jonas Toby, purser aboard the frigate *Euryalus*. Her position just to port of Nelson's flagship *Victory* provided him with an excellent view of the developing battle. It was *Euryalus* that had brought the news to England on 1 September for which Nelson had been waiting. The Franco-Spanish squadron under Villeneuve had been spotted entering Cadiz. A British squadron under Vice Admiral Collingwood was already lying in wait there and a message was sent back to England to inform Nelson and summon reinforcements.

On 15 September, Nelson arrived off Cadiz aboard *Victory*. He wanted to lure Villeneuve into an engagement which he was sure superior British seamanship, gunnery and morale would win. At first the French and Spanish merely probed and did not take the bait. Then on 19 October, Villeneuve, who had learned that Napoleon was relieving him of his command, decided to put to sea.

The winds were light and it took over a day to get his 33 battleships and 5 frigates out of harbour. Intelligence of their departure quickly reached Nelson and he ordered a

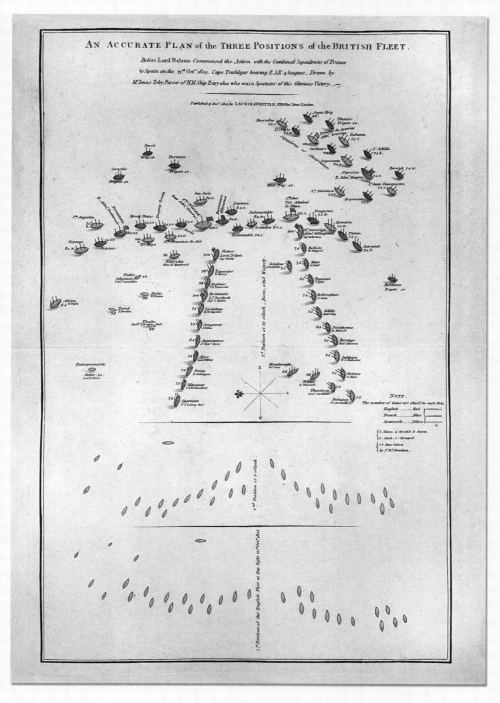

OPPOSITE This portrait, by Lemuel Abbott, shows Nelson in the dress uniform of a Rear Admiral. In his hat he wears the diamond chelengk, an Ottoman military decoration from Sultan Selim III; and on his jacket, the stars of a Knight of the Bath and of the Neapolitan Order of Saint Ferdinand and of Merit.

ABOVE This map of the battle was drawn up by Jonas Toby, purser aboard HMS *Euryalus*, the ship just to the left of Nelson's flagship *Victory*.

pursuit to stop Villeneuve escaping. Early on 21 October British lookouts sighted the French and Spanish fleet. Nelson had made a dramatic decision. He would not attack in a long line parallel to the enemy, as was customary. This was the cautious traditional tactic: the fleet could bring its whole firepower to bear in an orderly line and respond to orders from the commander to alter course or withdraw.

Instead, Nelson drew up his 27 battleships in two parallel columns. *Victory* was at the head of one, Collingwood in *Royal Sovereign* commanded the other. These would penetrate the French line, cut it in three and enable the British to annihilate the isolated enemy ships. The risk was that in approaching one by one, the British ships would at first be exposed to fire from more than one enemy ship at a time. But Nelson was confident that his fleet would survive the initial ordeal and eviscerate the enemy fleet. With history's most famous signal: "England expects that every man will do his duty" fluttering in his rigging, he led the attack.

At midday Collingwood's *Royal Sovereign* tore into the Combined Fleet's line near to the 112-gun *Santa Ana*. A duel erupted between the two ships, which became even fiercer as *Belleisle* and other following ships in Collingwood's column punched through, allowing them to fire broadsides at the enemy vessels. By now, Nelson in *Victory* had made contact with *Redoutable* and a similar running battle broke out involving his column.

Masts toppled as cannon fire crashed into the rigging, and musket-fire raked the decks. But Nelson's tactics had worked and, at close quarters the French and Spanish were proving no match for the British fleet. At around 1.15 p.m., as *Redoutable* engaged in a fierce duel with *Victory*, a French musketeer spotted Nelson's admiral's uniform and shot him through the chest. Nelson was taken below deck, but his injury was too severe and about three hours later he died.

Nelson survived long enough to be told that victory was his. The French fleet had been badly mauled: they had lost 22 ships, of which 18 had been captured by the British (including Villeneuve aboard his flagship *Bucentaure*), and suffered 7,000 dead or wounded. In contrast, though half of the British ships were damaged, none had gone down.

Collingwood, who had assumed command on Nelson's death, sent the news back to England on the little schooner *Pickle*, which reached Falmouth three weeks later. While there was rejoicing at the scale of the British victory, Nelson's death caused anguish. *The Times* remarked on the loss of "the darling of the British navy, whose death has plunged a whole nation into the deepest grief". But Nelson had sacrificed his life in a decisive victory that was to leave the French navy cowering in port for the remaining decade of the Napoleonic War. In life a talented naval commander, Nelson in death underwent an apotheosis to become an untouchable symbol of all that was great about Britain.

RIGHT On 22 November 1805 the printmakers Boydell offered a prize of 500 guineas for the best depiction of the death of Nelson "in the manner of the Death of General Wolfe". One of the entrants was this painting by Benjamin West, who had met Nelson in 1801. It inaccurately depicts his death on the quarterdeck rather than below decks.

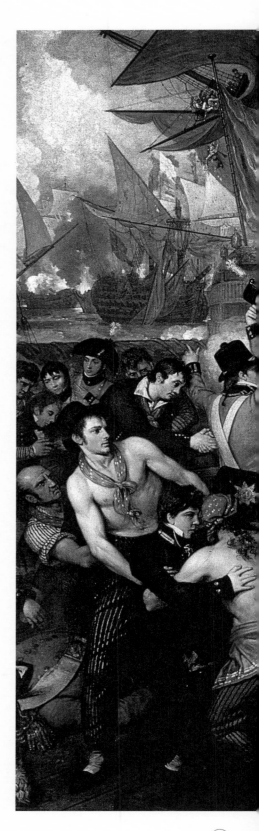

21

Wellington's Waterloo Dispatch

This is – for us – one of the most precious documents in Britain's entire historical record. It is the dispatch the Duke of Wellington penned – in his very clear, efficient handwriting and his cool, restrained style – to report one of the most decisive victories of all time. Here is the commander of the British and allied army at Waterloo writing in the very early hours of 19 June 1815 – after four days in which he had managed to snatch only a few moments of sleep. He is explaining with hardly any emotional embellishment how he has destroyed once and for all the armies of the French Emperor Napoleon. It was a victory that left Europe free of another continent-wide war until 1914 and established the myth of British military invincibility and of his own particular genius as a general.

It was a battle the allies, who had been fighting France for a quarter of a century, had not dreamt would occur. The oxygen had been squeezed out of France's war effort by a crushing defeat at Leipzig in 1813 and the remorseless advance of Wellington's troops out of Spain. In April 1814 Emperor Napoleon had abdicated. He was exiled to the island of Elba not far from the south of France. To the horror of the rest of Europe, he escaped and was back in Paris in March 1815.

The allies promptly declared him an outlaw and sent Wellington ahead to contain the new threat, promising to send reinforcements. But Napoleon was too quick for them. He had returned to a triumphant welcome from his supporters, collected an army and crossed the Belgian frontier in the early hours of 15 June.

It was a remarkable strategic coup. He was faced with two separate allied armies, Wellington's in Brussels with around 100,000 men, and Marshal Gebhard Blücher's with another 100,000 Prussians off to the east. Both were caught by surprise. Wellington was preparing to attend the Duchess of Richmond's ball, and he failed to move his army in time to join the Prussians.

Napoleon moved swiftly to defeat Blücher at the Battle of Ligny the following day, while Wellington desperately sent his men forward to hold the French back successfully at the crossroads of Quatre Bras. But with Blücher's defeat, Wellington was forced to withdraw to a position further north, on a ridge across the Brussels road near Waterloo.

On the morning of 18 June, Wellington's 67,000 men faced a slightly superior French force of 72,000. Wellington was worried that his army, which was only one-third British, would fail him – but in the battle that followed, it fought magnificently. Wellington's tactics were to absorb anything that Napoleon threw at his line on the ridge, while awaiting the support which he hoped would come from the Prussians. During the morning British troops and allies from the German state of Nassau defended the farm at Hougoumont (described on pages 7 and 8 of the dispatch). The main engagement didn't begin until around noon, as Napoleon had been slow to bring up his guns in very wet weather. An initial French infantry assault was beaten back after the British cavalry smashed into their ranks. But the British overreached themselves and almost half their cavalry was lost to a counter-attack.

The French horse then advanced, but the impetus of their charge was absorbed by British infantry squares. Even so, by early evening, Wellington's position was in peril. The French captured the farm of La Haye Sainte just forward of his main line. But by now Marshal Blücher had come to the rescue, his army miraculously recovered from their reverse at Ligny. He threw some 40,000 men into attacking the French right and Napoleon had to commit much of his reserve, including half his Imperial Guard, to hold them back. Then, well into the evening, he sent in the rest of the Guard in a final desperate bid to break Wellington's line. Wellington describes what happened at this critical moment on page 10 of his dispatch.

Scythed down by volleys from the British infantry which sprang up from behind a slope, the Guard did the unthinkable. They turned and fled. Seeing this, French morale collapsed and only a core around the Emperor stood fast to shield his retreat. Wellington and Blücher shook hands and Wellington went out of his way to thank Blücher for his help.

Napoleon fled pell-mell to Paris and a humiliating abdication on 22 June. Wellington was left to survey the carnage of the battlefield, where some 45,000 on all sides lay dead and wounded.

While the deposed Emperor languished the rest of his life in the safely remote prison-island of St Helena, Wellington enjoyed adulation and a stint as prime minister. Most of all though, he ensured Britain's primacy as a military power for the next century and a half, and his own position as its most famous general.

OPPOSITE David Wilke's portrait of Wellington shows him with his beloved horse Copenhagen, whom he rode at Waterloo.

BELOW Lady Elizabeth Butler's 1875 painting shows the 28th Regiment of foot resisting the advance of the French cavalry at Quatre-Bras, two days before Waterloo. Wellington mentioned the regiment in his Dispatch for its gallantry in this action.

FOLLOWING PAGES The Duke of Wellington's Waterloo Dispatch begins with the preliminaries to the battle. Pages 3, 8, 9 and 10 (included here) cover key moments in the battle. Page 3 describes the engagements at Quatre Bras and Ligny, where the "Prussian army maintained their position with their usual gallantry and perseverance against a great disparity of numbers". The climax of the battle comes on page 8, when the farm at La Haye Sainte is taken amid "a very heavy cannonade upon our whole line". The last desperate French attacks "with cavalry and infantry, supported by the fire of artillery" are described on page 9. The Prussian advance and the final breaking of the French line are recounted by Wellington on page 10.

Blücher's Position.

In the mean time I had directed the whole Army to march upon les Quatre bras, and the 5th Division under Lt. General Sir Thomas Picton arrived at about half past two in the day, followed by the Corps of Troops under the Duke of Brunswick and afterwards by the Contingent of Nassau

At this time the Enemy commenced an attack upon General Blücher with his whole force, excepting the 1st and 2nd Corps and a Corps of Cavalry under General Kellerman, with which he attacked our Post at Les Quatre bras.

The Prussian Army maintained their Position with their usual gallantry and Perseverance, against a great disparity of numbers, as the 4th Corps of their Army under General Bulow had not joined, and I was not able to assist them as I wished, as I was attacked myself, and the troops the Cavalry in particular which had a long distance to march had not

arrived

Brigade of Guards which was in
position in its Rear, and it was
for some time under the Command
of Lt. Colonel Macdonald and
afterwards of Coll. Home, and I am
happy to add that it was maintained
throughout the day with the utmost
Gallantry by these Brave Troops not-
=withstanding the repeated efforts
of large Bodies of the Enemy to obtain
possession of it.

His attack upon the Right of
our Centre was accompanied by a very
heavy Cannonade upon our whole Line,
which was destined to support the
repeated attacks of Cavalry and Infantry,
occasionally mixed but sometimes
seperate which were made upon it
In one of these the Enemy carried the
farm House of La Haye Sainte, as
the Detachment of the Light Battalion
of the Legion which occupied it had
expended all its Ammunition and
the Enemy occupied the only communication there was with them.

The

The Enemy repeatedly charged our
Infantry with his Cavalry but these
attacks were uniformly unsuccessful;
and they afforded opportunities to our
Cavalry to charge, in one of which
Lord Edward Somerset's Brigade consist-
-ing of the Life Guards, Royal Horse
Guards and 1st Dragoon Guards,
highly distinguished themselves as
did that of Major General Sir W.m
Ponsonby having taken many
Prisoners and an Eagle.

These attacks were repeated till
about 7 in the Evening when the Enemy
made a desperate Effort with Cavalry
and Infantry supported by the fire
of Artillery to force our Left Centre
near the farm of La Haye Sainte
which after a severe Contest was
defeated; and having observed that
the Troops retired from this attack in
great Confusion and that the march
of General Bulows Corps by Frischerman
upon

upon Planchenoit and la belle Alliance
had begun to take effect and as I
could perceive the fire of his cannon,
and as Marshal Prince Blücher
had joined in person with a Corps
of his Army to the left of our Line
by Ohain I determined to attack
the Enemy; and immediately advanced
the whole line of Infantry supported
by the Cavalry and Artillery — The attack
succeeded in every point. The Enemy
was forced from his Positions on the
heights and fled in the utmost confusion,
leaving behind him as far as I could
judge 150 pieces of Cannon with their Ammunition
which fell into our hands. I continued
the pursuit till long after dark; and
then discontinued it only on account of
the fatigue of our troops who had been
engaged during 12 hours, and because
I found myself on the same Road with
Marshal Blücher who assured me
of his Intention to follow the Enemy
throughout the night. He has sent me
word this Morning that he had taken

60

22

Stephenson's Patent for a Steam Engine

For us this is one of the most striking images of the Industrial Revolution. The carefully delineated lines of tubes and pistons in George Stephenson's patent application of 21 May 1822 mark an incremental improvement in the steam engine which he had been working on for over a decade. More importantly, they helped set off a transport revolution that led to the beginning of the world's first inter-city passenger railway line. It transformed a world in which, until then, most people had never travelled more than 30 miles (50 kilometres) from the place of their birth.

Stephenson was the son of a Yorkshire miner. He seemed destined to follow his father in feeding the growing hunger of the Industrial Revolution for coal to fire its factories – and avoided that fate thanks to steam. Those underground coal seams were prone to flooding and needed pumps to remove the water. Steam power was first harnessed to operate pistons by Thomas Newcomen in 1712. James Watt and Matthew Boulton created hugely improved steam engines in the 1770s, which also allowed the reciprocal action of pistons to be converted into a rotary action to operate wheels for milling and weaving. This led to the rapid spread of steam-driven pumps in mines.

In 1798 Stephenson escaped the coal seam by becoming minder of a steam pump and ultimately the engine-wright at Killingworth colliery, in charge of all the mine's engines. By this time, engineers had begun constructing locomotives to haul coal from mines and iron works on wooden or metal rails to canals or seaports, from where they would be transported by barge or ship. In 1813 Stephenson built his own freight locomotive, which came to be known as *Blücher* after Wellington's Prussian ally at the Battle of Waterloo. It managed just 4 miles per hour (6.5 kilometres per hour).

Steadily, Stephenson refined his engine: in 1815, he patented a system to discharge used steam into the chimney, doubling the engine's power, and by 1816 further improved its efficiency by carrying its weight on the

pistons. His 1822 application modestly proclaims that his new version produces "a more perfect" result than "in the cylinder of a single or double powered Boulton and Watts engine". Meanwhile commercial interest was growing in freight steam locomotives, and in 1821 Stephenson was appointed by the Stockton and Darlington Railway company to survey a new line in the face of bitter opposition from the citizens of Darlington, who favoured a canal. The short line opened in September 1825 and it became the world's first passenger service.

Interest was fired in the development of railway travel and in October 1829 the Liverpool and Manchester Railway (LMR) ran a series of trials at Rainhill to choose the locomotive that would carry passengers on the new route it planned. Stephenson and his son Robert had devised a new engine, the *Rocket*, to fulfil the stringent weight requirements laid down by the LMR. One of her competitors, the *Cycloped*, was a strange contraption powered by a horse-operated treadmill, which ended in farce when the beast fell through the floor of the engine. Two steam engines experienced mechanical problems and could not match *Rocket's* consistent speed of around 14 miles per hour (23 kilometres per hour).

The Stephensons earned a prize of £500 for winning the Rainhill trials and George was appointed chief engineer of the LMR. But his triumph was marred by the tragic death of William Huskisson, the MP for Liverpool (and a great supporter of the new

Rocket, shown here in an early photograph, was operated on the Liverpool and Manchester Railway from 1830 to 1834. After that the pioneering engine saw less glamorous service on a private freight railway belonging to Lord Carlisle until 1840. Donated to the Patent Office in 1862, it now forms part of the collection of London's Science Museum.

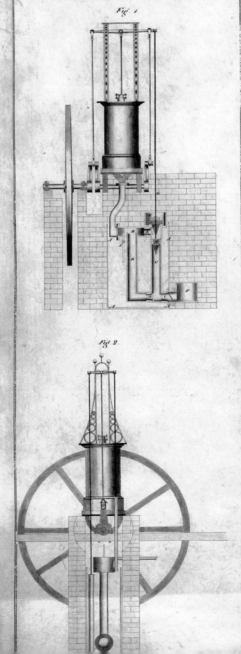

Fig. 1

Fig. 2

railways) on the railway's opening day of 15 September 1830. He was struck by *Rocket* as he attempted to enter the carriage occupied by the Duke of Wellington, who was also in attendance. The railways' first fatality did not stop their spread. Investors enthusiastically took up the new invention, which offered the prospect of easy profits, and Britain experienced a railways craze as new lines opened rapidly throughout the country.

By 1843, some 1,800 miles (3,000 kilometres) were in operation and a direct line had opened from London to York. By the close of the century, around a million kilometres of track had been laid, as railways spread swiftly throughout the industrializing world. Mine and quarry owners no longer had to rely on waterborne sources of fuel. Factory owners could now count on it being hauled cheaply to them over land. And passengers now experienced the freedom of mass long-distance travel. All of them thanks to George Stephenson and his meticulous improvements to his steam engine, which had made it all possible.

OPPOSITE George Stephenson's patent, granted on 21 March 1822, is for improvement in the vacuum in the condenser and cylinder of steam engines, a process carefully described and illustrated in the accompanying text and diagrams. Stephenson's improvements were first used on the Hetton Colliery Railway, near Durham, which in turn was the world's first purpose-built steam-operated railway.

RIGHT John Lucas's portrait of George Stephenson shows his subject in a landscape transformed by his invention: a railway line runs in the background on the left-hand side of the picture, itself traversed by a railway viaduct.

23

Darwin accepts a voyage on the *Beagle*

This is the letter that launched Charles Darwin's scientific career and which would ultimately lead to his development of the theories of natural selection and evolution. Yet it was a close run thing. The young Darwin had been offered the post of naturalist aboard HMS *Beagle*, which was about to embark on a survey voyage around South America, and had initially declined the role. His book *On the Origin of Species*, voted history's most important work of science, might never have been written.

In his letter, one of the founding documents of British science, Darwin writes that his refusal "was owing to my father not at first approving of the plan". Robert Darwin felt that the trip was another waste of time for his son, a young man who had so far shown little inclination to settle on a career.

Eventually, as Darwin noted, his father "has reconsidered the subject and given his consent" and so he was now in a position to accept the offer. Even then, however, Darwin nearly did not secure his berth aboard the *Beagle*. Her captain, Robert FitzRoy, had wanted a gentleman companion to ease the social isolation of the voyage. An apparently feckless Cambridge arts graduate was not what FitzRoy had in mind and so he initially rejected Darwin.

Charles, though, charmed FitzRoy when they met, and so, in the summer of 1831, he began preparing for the trip. When the ship set sail on 27 December, his baggage included the scientific instruments he would need – among them a microscope, geological compass, clinometer and hygrometer – as well as a geologist's pick, two pistols, a rifle,

12 shirts and a pair of slippers. Perhaps most importantly, he brought aboard a trove of books, including Charles Lyell's *Principles of Geology*, published in 1830. In it Lyell argued that the form of the Earth's surface has been shaped by physical and chemical forces acting over a long period of time and was not created in the form it exists today. This was a theory that was to have a profound effect on Darwin.

The first part of the voyage was a trial for Darwin; he suffered from incessant seasickness and clashed with FitzRoy over discipline (the captain had ordered the crew flogged for drunkenness) and about his ardent defence of slavery, which the young naturalist found abhorrent. Still, when the *Beagle* arrived in Brazil in February 1832, Darwin settled into a routine of shore visits and more extended expeditions in search of animal and plant specimens and geological samples which would keep him occupied for the next four years.

Periodically Darwin sent batches of specimens back to his mentor John Stevens Henslow, Professor of Botany at Cambridge, including a group of large fossil quadrupeds he found at Bahia Blanca, south of Buenos Aires. These included *Megatherium*, a gigantic sloth, which led Darwin to muse on the similarities between these extinct creatures and very similar (but smaller) animals he could see on his sallies ashore.

The ship made for the Galápagos Islands, where Darwin collected more specimens, including 13 different types of finch. He made little of these at first: he was kept busy with other distractions as the *Beagle* made its return journey via Tahiti, New Zealand, Mauritius and Cape Town, and only arrived at Falmouth on 2 October 1836.

Darwin was slow to process the results of his voyage – only in 1837 did it become apparent that his Galápagos finches were all of separate species and showed slight variation, particularly in their beaks, which were adapted for the foodstuffs available on the different islands on which they were found. Darwin began to realize that if a member of a species acquired a variation by chance – in the shape of its beak, for example – which favoured it over others of the species, then the variation might spread.

By 1842, Darwin had refined this to become the first version of his theory of Natural Selection, which proposed that all species are in a constant struggle for survival and that those with favourable variations will survive and have more offspring, passing on those variations. Species, therefore, gradually change or "evolve" over time.

Darwin waited some time before he fully set out his ideas: *On the Origin of Species* was published in November 1859 to a wave of acclaim from his supporters and a storm of derision from opponents (which became worse in 1871, when he applied the theory to the evolution of mankind, leading to accusations that he believed men were little better than apes). The scientific phenomenon that was Darwinism, however, would never have come about had Charles Darwin taken his father's advice and said "No" to the voyage on the *Beagle*.

OPPOSITE George Richmond's portrait of Charles Darwin shows him in 1840, not long after his return from the *Beagle* voyage. It would be 19 more years before he published *On the Origin of Species*, his great work on evolution.

ABOVE Galápagos mockingbird (*Mimus melanotis*) collected on James Island. Darwin noted at the time that there were distinct mockingbirds on different islands.

FOLLOWING PAGES Darwin is writing to Francis Beaufort, the Admiralty's Chief Hydrographer, who was in charge of assembling the expedition. In line 6 he writes that Beaufort may already have received a letter "stating my refusal" from George Peacock, a mathematics lecturer at Cambridge whom Beaufort had asked to find a likely companion for Captain FitzRoy on the long voyage to South America. "If the appointment is not already filled up," Darwin adds, he is now happy to accept it.

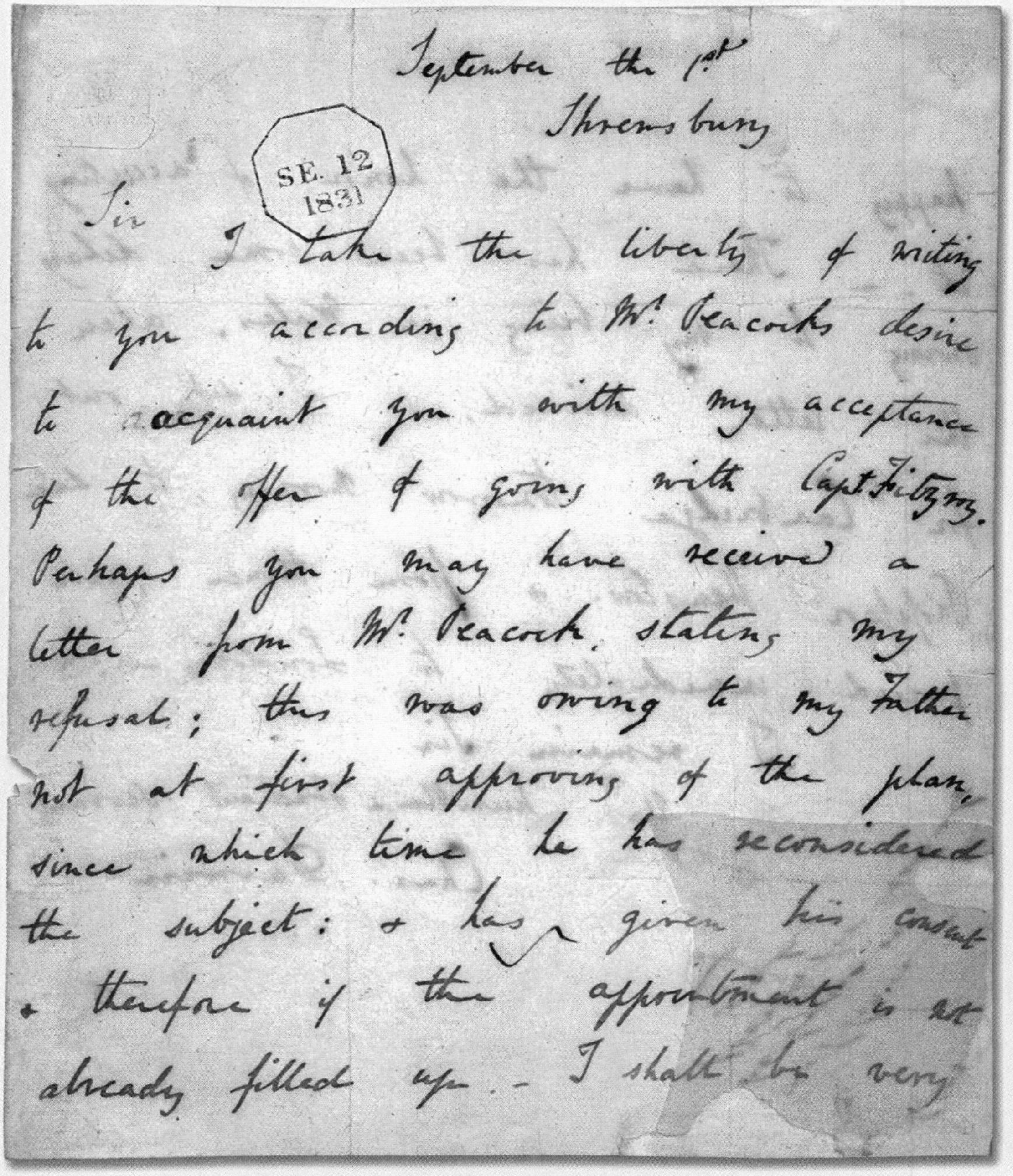

September the 1st
Shrewsbury

SE. 12
1831

Sir
I take the liberty of writing
to you according to Mr Peacocks desire
to acquaint you with my acceptance
of the offer of going with Capt Fitzroy.
Perhaps you may have received a
letter from Mr Peacock, stating my
refusal; this was owing to my Father
not at first approving of the plan,
since which time he has reconsidered
the subject: & has given his consent
& therefore if the appointment is not
already filled up. — I shall be very

happy to have the honor of accepting it. — There has been some delay owing to my being in Wales, when the letter arrived. — I set out for Cambridge tomorrow morning, to see Professor Henslow: & from thence will proceed immediately to London. —

I remain Sir
Your humble & obedient servant
Chas. Darwin

24

Gladstone's payment from the Slavery Compensation Commission

The document records the payment by a British government commission of a sum of £10,278 to John Gladstone, whose fourth son William had recently been elected Tory MP for Newark (and would, in due course, serve four terms as prime minister). Such a large sum – around £8 million in today's terms – paid to a politician's family might raise eyebrows at any time. Remarkably, though, Gladstone senior was being compensated for the losses he had suffered in 1833 when slavery was abolished in the British Empire.

The Society for the Effecting of the Abolition of the Slave Trade's two-decade campaign for the outlawing of the trade in human beings was crowned with success in 1807. The trade in humans was now outlawed, yet despite the efforts of William Wilberforce and other abolitionists, slavery itself remained legal in the British empire. A slave could not now be bought or sold, but more than 800,000 people of African descent remained unfree, mostly as the chattels of plantation owners.

Owning slaves in the Caribbean was widespread among the British middle and upper classes. From major landowners who controlled thousands of slaves to shopkeepers and widows who had just a couple whom they rented out to others, there was a ready-made lobby in support of maintaining the status quo. The most important of all was John Gladstone, a Liverpool merchant who had begun as an agent for absentee plantation owners. He bought his first land and slaves in the West Indies in 1812. Twenty years later, he owned 2,500 slaves on nine different plantations, and was, unsurprisingly, a vociferous opponent of the early abolition of slavery.

John Gladstone's argument was that the time was simply not right. The level of education and economic prospects of slaves needed to be improved before they could be cut loose from the alleged security of being owned by another. It was a theme taken up by his fourth son, William, when he entered Parliament in 1832. His hustings speech to the voters of Newark had pledged "measures for the moral advancement and legal protection of our fellow subjects in slavery", by which he decidedly did not mean their emancipation.

William Gladstone's maiden speech, and most of his parliamentary work for the next decade, was taken up in securing the interests of plantation owners, and in particular those involved in the sugar trade. His position became increasingly difficult to defend after a widescale slave revolt in Jamaica in December 1831. This coincided with a slump in sugar prices, which demoralized the planters and disheartened supporters of slavery, who feared the prospect of a succession of such revolts. Public pressure grew too; in 1830–31 more than 5,000 petitions were presented to Parliament calling for slavery's abolition.

After two parliamentary inquiries, Lord Stanley, the Colonial Secretary, presented a bill to do just that. Gladstone and his allies shifted ground, lobbying for a high level of compensation to be paid to slave owners for the loss of their property. Conceding the compensation was the only way for the government to muster enough votes to get the bill through, it gave way. The enormous sum of £20 million was set aside, representing around 40 per cent of the state's annual budget, and a commission established to take evidence to establish the sums each slave-owner would receive.

An additional concession was made, which caused outrage in the West Indies, where most slaves were concentrated. The slaves were not in any real sense to be freed – at least, not at first. Instead, those over the age of 5 were obliged to serve for six years as "apprentices", giving 45 hours of labour a week free to their former masters. The plantation owners were thus doubly compensated and the British public made to pay for it by increased sugar import duties, which led to higher prices. The bill comfortably passed its third reading in the House of Commons on 26 July 1833, just days before William Wilberforce died.

John Gladstone received a total of £106,769 from the Commission, which paid out on any slaves on an owner's books in July 1835. William, who became prime minster (for the first of four administrations) in 1868, received £150,000 from his father, funds which derived from his investment in slavery. The descendants of those who benefited from the biggest bail out in British financial history before the 2008–9 banking crisis are legion. They included the great-grandfather of George Orwell, author of *Nineteen Eighty-Four*, who received £4,442.

The huge payments to buy off slave-owners may appear to have the taint of corruption. The way people like the Gladstones were converted from being supporters of gradual emancipation to advocates of freeing slaves with compensation for their owners smacks of hypocrisy. Yet it was effective. There was very little violence, and in 1838 even the requirement of "apprenticeships" for former slaves was dropped. As the American abolitionist Frederick Douglass remarked in 1848: "We have discovered in the progress of the anti-slavery movement that England's passage to freedom is not through rivers of blood."

OPPOSITE Large numbers of slaves were transported from the West Coast of Africa to work on British-owned sugar plantations in Antigua. This 1823 print shows the sugar harvest, supervised by a European overseer at a time the slave trade itself had been abolished but slave-owning was still legal.

ABOVE The Slavery Compensation Commission's award lists a payment of £10,278 to John Gladstone, father of the future prime minister William Gladstone. This amount, for one particular plantation, was a little over a tenth the total compensation he received. The number to the right of his name represents the number of slaves, 193, that he was being compensated for. None of them are named.

LEFT George Frederic Watts' 1859 portrait of William Gladstone shows the politician in his prime. At 50, he had just become Chancellor of the Exchequer for the second time. He had also abandoned his roots as a member of Peel's Conservative party, and joined the Liberals.

25

The Penny Black Stamp

It is a tiny piece of paper, just ¾ inch × ⅞ inch, and it launched a communications revolution. The Penny Black, first issued in 1840, became the world's first postage stamp, sweeping away a complex and expensive set of tariffs that had cost up to a day's pay and made letter-writing a hobby for the rich or desperate.

Although Britain's monarchs had long had their own mail service, this was opened up to the public only in 1635 as a means of raising revenue – and more easily intercepting seditious letters. Almost inevitably a thicket of regulations sprang up about fees for letters. Costs rose over time, scaled by weight and distance and almost always payable by the recipient. Attempts were made to circumvent these, notably by the establishment of private mail services: among the most successful was the London Penny Post set up in 1680 by merchant William Dockwra. Its advantages, its flyers explained, included that "Parents may Converse with their absent Children at Boarding-Schooles". But it was too successful for the taste of royal officials and the Postmaster-General ordered the confiscation of its assets in 1682, in an early example of nationalization.

By the 1830s the charge for sending a letter from London to Edinburgh had risen to more than a shilling and corruption was rife. Postmasters did not always hand over the money they received. Envelopes that had been franked were reused to avoid paying again. The wilier took to writing secret codes on the envelope, so that the recipient could understand the message and then refuse to receive the letter.

Rowland Hill, the son of a Kidderminster schoolmaster, became passionate about reforming the system at an early age. He was said to have seen his family pay three shillings for the delivery of a bundle of mail. He calculated that the real cost of a letter from London to Edinburgh was just $1/_{36}$ of a penny.

In 1837 Hill produced a pamphlet, *Post Office Reform*. It argued that a flat-rate penny postage would be fairer and should, within five years, lead to such an increase in letter-writing that the Post Office would recoup any revenues lost by a reduction in its charges. Because the postman would no longer have to deliver letters in person in order to collect the fee, the service would also be faster and cost less to run. Additionally, Hill proposed the introduction of "A piece of paper just large enough to bear the stamp, and covered at the back with a glutinous wash, which the bringer might, by applying a little moisture, attach to the back of the letter."

In 1837 a Select Committee on Postal Reform was set up, and by 1839 it had partially approved Hill's proposals, establishing first a Fourpenny Post. This began operation on 5 December 1839, but was so successful that after 36 days the price was cut to the originally envisaged single penny. Hill rushed to get the "stamps" designed, enlisting a firm of bank note printers to produce them. After 2,600 suggestions were submitted, he chose a design that featured Queen Victoria's head based on an engraving of her as a 15-year-old by William Wyon. This image of her as a teenager remained the portrait on British stamps issued right up to her death at the age of 81.

The first Penny Blacks were printed by early May 1840 in sheets of 240 stamps, which had to be cut by hand (perforation was introduced in 1854). Hill already knew it was going to be a success: on 10 January, the first day of the Penny Post (before the stamps became available) 112,000 letters were posted. In 1840 the number of letters the Post Office carried reached 168 million, almost double the level of the previous year. Post office counters were besieged by customers wanting to buy stamps and avoid the double tariff paid by recipients if a letter was unstamped.

There were teething problems; stamps were cancelled by a Maltese cross frank that was initially easy to remove (made from red ink mixed by postmasters from printer's ink, linseed oil and "droppings of sweet oil"). This allowed the stamps to be reused, while the black frank which replaced it could not be seen against the Penny Black's colour. In 1841, after just a year in circulation the Penny Black was retired and replaced by the more practical Penny Red. Some 68 million had been printed. Despite its ephemeral career the Penny Black is the most famous stamp

of all time, a symbol of Britain's place at the forefront of innovation in communications in the nineteenth century and, for some, a melancholy reminder of a time when people actually wrote letters, rather than sent emails.

OPPOSITE London's first pillar box on the corner of Fleet Street and Farringdon Street, designed by A.E. Cowper in 1855–7. Pillar boxes were introduced after the novelist Anthony Trollope, who was Postal Surveyor for the Western District, saw them in use in France. At first they were green; red was introduced as the standard colour only in 1874.

ABOVE LEFT The Penny Red was first issued in 1841 to replace the Penny Black, on which franking marks had been difficult to make out. It became the first perforated postage stamp in 1854. In 1880 the Penny Red was superseded by the Penny Venetian Red and then, in 1881, by the Penny Lilac.

LEFT A Penny Black stamp with a Maltese cross frank. The letters in the bottom corners indicate the stamp's position on the printing sheet (with AA at the top left and TL at the bottom right of the 240-stamp sheets).

BELOW The Edinburgh–London Royal Mail coach. Mail coaches bore a distinctive livery of maroon doors and lower panels, black upper panels and Post Office red wheels. The names of the towns at either end of the journey were painted on the doors.

26

Brunel's notebooks

If Isambard Kingdom Brunel was the high priest of Victorian engineering, this is a plan for one of its temples. The roof of the engine shed of the new Great Western Railway terminus at Paddington is sketched out here in meticulous detail. The careful lines of formulae show the unbending precision of a mind assessing each strut in the web of iron and glass that will encase one of his most brilliant masterpieces.

Engineering was in Brunel's blood. His father, Marc, was a French civil engineer, who ruined the family's fortunes by unwise investments. In 1825, though, he managed to win the contract to drive a tunnel under the Thames from Rotherhithe to Wapping. Young Isambard, then only 19, cut his teeth on the project as assistant engineer. The tunnel proved unstable, and in June 1828 work on it was suspended after a serious breach in which Isambard himself almost drowned.

While convalescing in Bristol, he submitted a design for a new bridge to span the Avon Gorge at Clifton. Brunel's plan was initially rejected by a committee that included the notable bridge-builder Thomas Telford. He argued for his own design, which flaunted huge ornately decorated Gothic towers. To Telford's chagrin Brunel's plan was preferred, though he had to accept the shortened span that a sulky Telford insisted upon. The project was then abandoned altogether after a riot in favour of the Reform Bill caused a loss of confidence among investors. Construction was not completed until 1864, after Brunel's death.

Until 1833 Brunel had few real successes. His appointment that year as chief engineer of the Great Western Railway allowed him to undertake projects on a truly imperial scale, using steam and sheer size to defy nature. Brunel's vision was grandiose – he dreamt of a railway taking passengers all the way to the Americas. It would transport them from London by train and embark them on steam-driven liners to cross the Atlantic.

The railway received Royal Assent in 1835 and Brunel boldly drove his tracks west as straight as he could. That meant edging them north of the Marlborough Downs through comparatively unpopulated areas via Didcot and Swindon. Along the way he had to bridge a 100-yard (91-metre) width of the Thames at Maidenhead, which he solved with twin spans of 128 feet (39 metres) and abnormally flat brick arches. He also drove through 2 miles (3 kilometres) of solid rock

to dig the Box Tunnel. It involved the work of a thousand navvies over five years and consumed a ton of gunpowder a week.

Brunel's railway was complete by 1842, but it still lacked a suitably grand terminus. In 1850 he began to design a new station to replace the temporary sheds that had been thrown up at Paddington in 1840. Taking inspiration from Joseph Paxton's "Crystal Palace" which housed the Great Exhibition in 1851, Brunel modified his initial plans and came up with something very similar: a shell of iron-ribbed glass that would allow light to stream onto the platforms. Passengers would alight at a monument to Britain's – and Brunel's – engineering prowess.

By the time the new Paddington terminus opened fully in 1854, Brunel had almost completed the second stage of his project. In 1836 the Great Western Steamship Company

was established to pioneer a route from Bristol to New York. Brunel became its chief adviser, and designed the SS *Great Western*, a huge vessel of 1,400 tons. He explained that a larger ship would be more fuel-efficient, as it would cut through the water with less resistance. On Great Western's maiden voyage in April 1838 he was proved right, as she arrived in New York with a third of her coal unused. Bolder yet was the SS *Great Britain*, which he designed to be the first steam-powered vessel built of iron. When its keel was laid down in 1839, few save Brunel understood the engineering challenges of constructing her: every iron plate had to be individually forged and the sheer novelty of the enterprise meant constant tinkering with the shape of the hull.

On 26 July 1845 Brunel's iron dream took to the waters, making her maiden voyage from New York to Liverpool. Yet the greatest passenger vessel of the age had a short career, running aground off Northern Ireland when her captain lost his bearings. Salvaged in 1852, she was employed for 30 years carrying emigrants to Australia. Brunel's next venture failed too: the even larger SS *Great Eastern* proved to be commercially unviable when iron prices rocketed after the outbreak of the Crimean War in 1854. She ended up as a cable-laying ship.

The sheer breadth of Brunel's ambition ensured that his reputation survived and the solid achievement of his bridges, tunnels and stations more than made up for the imperial hubris of his steamships. And underpinning those – with the flair and genius that allowed him to dare what others would not – was the attention to detail that his Paddington Station drawings display.

OPPOSITE Brunel stands in front of the launching chains tethering his steamship, the *Great Eastern*, during her construction at Millwall on the Thames, November 1857.

ABOVE Paddington Station, the London terminus of the Great Western Railway, 1854. The illustration shows the roof, a shell of iron-ribbed glass supported on cast iron pillars. Brunel made the arches semi-circular to avoid ruining their effect with horizontal lines. As he wrote to his assistant, the architect Matthew Digby: "I am going to design, and I believe to build, a station after my own fancy."

FOLLOWING PAGES Brunel's sketches for the engine shed at the new Great Western Terminus at Paddington contain detailed calculations of the strain each element in the design would have to bear. At the end (on the second page) he calculates that the total weight of the roof, which its structure would have to support, was 17 tons and 10 hundredweights (17.5 tons).

G.W. Railway Swindon Station

Diagram of Centre Roof for Engine & Tender drawing Shed

Mr Brodie Sept 12 1841

$a = \frac{1}{2}$ the weight between A & C or C & E.

$2h = \frac{1}{2}$ — — — — — — — B & D.

(a) acting downwards at B & D & (2h) acting downwards at C

will be balanced by (a + h) acting upwards at A & at E

Draw B.M. B.K. B.L. & C.N. perpendiculars

Considering A.B. as a Lever and h the fulcrum

∴ Strain on A.F × B.L = (a + h) A.M. ∴ Strain on A.F = (a+h) $\frac{am}{B.L}$

Considering A.B.F. as a Lever & B as Fulcrum

∴ Strain on F.G × B.K. = (a + h) A.M. ∴ Strain on F.G = (a+h) $\frac{AM}{B.K}$

Considering A.B.C.G.F. as a Lever and C as Fulcrum

∴ Strain on B.D × C.O + a (at B) × B.O. + Strain on G.H × C.N = (a+h) A.P.

∴ Strain B.D × C.O = (a+h) A.P. − a B.O − (a+h) $\frac{A.M}{B.K} \times C.N$

∴ Strain on B.D = a $\frac{B.O}{C.O}$ + h $\frac{A.P}{C.O}$ − (a+h) $\frac{A.M}{B.K} \times \frac{C.N}{C.O}$

Produce B.F & draw 2.F parallel to G.H & G.K & A.F

∴ Strain on B.F : Strain on F.G = F.K : H.G ∴ Strain on B.F = (a+h) $\frac{AM}{BK} \times \frac{FK}{HG}$

∴ Strain on C.G : Strain F.G = G.2 : H.G ∴ Strain on C.G = (a+h) $\frac{AM}{BK} \times \frac{G2}{HG}$

If F.G represent the Strain on F.G then

G.K. F.K. 2.G will represent the strain on A.F

B.F & C.G respectively.

For Plan shewing position of Ties & when proved

see Tracings Vol. 2 page 80.

Great Western Railway – Paddington – Proving of New Engine House Roof
J. H. Bentham Sept 1. 1846

Two principal frames of the Roof were placed at the
distance of 12 feet the ridge D. & Purlins B.C &c were firmly
fixed & the whole kept upright by struts fixed to Parallel
uprights so that the frames might sink freely but could
not give sideways (see Fig. 1) A Platform was then slung
by Chains from the Points B.C.E. & F and the load applied gradually & as nearly
in proportion to the ultimate arrangement as possible most weight being thrown
on the points C & E on account of the lantern &c – The Calculation of the
testing weight is as follows – Openings 12 feet – Measurement over ridge
say 80 feet from side to side – For 2 frames 2/80×12/ =1920 sup feet
Weight of Principals Iron &c (without boarding & Zinc) say 16 lb per foot.
Whole testing weight required 80 lb per foot.

$$\frac{1920 \times 20}{112} = 343 \text{ Cwt or } 17 \text{ Tons } 3 \text{ Cwt nearly}$$

Whole weight applied including Platforms Chains &c (but exclusive
of frames of roof) 15 Tons 10 Cwt.

Part of roof supported by Purlins H & K not represented in weight
placed on Platform & half of this will be carried by the Walls say ⅔ of the weight

$$\frac{17 \text{ Tons}}{8} = \text{say 2 Tons.}$$

Tons
15 . 10
2 . 0
Whole Test applied 17 . 10

Fig 2.

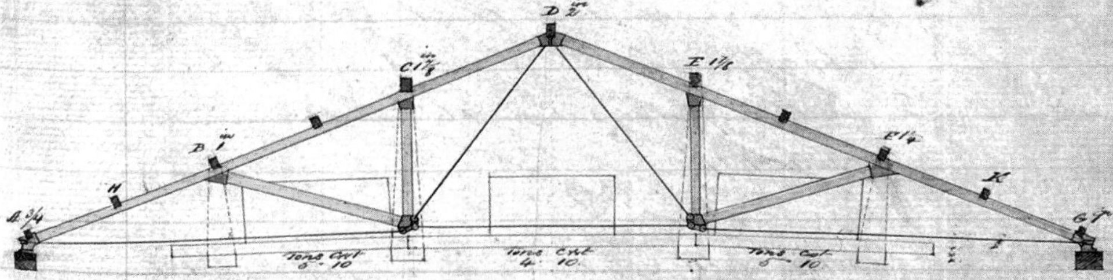

Amount of Deflection marked in inches at B & C the amount is marked as
sinking in supports which ofcourse must be deducted from the other amounts
these are accounted for by the Joints coming home & the points did not rise till the ...
relieved

(Cont.)

Ada Lovelace's letter to Charles Babbage

The note from a Victorian lady to her mathematician friend seems unassuming enough, although its emphatic underlinings indicate a certain force of personality. Yet Ada Lovelace's 1843 letter to Charles Babbage is the work of an underrated genius.
In it she hints how she has devised a method by which the calculating machine that Babbage has been working on may be instructed to calculate an implicit function "without having been worked out by human head or hand first". It is, in short, the first computer program. Ada, a century before Alan Turing and 150 years before Bill Gates, was the first computer programmer.

Ada Lovelace had an unusual family background. Born the only legitimate child of the poet Lord Byron, she never knew her father, who abandoned the family when she was only five weeks old. Her mother, Annabella Milbanke, was a talented mathematician. Byron referred to his wife as his "Princess of Parallelograms" – and she encouraged her daughter in scientific and mathematical pursuits to steer her away from her father's wild poetic path.

Ada had a passionate, voracious intellect. By her early teens she had taken a fancy to flying and tried to devise functioning wings from various materials, including silk. In 1833, aged 17, she met Charles Babbage, a mathematician and inventor who had been working for the best part of a decade on a calculating machine he called the Difference Engine. Ada was fascinated. Babbage was intrigued by the girl who seemed to have an insight into his work, which others entirely lacked. They were more taken by a mechanical dancing ballerina he often demonstrated.

Ada's mathematical correspondence with Babbage was interrupted by her marriage, then by motherhood and an illness that followed. In 1839 Ada renewed contact with Babbage when she asked him to find her a mathematical tutor so that she could resume her studies.

Babbage's Difference Engine was a complex array of tubes and gears which could perform basic mathematical functions. The level of precision necessary to build it had defied engineers and frustrated craftsmen who tried to interpret his complex instructions. By the early 1840s there was still no working model. Undeterred, Babbage had moved onto greater things and designed the Analytical Engine. This used the principle devised by Joseph Jacquard, who in 1801 created a loom that varied the pattern woven according to a template imprinted on wooden punch cards. Babbage's engine could, therefore, in principle be "programmed" to carry out an operation by inserting differently punched cards.

The problem remained that he could not find anyone to build it or even to understand fully how it worked. In 1840 Babbage gave a series of lectures in Turin. From these Luigi Menabrea, a keen engineering student – and future Italian prime minister – took notes, which he compiled and published in French.

Babbage was keen that this explanation of his work be available in English and he asked Ada to translate it.

Ada did more than this. She added a series of notes labelled A to G which expanded on Menabrea's text and explained the Analytical Engine's operations in more detail. Note G concerned a method by which the Engine could be instructed to calculate Bernoulli's numbers, a sequence of numbers with important applications in trigonometry and number theory. Ada worked furiously to get the calculations right. In her letter she asks Babbage to "Give me the necessary data and formulae" to complete her work and suggests that delaying publication by a week or two to allow her do so would be well worth the wait.

Ada's Note G to Menabrea's Notes on the *Analytical Engine of Mr Charles Babbage* contained the first computer program, although as the Analytical Engine (just like the Difference Engine) was never built, it was never run. Ada's notes were only signed with her initials, AAL, at Babbage's insistence and her work was largely

forgotten for a century. She tried to take up other scientific projects, musing in 1844 that she wanted to devise a "calculus of the nerves" to explain how thoughts were generated by the brain. But her health failed her and in 1852, aged only 36, she died of cancer.

Babbage kept plugging away with the Analytical Engine, but the task overwhelmed him and he became bitterly engrossed in documenting minutiae. In 1867 he spent months working up his "Table Of The Relative Frequency Of Occurance Of The Causes Of Breaking Plate Glass Windows" which analyzed the causes of window breakages in a factory (including boys throwing stones at each other and runaway sheep).

Without the inspiration of the woman he called the "Enchantress of Numbers", Babbage was adrift. It had taken Ada's combination of poetic fancy, logic and determined application to squeeze that first computer program out of his grandiose labyrinth of a project. In this she provides an excellent role model for today's programmers.

OPPOSITE ABOVE Alfred Edward Chaton's engraving of Ada Lovelace is one of the few images of her that survive. It was turned into a mass-produced print by William Henry Mote, one of Victorian England's most prolific etchers.

OPPOSITE BELOW An 1871 engraving of Babbage from the *Illustrated London News*, just after his death. He was a prolific inventor. As well as the Difference Engine, he created the cow-catcher for locomotives, the first train speedometer and an early form of ophthalmoscope.

ABOVE A reconstruction of Babbage's Difference Engine No. 2, completed by the Science Museum for the bicentennial of his birth in 1991. The calculating section of the Engine weighs 2.6 tons and has 4,000 separate parts (and the whole Engine twice that amount).

FOLLOWING PAGES Ada Lovelace's July 1843 letter to Charles Babbage contains the first reference to what was in effect a computer program. In the final paragraph she writes, "I want to put in something about Bernoulli's number, in one of my notes, as an example of how an important function may be worked out by the engine, without having been worked out by human hand."

will send down to the Square before tomorrow evening, Brodie's Formulae, & also the Reports of the Royal Society on your machine. I suppose you can get it easily, & I particularly want to see it, before I see you on Wed^{dy} Mon^g. —

It appears to me that I am working up the Notes with much success; & that even if the book be delayed in it's publication, a week or two, in consequence, it would be worth Mrs Taylor's while to wait. I _will_ have it _well_ & _fully_ done; or not at all.

I want to put in something about Bernoulli's Numbers, in one of my Notes, as an example of how an implicit function may be worked out by the engine, without having been worked out by ~~the~~ human head & hands first. Give me the necessary data & formulae.

Yours ever
A. A. L.

28

Design for the Great Exhibition

The floor plan of the Great Exhibition, the glorious celebration in 1851 of inventiveness, internationalism and the variety of human endeavour, bears witness to the process of globalization that was shrinking the world. It also makes clear – with only the merest hint of triumphalism – that Britain was the engine powering the process. Over half the exhibition space is given over to British exhibitors, with foreign stalls safely sectioned off in the eastern half of the building.

Britain was conscious of its industrial might, and increasingly of its imperial power. As a result, the proposal put forward in 1845 by the worthies of the Royal Society for the Encouragement of Art, Manufacture and Commerce for an exhibition to showcase the country's most innovative products was eagerly taken up. Its most enthusiastic proponent was the society's patron, Prince Albert, who was in desperate search of a meaningful project to compensate for his disappointingly meagre duties as Prince Consort.

After four years mired in committees, the Great Exhibition – as it came to be known – began to take shape with the choice of Joseph Paxton as the building's architect. Whereas the first proposal, drafted by Isambard Kingdom Brunel, had been for a solid brick monolith, more railway terminus than fairground, Paxton – fittingly for a man who had designed the Duke of Devonshire's greenhouses – opted for a palace of glass that would blend with the greenery of Hyde Park and encompass three of its elm trees within its 180-foot (55-metre height).

The construction took little more than six months. When the exhibition finally opened on 1 May 1851 – amid some concerns that the lower orders might riot – the 300,000 spectators who gathered were treated to a spectacle for all the world like a coronation of British industrial prowess. The imperial establishment was in attendance: archbishops, ambassadors, Prince Albert in full highland dress and a medal-bedecked Duke of Wellington, celebrating his 82nd birthday.

The well-heeled forked out three guineas for a season ticket, while those of more modest means entered for just a shilling on weekdays. But the 42,000 who came each day were all treated to the same extravaganza, half-bazaar, half-cathedral, where the wares of Britain's merchants – and of the foreign nations brought in for ballast – could be worshipped, gawked at or even bought. The interior space was laid out like a church – the central spine was even referred to as the "nave" – and the walkways were lined with statues and fountains, including a 27-foot (8-metre) leviathan of coloured glass.

The exhibits spanned an astounding range. The solid virtues of industry were on display, from weaving frames, to a diorama of the Liverpool docks and a 500-foot (152-metre) stretch of railway track with all the latest engines lined up. The Koh-i-Noor diamond was one of the exhibition's centrepieces and attracted queues several hundred long to view the monstrous 186-carat gem which had arrived in Britain from India the year before. But it was the exotica that caught the eye. Queen Victoria commented in her diary on the piano keyboard on which a quartet could play. Also pulling in the crowds were Theophilus Carter's alarm bed, which tipped out the unfortunate sleeper from his mattress

at the allotted hour, and a buttonless shirt aimed at bachelors.

Many also made their way to the foreign section, perhaps pausing to take tea in one of the three cafés whose reputation for high prices and poor service led to the exhibition's aisles becoming clogged with sprawling picnickers. The French showed off their textiles and a prototype submarine, the Austrians' emphasis on agriculture made them look like country bumpkins. Reflecting political turmoil back home the comparative minnows of Mecklenburg-Strelitz, Hamburg and Bremen refused to share a joint space with the Prussians, and most of their leading industrialists (apart from Meissen's porcelain) stayed at home. Other German states were happy to attend as members of the Zollverein, the Prussian-led customs union that was a forerunner of a unified Germany. The Americans, who came close to inviting mockery with their stuffed squirrel and giant eagle suspended from the ceiling, had an inventive selection on show, including

a range of unpickable locks. Did onlookers realize that the British had reached their zenith, as other nations scrambled to catch up? The future belonged to the Americans and the Germans, soon to overtake the British. Success had bred complacency and Britain's second generation of industrial magnates were often more comfortable in London clubs and country estates than at railheads or on factory floors.

In October, the gates finally closed and the "Crystal Palace" was dismantled and re-erected in South London. The Great Exhibition's profit of £186,000 was used to fund "Albertopolis", the complex of museums in South Kensington that would include the Victoria and Albert, Natural History and Science Museums. Among those who left the show most satisfied were the winners of the coveted Council Medal, including Prince Albert, who was recognized for the excellence of his "sample of beans and winter oats". That British industry might have kept a closer eye on its competitors is indicated by

the grudging award of "Highly Commended" to American gun-maker Samuel Colt for his new line of revolvers, destined to be rather more influential than Prince Albert's oats.

OPPOSITE This 1842 portrait of Prince Albert by Franz Winterhalter shows him in field marshal's undress uniform. He wears the Garter star and the insignia of the Golden Fleece, a Spanish order of chivalry. Without his enthusiastic support, the Great Exhibition might not have happened.

ABOVE Interior view of the "Crystal Palace", site of the Great Exhibition in Hyde Park.

FOLLOWING PAGES The exoticism of Joseph Paxton's glass design for the Great Exhibition building lent it the nickname "The Great Shalimar", after a series of Mughal-era gardens in India. To match the year of its inauguration it was precisely 1,851 feet (just over 564 metres) long. Also called "The Crystal Palace" it was dismantled and moved to a site in Sydenham, South London, where it stood until destroyed by a fire in 1936.

PLAN OF

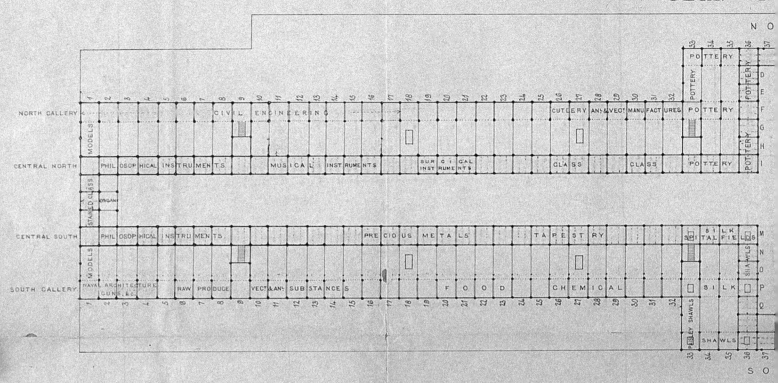

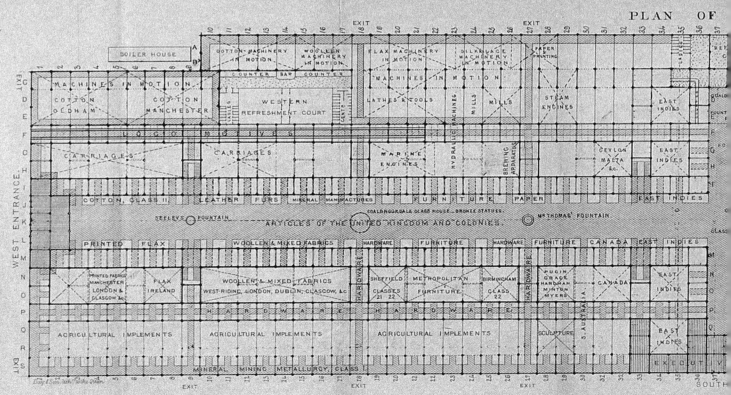

PLAN OF

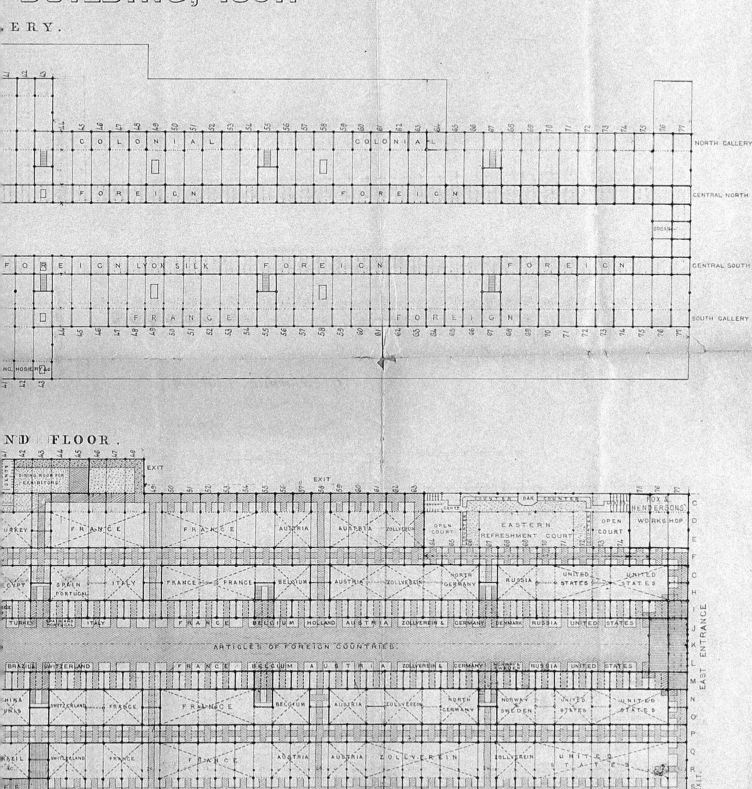

BUILDINC, 1851.

...ERY.

COLONIAL ... COLONIAL — NORTH GALLERY

FOREIGN ... FOREIGN — CENTRAL NORTH

ORGAN

FOREIGN LYON SILK ... FOREIGN ... FOREIGN — CENTRAL SOUTH

FRANCE ... FOREIGN — SOUTH GALLERY

...NG, HOSIERY &c.

...ND FLOOR.

DINING ROOM FOR EXHIBITORS

EXIT

OYSTER BAR COUNTER

FOX & HENDERSONS

...URKEY | FRANCE | FRANCE | AUSTRIA | AUSTRIA | ZOLLVEREIN | OPEN COURT | EASTERN REFRESHMENT COURT | OPEN COURT | WORKSHOP

...EGYPT | SPAIN PORTUGAL | ITALY | FRANCE | FRANCE | BELGIUM | AUSTRIA | ZOLLVEREIN | NORTH GERMANY | RUSSIA | UNITED STATES | UNITED STATES

TURKEY | SPAIN AND PORTUGAL | ITALY | FRANCE | BELGIUM | HOLLAND | AUSTRIA | ZOLLVEREIN & GERMANY | DENMARK | RUSSIA | UNITED STATES

ARTICLES OF FOREIGN COUNTRIES.

BRAZIL | SWITZERLAND | FRANCE | BELGIUM | AUSTRIA | ZOLLVEREIN & GERMANY | NORWAY SWEDEN | RUSSIA | UNITED STATES

CHINA ...UNIS | SWITZERLAND | FRANCE | FRANCE | BELGIUM | AUSTRIA | ZOLLVEREIN | NORTH GERMANY | NORWAY SWEDEN | UNITED STATES | UNITED STATES

BRAZIL &c. | SWITZERLAND | FRANCE | FRANCE | AUSTRIA | AUSTRIA | ZOLLVEREIN | ZOLLVEREIN | UNITED STATES

EAST ENTRANCE

EXIT | EXIT | EXIT

Feet

26TH FEB. 1851.

29

The Charge of the Light Brigade Order

Of all the orders dashed off on a piece of paper in the heat of battle, this one strikes us as the most poignant of all. it is hastily written, its command to attack tailing off into a scrawl. Issued by Lord Raglan, commander of the British land forces during the Crimean War, it is also fatally ambiguous, ordering its recipient to "prevent the enemy carrying away the guns", without specifying which guns he meant. The resulting Charge of the Light Brigade, on 25 October 1854, became one of the most notorious episodes in British military history, a fiasco in which nearly 300 cavalrymen lost their lives.

The origins of the Crimean War lay in an obscure dispute over religious freedom. Russia sought to exert its right to protect Orthodox Christians in the lands of the Ottoman sultan and this drew in France and Britain on Turkey's side, neither of them keen to see Russia's position in the Balkans strengthened. A large Anglo-French expeditionary force, which landed in the Crimea in September 1854 to confront Russia, soon made for the strategic port of Sevastopol and laid siege to it.

The allied approach to Sevastopol was slow and allowed the Russian defenders to seize a series of redoubts around Balaklava to the southeast of Sevastopol. The attempt to recapture these – and to stop the Russians hauling off the guns which the Turkish defenders had abandoned – led to the Battle of Balaklava on 25 October.

The fight to stop the Russians advancing beyond the redoubts towards Balaklava went well for the Allies. The first Russian attacks were repelled by Major-General Colin Campbell's 93rd Highlanders, whose bravery in facing the cavalry assault led to their being immortalized as the "Thin Red Line". The Russian cavalry were further disordered by an attack from the British Heavy Brigade of cavalry, whose charge smashed into the Russian horse regiments and threatened to carry the day for the allies.

Then Lord Raglan, high up on the hills overlooking the battlefield, spotted what he thought was an attempt by the Russians to move the captured guns from the redoubts. Keen to forestall their use in Sevastopol's defence, he barked an order which was hurriedly scribbled down by General Richard Airey, the Quartermaster General, and then passed to Airey's aide-de-camp Captain Nolan to be carried to Lord Lucan, commander of the cavalry brigade.

Minutes later the order was in the hands of Lucan, who struggled to understand it. He could not see the guns on the redoubts; the only artillery visible to him were the Russian guns at the far end of a valley to the north. To charge its full length under Russian fire would clearly be suicidal, but when Lucan asked which guns were meant, Nolan merely gestured right down the valley and proclaimed: "There, my Lord! There is your enemy! There are your guns!"

Lucan felt he had no choice but to comply. He ordered Lord Cardigan's Light Brigade to attack the Russian batteries. The 600 men formed up and moved forward, first at a trot and then at a charge. Riders and horses crashed to the ground, torn apart by the Russian guns stationed on three sides, but against the odds many reached the end of the valley, where the Russian gunners turned tail and fled. The sheer impetus of their charge took the Light Brigade beyond the line of guns and straight into units of Russian hussars and Cossacks, who drove them back. The fleeing British were forced once again to run the gauntlet of the Russian guns before a counter-attack by the French Chasseurs d'Afrique allowed the survivors to reach the safety of the British lines.

Or at least half of them did. Nearly 300 men were lost in the charge and the Light Brigade was shattered as a force for the rest of the war. The French General Bosquet, who witnessed the charge from the Sapoune Heights, acidly remarked, "C'est magnifique, mais ce n'est pas la guerre: c'est de la folie" ("It is magnificent, but it is not war: it is madness"). The debacle also inspired Alfred, Lord Tennyson, to write a poem memorializing the futile sacrifice of "the noble six hundred" who rode "into the valley of Death".

Despite the British losses, the Russians were still trapped in Sevastopol and they remained so until the city's fall in September 1855. The conflict was brought to an end when none of the combatants saw any future in further fighting, and the peace signed with Russia in March 1856 made only minor frontier adjustments. The greater result of the war, perhaps, was the scar inflicted on the British military psyche by Lord Raglan's order and the carnage it had caused.

OPPOSITE Richard Caton Woodville's vivid depiction of the Charge of the Light Brigade depicts the British cavalry at the beginning of the charge, before their ranks were decimated by the Russian guns on each side of them.

BELOW The Charge of the Light Brigade order, dictated by Lord Raglan and scribbled in haste by his Quartermaster-General Richard Airey reads: "Lord Raglan wishes the Cavalry to advance rapidly to the front. Follow the enemy and try to prevent the enemy carrying away the guns. Troop Horse artillery may accompany. French cavalry is on your left. Immediate." Raglan may have understood his order but, tragically, those who received it did not.

LEFT Lord Raglan – here shown in an engraving by Joseph Edwards – did not long survive the debacle of Balaklava. His health was weakened by depression caused by criticism of his handling of the campaign. In June 1855 he died of dysentery while still besieging Sevastopol.

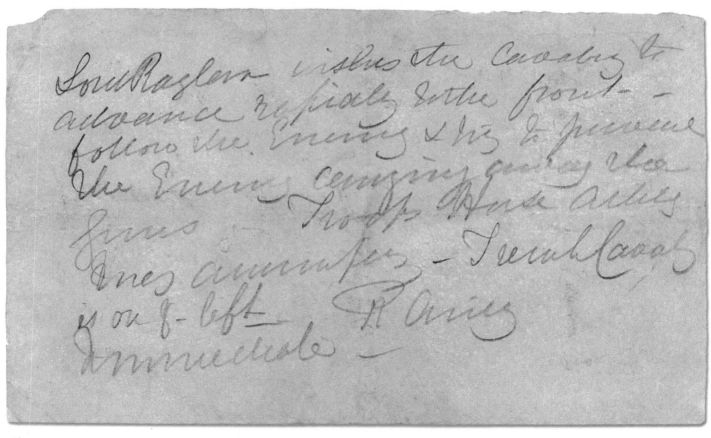

30

Gordon's letter from Khartoum

It is one the last letters of the British empire's most romantic martyr. General Charles Gordon, warns directly that Khartoum, the town he has been defending against Mahdist rebels, can hold out for only five to seven more days, after which it "may, at any time, fall". His death a month later, defending the governor's palace, transformed him into a very British hero and made him a role model for the empire's defenders.

Gordon's career had begun conventionally enough with service as a combat engineer in the Crimean War in 1854–5. But a transfer to China in 1860 led to his elevation. He became a general in the Ever Victorious Army, a mercenary force loosely allied with the Chinese government in their struggle against the Taiping Rebellion.

With the nickname of "Chinese Gordon" and a reputation for getting things done, he ran through a number of roles unequal to his energy and vision before becoming attached to the service of the Khedive of Egypt in 1874. Egypt was in the process of detaching itself from the Ottoman empire and its hold on its southern neighbour, Sudan, was shaky. Having proven his worth, Gordon was made governor-general of all Sudan. He surprised everyone by being impervious to bribery and made enemies through his opposition to the slave trade, but he was unable to achieve any lasting reforms.

By 1883 the Egyptian hold on Sudan was failing. An Islamic revivalist movement, led by Muhammad Ahmed, who called himself the Mahdi ("the Expected One"), had attracted thousands of followers, seized forts and now threatened Khartoum. Gladstone's British government decided to abandon the Sudan. Gordon was summoned back and ordered to evacuate the remaining Egyptian garrisons.

He arrived in Khartoum in January 1884 and promptly began to act like a man possessed. Far from ordering what he saw as an inglorious retreat, he disobeyed his orders and decided to hold on in Khartoum in spite of the odds against him. He remitted taxes, emptied the jails of wrongly imprisoned men, and made plans to take on the Mahdi. "If Egypt is to be quiet," he explained to his masters in London, "the Mahdi must be mashed up."

The last thing the Gladstone government wanted was an expensive war. Egypt was practically bankrupt and the costs of a campaign against the Mahdi would inevitably

fall on Britain. Gordon caused irritation by his increasingly strident appeals for reinforcements: he asked first for a regiment of Ottoman infantry; then of Muslim troops from the British Indian army; and finally for British regulars. All were ignored.

Gordon in turn stood firm. He began to fortify Khartoum and its outlying forts. When the post at Berber was taken and the telegraph line cut by the Mahdists in March 1884, he found himself under a partial siege. Communication was still possible using one of the small flotilla of Nile steamers which Gordon commanded, but food supplies began to run low.

Pressure mounted on Gladstone to help Gordon. Criticism in the House of Commons, a campaign in the press marshalled by *The*

ABOVE Gordon wearing the uniform of an Egyptian general, with tarboush and abundant gold brocade. Most of the garrison Gordon commanded at Khartoum were Egyptian soldiers, and in theory he answered to the khedive of Egypt rather than the British.

OPPOSITE On 14 December, as Khartoum seemed doomed, Gordon composed a final batch of letters to send out on the Nile steamer *Bordeen*. In this one, to the Chief of Staff of the Relief Force, he warns "without any feeling of bitterness" that "should the town fall, it will be questionable whether it will be worth the while of HMG to continue its expedition".

Copy.

Inclosure of 7700/1522

Kartoum
14. 12. 84

Sir

I send down the steamer "Bordein" tomorrow with Vol VI of my Private Journal containing account of the events in Kartoum from 5 Nov to 14 Dec. The state of affairs is such that one cannot foresee further than 5 to 7 days, after which the town may at any time, fall. I have done all, in my power to hold out, but I own, I consider the position is extremely critical, almost desperate, & I say this, without any feeling of bitterness, with respect to H. M. Gov't, but merely as a matter of fact. Should the town fall; it will be questionable whether it will be worth the while of H. M. ✗✗✗ G. to continue its expedition, for it is certain, that the fall of Kartoum will insure that of Kasala & Sennaar.

I have &c.

(sd) C. G. Gordon.

The Chief of Staff
Soudan Expedy Force

Times correspondent Frank Powers, who was in Khartoum, and lobbying from Queen Victoria finally forced him to act. But the relief force, under Sir Garnet Wolseley – which included our ancestor, Thomas Snow, then a young lieutenant – was only authorized to move south from Cairo on 25 September. Its progress was glacial; Wolseley insisted on waiting for specially built boats to arrive from Canada before embarking on the Nile. Gordon repeatedly warned that he could not hold out. On 14 December he sent out a last batch of letters, together with his diary, which he wanted to survive as a record of his ordeal. He hints "without any feeling of bitterness, with respect to Her Majesty's Government" that the relief expedition might as well turn back in the event of Khartoum's fall. Whatever the failings of the efforts to rescue him, Gordon can find no fault in his own conduct, writing: "I have done all in my power to hold out".

It was mid-January before the relief column came within striking distance of Khartoum. The Mahdi decided he had to act before Wolseley could arrive. Already the outlying forts had fallen and on the night of 25/26 January the Mahdists took advantage of the low level of the Nile to outflank the city walls and break into Khartoum. The exhausted garrison put up little resistance as tens of thousands of Mahdist warriors flooded in. Gordon and his bodyguards fired on the rebels from the roof of the governor's palace. But that didn't stop them. He then went out to confront them, pistol and sword in hand.

It was a brave, but futile gesture. Several spear-thrusts and Gordon fell, fatally wounded. His head was severed and sent as a trophy to the Mahdi. The relief column, on hearing of the disaster, veered away from Khartoum and the British evacuated Sudan. Thomas Snow brought back unopened the bottle of champagne* he had hoped to crack open when they relieved Gordon in Khartoum. Back home the nation fell into a paroxysm of grief and Gladstone, previously the GOM

("Grand Old Man") was reviled as the MOG ("Murderer of Gordon").

Britain had to wait for its revenge until Lord Kitchener smashed a Mahdist army at Omdurman in 1898 and marched back into Khartoum. But it had acquired a hero – and one whose sense of the right thing to do and

refusal to retreat, no matter what, made him into the closest thing Victorian imperialism had to a saint.

* Peter Snow's grandfather, later Lt-General Sir Thomas Snow, was to command a Corps at the Battle of the Somme in 1916. The unopened bottle is still on show at the Somerset Light Infantry Museum in Taunton.

ABOVE Members of the Gordon Relief
Expedition haul the armed steamer *Nasaf
el-Khair* over the Second Cataract of the
Nile at Wadi Halfa in the far north of Sudan.
The expedition's slow progress meant
its vanguard arrived on the outskirts of
Khartoum two days after the city's fall and
Gordon's death.

31

Jack the Ripper "Dear Boss" letter

On 27 September 1888, a letter was received at the Central News agency, claiming to be from "Jack the Ripper", whose murder of two prostitutes had kept London's East End in a state of terror for weeks. The writer taunts the police for their failure to catch him, saying: "they wont fix me just yet" and joking that the blood from his victims "went thick like glue and I can't use it" as ink. It is a document from the dark underbelly of Victorian London, an age of cheap literacy in which crime sold newspapers, and it provoked feverish speculation in the burgeoning press.

The number of the Ripper's victims is uncertain – five are generally accepted, and there may have been several more. Some had been respectable women who fell on hard times and were sucked into a life of prostitution at the violent edges of Victorian society. The first to die was Mary Anne Nichols, whose body was found in a Whitechapel alley in the early morning of 31 August 1888. Her throat had been cut and her abdomen slashed open, leaving her corpse in a pool of blood. The murder of prostitutes was not an especially unusual occurrence in Victorian London, but even before the inquest on Nichols was complete, an event took place which left the East End in a state of shock and galvanized the press into strident calls for immediate action.

The body of Annie Chapman, who was killed on the night of 7/8 September, bore the hallmarks of the same killer; the throat was cut, the body slit open, and parts of it sliced off, apparently carried away by the murderer. The police did their best,

interviewing witnesses to the last hours of the victims, whose testimony produced nothing but shadowy leads and tantalizing hints. In the days before the establishment of forensic science, the Metropolitan Police could not rely on fingerprinting, DNA profiling or chemical analysis, and were forced instead to gather witness statements, hoping to identify a suspect, who could then be persuaded to confess.

Little progress had been made by the time two more mutilated corpses were found on 30 September. Elizabeth Stride and Catherine Eddowes bore the same marks as the others; first strangled, then their throats cut and finally mutilated in a ghoulishly efficient manner that made some think a surgeon or butcher might be responsible. Eddowes' earlobe was sliced off, just as the "Dear Boss" writer had promised he would do to his next victim, leading the police to believe the letter was genuine.

The discovery of the mutilated body of Mary Jane Kelly on 9 November provided no definitive new evidence of the killer's identity. The inquest on Kelly was carried out in unseemly haste, concluded within a day, and there the Ripper's trail went cold. His last certain victim was the career of Sir Charles Warren, Commissioner of the Metropolitan Police, who resigned in November after being pilloried in the press for his lack of success in bringing the killer to justice.

There was never any shortage of suspects, some plausible, many sensational, for the Ripper murders. They included three identified by Sir Melville Macnaghten, the Chief Constable in 1894: M.J. Druitt a barrister turned teacher, who committed suicide in December 1888, providing a convenient explanation for why the killings stopped abruptly; Aaron Kosminski, a Polish Jew who ended up in a lunatic asylum; and a conman named Michael Ostrog. During the more than a century since, other names have emerged, as the hunt for the Ripper's identity continued unabated, extending even to the accusation that Queen Victoria's grandson, the Duke of Clarence, was the knife-wielding murderer.

No one was ever brought to court, let alone convicted of the murders. The Ripper must have died unidentified and free of blame, though whether months, years or even decades after his killing spree we will never know. All that remains of the most notorious killer of the Victorian era are a collection of letters, with their chilling, mocking lines that resonate through the century in between.

THE MILLER-COURT MURDER, WHITECHAPEL: SITE OF MARY KELLY'S LODGINGS.

OPPOSITE An illustration of the High Street, Whitechapel, showing how it would have looked at the time of the murders. The bustle and apparent prosperity of the main street belies the appalling poverty that festered in the alleyways and courts that led off it.

ABOVE A contemporary engraving of Miller Court, a series of tenement buildings off Dorset Street in Spitalfields. Mary Kelly, the last of the Ripper's confirmed victims, lived in a small room at Number 13. Her body was found by her landlord's agent when he came to collect overdue rent.

FOLLOWING PAGES This "Dear Boss" letter was received at the Central News Agency on 27 September 1888. Written in red ink, with reddish stains, the writer jokes that he wanted to use the blood of his victims as ink. The signature contains the first known reference to "Jack the Ripper"; the writer apologizes for "giving the trade name".

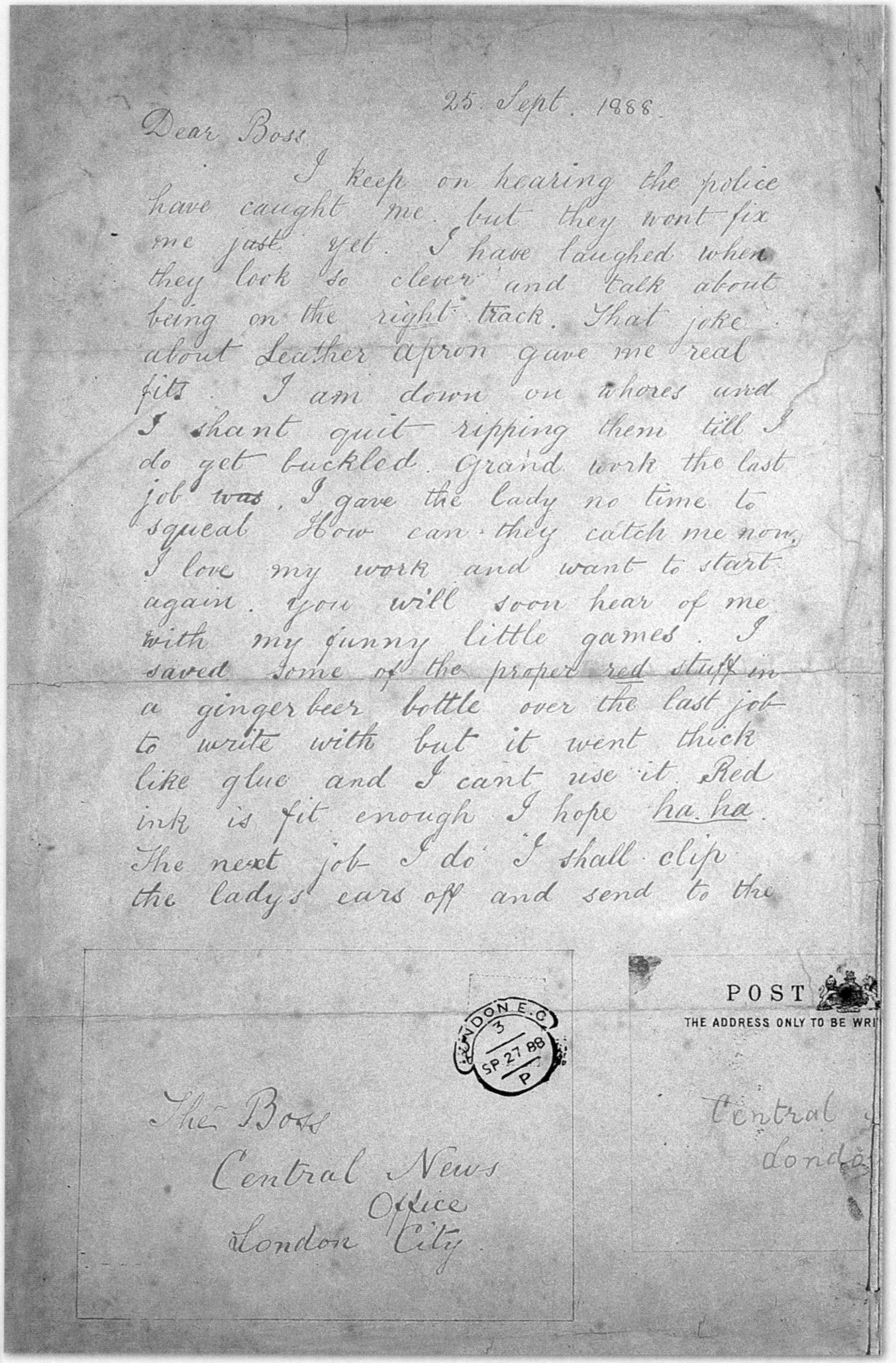
25. Sept. 1888.
Dear Boss
I keep on hearing the police
have caught me but they wont fix
me just yet. I have laughed when
they look so clever and talk about
being on the right track. That joke
about Leather Apron gave me real
fits. I am down on whores and
I shant quit ripping them till I
do get buckled. Grand work the last
job was, I gave the lady no time to
squeal. How can they catch me now,
I love my work and want to start
again. You will soon hear of me
with my funny little games. I
saved some of the proper red stuff in
a ginger beer bottle over the last job
to write with but it went thick
like glue and I cant use it. Red
ink is fit enough I hope ha. ha.
The next job I do I shall clip
the ladys ears off and send to the

LONDON E.C.
3
SP 27 88
P
The Boss
Central News
Office
London City
POST
THE ADDRESS ONLY TO BE WRI
Central
Londo

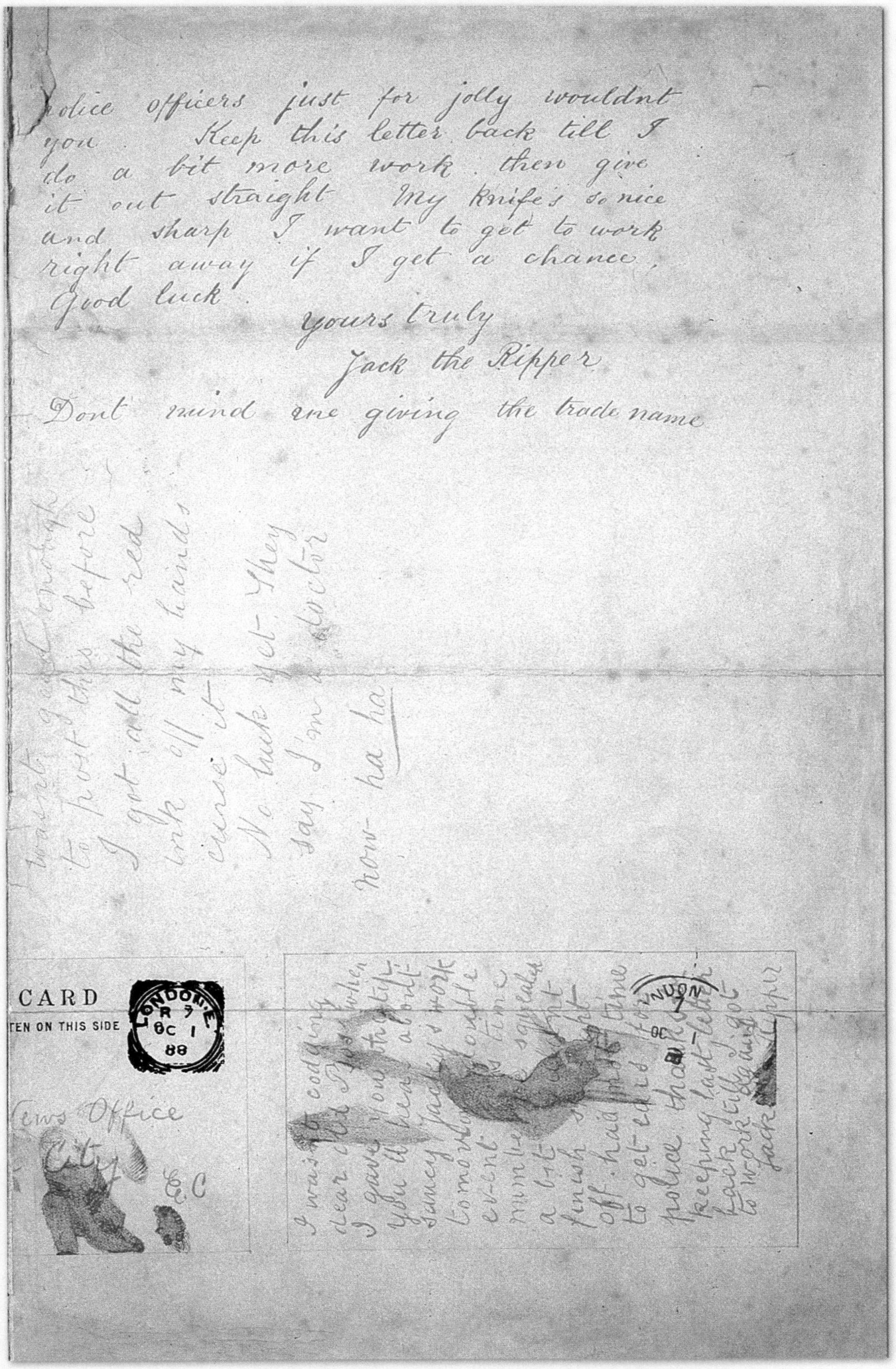

police officers just for jolly wouldnt
you. Keep this letter back till I
do a bit more work. then give
it out straight. My knife's so nice
and sharp I want to get to work
right away if I get a chance.
Good luck.

Yours truly

Jack the Ripper

Dont mind me giving the trade name

wasnt good enough
to post this before
I got all the red
ink off my hands
curse it
No luck yet. They
say I'm a doctor
now. ha ha

CARD
TEN ON THIS SIDE

LONDON E
OC 1
88

News Office
City
E.C

I was not codding
dear old Boss when
I gave you the tip.
you'll hear about
saucy Jacky's work
tomorrow double
event this time
number one squealed
a bit couldnt
finish straight
off. had not time
to get ears for
police thanks for
keeping last letter
back till I got
to work again.
Jack the Ripper

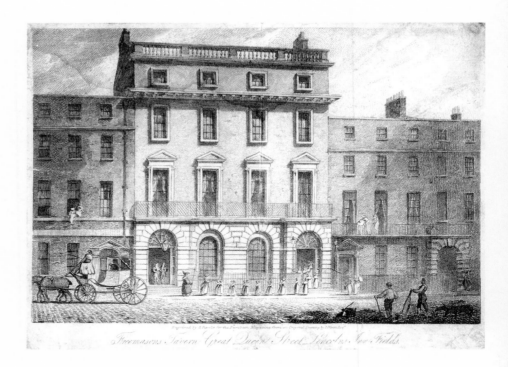

Freemasons Tavern Great Queen Street Lincoln's Inn Fields.

32

FA Cup design

It is an iconic shape, lifted in triumph each year in front of tens of thousands of football fans and coveted by millions more. The 1910 design for the FA Cup encompasses much that has characterized (or afflicted) the game of football ever since: the struggle between sporting elites and the grass roots for its soul; the tug of war between the purity of sport and the corrosive power of money; the sheer glamour of victory; and tragedy, in the First World War that would cut short the lives of professional footballers.

Team ball games of a sort have an ancient pedigree, arguably dating back to Han China. A type of football provoked medieval legislation, notably by Edward III, who sought to ban it for the disorder it promoted and the time it took enticing men away from more useful pursuits such as the practice of archery. By the early nineteenth century, though, football had begun to wither as a popular pastime, only to be saved by two contrasting trends. The first was the urge in Britain's public schools and universities to codify the rules for the ball games they favoured. The chaos of fixtures with each side playing to competing rules did not please the tidy minds of Victorian educationalists. The second was the increase in leisure time for the working classes, who from the 1840s began to enjoy a half-day's holiday on Saturday and sought entertainment to fill those idle hours.

Cambridge University codified its rules in 1848, though a variety of codes still abounded, emerging as the ancestors of Rugby League, Rugby Union, Association

Football and the Eton Wall Game. For a while, public school and university teams dominated the Football Association that was founded in 1863 to bring order to the fledgling world of the new sport. Before long, though, clubs began to spring up in working-class areas, nurtured by schools, churches, YMCAs and factories. What would become Manchester United grew

ABOVE An engraving of The Freemason's Tavern, Great Queen Street, London, where the Football Association was founded on 26 October 1863. The meeting was called to draw up an agreed set of rules, which almost foundered when one of the dozen clubs attending tried to insist that "hacking" (kicking an opponent's legs) be allowed. Of the 12 clubs at the meeting, only one, Civil Service FC (known as War Office in 1863), survives today as a football club.

OPPOSITE The 1910 FA cup design by Fattorini & Sons of Bradford had to meet a brief that the final cost should be no more than 50 guineas. The cup was used until 1992, when a replica was made. This in turn was replaced in 2014 by a second replica.

out of the Newton Heath railwaymen's club and Arsenal was born from the Woolwich munition workers' team.

By 1871 a national competition, the FA Challenge Cup, had been established. Its early tournaments were still dominated by a narrow social elite; half the players in the inaugural final had been educated at either Eton or Harrow. But after Blackburn's historic win over the Old Etonians in 1883, a public school side never again raised the "little tin idol". The first FA Cup was stolen in 1895 from a Birmingham shoe shop, where it was being displayed after Aston Villa's triumph in the final that year. By then, professionalism had entered the game. Public school purists in the FA tried to ban teams from playing fixtures against anyone who paid their players. But this barred those of humbler means from participating, and in 1885 they gave way and allowed wages (and transfer fees) to be paid.

The FA commissioned a replica cup, but in 1910 found to its embarrassment that it could not act against pirated versions because it did not own the copyright. A competition for a new version was ordered, and hundreds of designs flooded in. Most conformed to the age-old design of a trophy, with a bulging centre and arms on a narrow pedestal, harking back to the ancient Greek and Roman custom of a *tropaeum*, by which a victorious general hung the arms and armour of his defeated enemies on a tree-shaped frame. The winner, as it happened, came from an Italian family, who had moved to Yorkshire in the 1820s. So it was the design of Fattorini & Sons of Bradford – at 175 ounces (5 kilograms) and 19 inches (48 centimetres) high, fittingly decorated with classical bold fluting, bunches of grapes and vine leaves – that would be awarded to the victors of the 1911 tournament.

Antonio Fattorini, the firm's owner and also a director of Bradford City, must have been delighted when his team reached the

final. No doubt he was doubly so, when, after a replay against Newcastle in front of a crowd of over 60,000, Bradford's captain Jimmy Speirs thumped home the winning goal. The fans were delirious as a Bradford team lifted a Bradford-made trophy in the

club's only FA Cup triumph before or since. It was Speirs' finest hour, too. Although Leeds bought him for the near-record sum of £1,400 in 1912, the outbreak of the First World War interrupted his career. Twice-wounded, Speirs died at Passchendaele in

August 1917, one of nine Bradford players to fall in the war, making it the worst affected of England's clubs.

Tinged with sadness, the FA cup competition was resumed in 1920 after its wartime suspension. Fattorini's trophy continued to be the prize until 1992 when, fragile after almost 70 outings, it was retired. So fixed in the mind of the public was its shape that the FA decided to retain the original design. The trophy, and the raw emotion it still inspires, were unchanged.

ABOVE At the FA Cup Final replay of 1911 between Bradford City and Newcastle United at Old Trafford, the winning goal is scored for Bradford City by Jimmy Speirs. The first match between the teams took place at Crystal Palace and ended in a 0-0 draw.

Scott of the Antarctic's last diary entry

They are the last words of a dying man, trapped by an Antarctic blizzard in his tent just miles from supplies that would have saved him. They are also the best example of a distinctly British taste for heroes who fail, as long as they are seen to do their duty. Robert Falcon Scott, whose final diary entry this is, was immortalized for the manner in which he failed to reach the South Pole ahead of a rival expedition mounted by the Norwegian Roald Amundsen. At key moments he chose chivalry over good sense, and amateur bravado over cool-headed professionalism. And he – and his men – died for it.

Scott was a career naval officer who had little interest in the Antarctic until a chance meeting with Clements Markham, the President of the Royal Geographical Society, led to his command of the *Discovery* Expedition in 1901–4. Although the expedition had scientific objectives, its clear goal was exploration in the Ross Sea area and, in particular, to reach as close as possible to the South Pole.

Scott's achievement was real enough – he and another veteran Polar explorer, Ernest Shackleton, trudged to within 500 miles (800 kilometres) of the South Pole before turning back. But, despite the lionizing he was subject to on his return, it was not enough for Scott, who determined to return for a second try. Annoyed that Shackleton had not included him in a new expedition in 1907 – which fell tantalizingly short of the Pole – Scott decided to mount another attempt himself.

Having raised the £50,000 needed, Scott bought the *Terra Nova*, a converted whaler, and began to assemble his team. He preferred enthusiasm over experience and two of its members, Henry Bowers and Lawrence "Titus" Oates, had never before set foot on Antarctica. Scott had learnt all the wrong lessons from the *Discovery* expedition. The dogs had let them down in 1904 and so he favoured the use of mechanical sleighs,

which proved unreliable, and ponies, which could not cope in the icy conditions.

It was only when the *Terra Nova* reached Melbourne in October that Scott found he was in a race with Amundsen. The Norwegian was a far more pragmatic leader, and both he and his men were expert skiers, knew how to handle their dogs and had a far more realistic assessment of the logistical effort required to reach the Pole.

After making base on Ross Island, Scott sent out teams to lay depots with supplies that would be needed on the return from the Pole. Fatally, the most southerly of these, "One Ton Depot", was 30 miles (55 kilometres) north of the intended point. This meant Scott's team would be dangerously low on supplies on the return journey before they reached it. On 1 November, Scott set out with 10 ponies, two dog teams and two motor sledges. The going was slow, the motor sledges broke down and the ponies had to be butchered, leaving the men hauling heavy sleighs up the steep Beardmore glacier in temperatures as low as -76°F (-60°C). Once on the Polar Plateau, Scott sent the remaining support party back and a five-man team (Scott, Edward Wilson, Lawrence Oates, Henry Bowers and Edgar Evans) made the final push to the Pole.

It was an exhausted and disheartened group that arrived there on 17 January 1912 to find

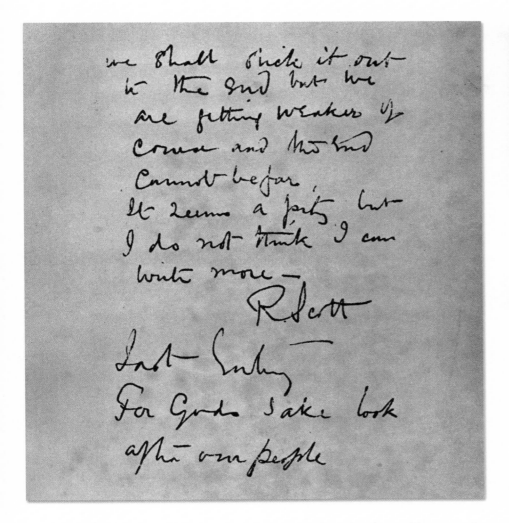

Amundsen had beaten them by more than a month. Having planted the Union Jack in a cairn to flutter alongside the flag of the victorious Norwegians, Scott and his men began the trek back to base. Bedevilled by bad weather, their progress was too slow. Evans grew steadily weaker and died on 17 February. Oates was suffering from severe frostbite and could hardly walk. On 16 March, seeing his condition was endangering the others, he walked out of his tent saying, "I am going outside, and may be some time." He never returned.

By 19 March, Scott and the two others were just 11 miles (17 kilometres) from One Ton depot, but were trapped by a blizzard. Out of food and hope, they sat in their sleeping bags and waited to die. Scott kept his diary until near the end. In the penultimate entry he wrote, "Had we lived, I should have had a tale to tell of the hardihood, endurance and courage of my companions which would have stirred the heart of every Englishman". But then, despair took him, and he scrawled: "It seems a pity, but I do not think I can write more", before returning to a hero's sense of duty with a final plea to those who might find his corpse: "For God's sake look after our people."

A search party found the bodies seven months later and recovered Scott's papers, geological samples and the team's diaries. At their base at McMurdo Sound, the remaining crew of the *Terra Nova* erected a cross in their leader's memory. On it was inscribed the last line of Tennyson's poem *Ulysses*: "To strive, to seek, to find, and not to yield." It was a fitting memorial to a hero, whose courage and refusal to turn back made him a model that Edwardian schoolchildren were exhorted to emulate. Amundsen, whose cool efficiency had made his race with Scott an unequal one and himself the victor, received none of the glory.

34

Distress call from *Titanic*

The telegram is brief, but chilling, bearing the shocking news that SS *Titanic*, the greatest passenger liner yet built, has struck an iceberg and is sinking. The loss of *Titanic*, in the early hours of 14/15 April 1912, claimed the lives of more than 1,500 passengers and crew and became the most famous maritime disaster in history.

It was supposed to be so different. *Titanic* was one of three new Olympic-class vessels built for the White Star Line as part of the race to create the fastest and most sumptuous ships for the ruthlessly competitive transatlantic passenger route. At 52,000 tons, she was the jewel in the crown of the company's fleet, offering unparalleled levels of comfort. First Class cabins were decked out in Empire style, and featured a gymnasium, squash court, swimming pool and Turkish spa.

The ship was only about half full for her maiden voyage from Southampton to New York. Some 1,300 passengers boarded, with prices ranging from £7/5s in Third Class to over £220 paid by John Jacob Astor IV, and Isidor Straus, the owner of Macy's department store, for their First Class cabins. Also on board was a massive store of supplies, including 75,000 pounds of meat, 40,000 fresh eggs, nearly 3 tons of tomatoes, 1,100 pounds of jam and 8,000 cigars.

Captain Edward Smith, who had been transferred from *Titanic*'s sister-ship *Olympic* – ironically because she had been involved in a collision – must have been confident in the ship's safety features. There were 16 watertight compartments, separated by bulkheads, to contain damage in the event of an accident. The ship was equipped with the latest in telegraph technology, supplied by the Marconi Company, to transmit rapid signals in case of distress (and also, an added luxury feature, to allow passengers to send and receive telegrams on board).

All this was to no avail. At 11.40 p.m. on the cold, clear night of 14 April, four days into the voyage and around 375 miles (600 kilometres)

ABOVE Jack Phillips was the Chief Wireless Officer on board *Titanic*. An experienced radio operator for Marconi, he had worked on White Star liners since 1906. When the ship hit the iceberg, Phillips and his assistant Harold Bride sent the first distress call and carried on transmitting until minutes before the ship sank.

OPPOSITE The first telegram was sent 5 minutes after *Titanic* hit an iceberg late on 14 April 1912. The ship's new telegraphy system had a range of around 1,000 miles (1,600 kilometres) and several nearby ships, including the SS *Birma*, the recipient of this one, received her distress calls.

The Russian East Asiatic S.S. Co.   Radio-Telegram.

S.S. "Birma".

No Words.	Origin.Station.	Time handed in.	Via.	Remarks.
bg to S.	Titanic	11 H.45M.April 14/15 1912.		Distress call Ligs Loud.

Cgd – Sos. from M. G. Y.

We have struck iceberg sinking fast come to our assis-tance.

Position Lat. 41.46 n. Lon. 50.14. w.

M.G.Y.

south of Newfoundland, the lookout spotted a large object in the water and immediately telephoned the bridge. Captain Smith ordered a full stop and put the engines into reverse, but it was too late; around 30 seconds later the iceberg struck the *Titanic* on her starboard side, ripping a 330-foot (100-metre) gash through six compartments.

As water flooded into the breach, Jack Phillips and Harold Bride, the radio operators, tapped out the first of dozens of telegrams. The distress call CQD – the modern version

SOS had not yet become established – was said to stand for "Come Quick Danger", while MGY was *Titanic*'s call sign. There were several ships in the area including, SS *Birma*, the recipient of this telegram; the SS *Californian*, which saw *Titanic*'s distress flares, but did not respond; and SS *Carpathia*, which rushed to the scene. *Birma* steamed to the rescue but was too late to be of any help.

The evacuation was almost leisurely. It took the captain 40 minutes after *Titanic* struck

the iceberg to order the lifeboats lowered. There was capacity in them for only 1,178 people, half the crew and passengers aboard. The order that women and children be given priority was largely obeyed and many men stood back as their families scrambled to safety. Among those who survived, though, was Bruce Ismay, managing director of the White Star Line. His senior position in the shipping company gave rise to criticism at the subsequent inquests that he should have stayed with the vessel.

The telegraph operators continued to transmit as deck after deck became submerged. At 1.27 a.m., they sent the message "We are putting the women in the boats" and then at 2.20 a.m. *Titanic* began to sink faster and to break in two. All the lifeboats had by now launched and those left clinging to the ship's side were plunged into freezing water as she slid 9,800 feet (3,000 metres) to the ocean bed.

Rumours and myths abound about the ship's last moments that terrible night. Many of them were passed on by petrified survivors who huddled in the lifeboats, sheltering from the freezing water that killed any who fell into it within minutes. The orchestra was said to have played to the last minute, its final number being the sombre hymn "Nearer, My God, to Thee". The industrialist Benjamin Guggenheim, seeing he had no place on a lifeboat, was said to have changed into evening dress, remarking, "We are prepared to go down like gentlemen".

Carpathia was first on the scene, about two hours later, and picked up around 700 survivors: three days later she landed them in New York. The subsequent American and British inquiries absolved Captain Smith — who died with his ship — of any fault, but the disaster shook the complacency of a shipping establishment that had viewed such vessels as all but unsinkable. *Titanic*'s sinking led to the establishment in 1914 of SOLAS, an international body to supervise maritime safety, the legacy, perhaps, of those final desperate messages, pleading for help that would come too slowly to save 1,500 souls.

OPPOSITE This 1911 Thomas Cook poster advertising Atlantic crossings on *Titanic* and her sister-ship *Olympic* stresses the sheer size (and, implicitly, the safety) of the vessels. Many passengers aboard *Titanic* bought their tickets through the company.

BELOW Survivors of the *Titanic* disaster about to be taken aboard *Carpathia*. The vessel was the first to answer *Titanic*'s distress call and reached the site at about 4 a.m. The quick action by Captain Arthur Rostron resulted in the saving of over 700 passengers.

35

Police Report on the death of suffragette Emily Davison

The report by a member of the constabulary about Britain's most famous race-course accident adopts a level, almost deadpan tone. It accords equal weight to the jockey and the woman who has just run in front of the king's horse at the Epsom Derby, an act which ended with both lying unconscious at the side of the track.

The only nod towards the significance of the moment is the policeman's reference to Emily Wilding Davison as a "well known militant suffragette". It was an accurate description, since Miss Davison, born to a well-to-do Kent family who moved to Northumberland, had become involved in the campaign to win women the right to vote in 1906, and had been jailed nine times for her activities.

She was part of a growing movement, largely composed of upper- and middle-class women who resented their exclusion from the nation's political life. Although they originally called themselves "suffragists", the term suffragette was coined by the *Daily Mail* as an insult to those who followed Emmeline Pankhurst's Women's Social and Political Union (WSPU). It argued for more radical tactics than those espoused by Millicent Fawcett's more gradualist National Union of Women's Suffrage Societies.

Forceful debate got the WSPU nowhere in shifting entrenched interests that opposed women's suffrage. From 1909 they became more militant, chaining themselves to railings, smashing windows and staging arson attacks, including burning down the seaside house of Arthur du Cros, the MP for Hastings, a vocal opponent of votes for women.

The authorities struck back, arresting hundreds of WSPU activists. When the women began to go on hunger strikes, they were ordered to be force fed. It wasn't until 1913 that the Cat and Mouse Act was passed, which allowed hunger strikers to be released from prison and then rearrested once their health was restored.

Emily Davison threw herself wholeheartedly into this maelstrom. Educated at St Hugh's Oxford, she was refused the chance to gain her degree there because this was an accolade still denied to women. She then took up a series of positions as governess for which she was clearly intellectually overqualified. In 1908 she adopted full-time activism and the next year was arrested for the first time as she tried to force her way into Parliament following a rally. She showed her mettle once in Holloway, where she smashed 24 panes of glass in the first two cells the warders put her in before someone wrestled away her hammer.

In October 1909 she was arrested again, this time for throwing a stone at Lloyd George's car, and while in Strangeways prison was force-fed for the first time. In 1912 she served yet another stretch for fire-bombing a postbox, and while at Holloway threw herself down the stairs in protest at being force-fed. Not long after, in an essay entitled "The Price of Liberty", she wrote: "The glorious and inscrutable spirit of liberty has but one further penalty written in its power:

OPPOSITE Emily Davison wears a graduation gown and a "Holloway Badge" showing she has been imprisoned for her suffragette beliefs. In a poignant irony, the college where she studied was Royal Holloway, which, though it allowed women to study, did not allow them to graduate formally.

THE LATE MISS E.W. DAVISON.

the surrender of life itself. It is the supreme consummation of sacrifice, than which none can be higher and greater."

No one knows if Emily Davison planned to die on 4 June 1913. She was at the front of the crowd, pressed against the rails at Tattenham Corner, and onlookers later related that she ducked under the fence as the leading horses came round the bend. She may have been holding a flag or scarf, possibly intending to pin a WSPU banner to the king's horse, Anmer. But she was knocked down by Anmer and as she fell, its hooves trampled her, fracturing her skull. The horse fell, too, taking with it the jockey, Herbert Smith. Attempts by bystanders to revive them failed, and they were taken to Epsom Cottage Hospital, where it turned out Smith only had concussion.

Despite attempts by her surgeon friend Charles Mansell-Moullin to operate to relieve bleeding in her skull, Davison died four days

later. The press reacted furiously, raging that both jockey and horse could have been killed, but the WSPU defended her. Emmeline Pankhurst's daughter Christabel wrote: "Miss Davison has died for women. She has died to call attention to their wrong and win them the vote." At her funeral in Bloomsbury on 14 June, thousands of women marched with a banner on which was emblazoned "Fight on and God will give the victory".

Victory did finally come, but only after most suffragette activity was suspended during the First World War. The limited suffrage granted in 1918 (to married women over 30) was seen as a reward for this support rather than directly forced by the militants' lobbying. The WSPU, though, had kept their cause in the public eye and the actions of Emily Davison on Derby Day 1913 made her a heroine of the movement and the suffragettes' only martyr. It wasn't until 1928 that women won the same voting rights as men.

ABOVE Suffragette leader Emmeline Pankhurst is arrested in Victoria Street, London on 13 February 1908. She was sentenced to six weeks' imprisonment for participating in a deputation to the House of Commons.

FOLLOWING PAGES The police report on Emily Davison's death is submitted on standard police note paper, in a matter of fact bureaucratic tone. On the second page the officer admits "I did not actually witness the accident". Conflicting reports by eyewitnesses made it later very hard to reconstruct exactly what happened and what Davison's real intentions had been.

Metropolitan Police.

Lee Road STATION. R DIVISION.

8th June 1913

With reference to attached Correspondence I beg to report that at about 3pm on 4th inst I was on duty on Epsom Race Course when the race for the Derby Stakes took place.

When the horses were rounding Tattenham Corner, Miss Emily Davison, a well known militant Suffragette suddenly rushed from under the rail immediately in front of "Anmer" a horse owned by H.M. The King, and ridden by Herbert Jones.

The woman was knocked down and rendered unconscious, the horse was thrown down and the Jockey also rendered unconscious.

Police of "N" Division were on duty at the spot and P.S. 4 NR Bunn 8 NR Burridge and P.C. 59 NR Eady promptly went to the assistance of the woman, and Insp Whitebread "N" with P.C.s 80 NR Brown, 84 NR Phillips and 85 NR Johnson attended to the

injured man. Dr Lane, who was
in the Crowd, at once volunteered
to render medical aid to the
woman and another medical
man attended to the man, who
was conveyed on the Police
Ambulance to the Ambulance
Station at the rear of the
Grand Stand and the woman
was taken in a motor car
to the Epsom Cottage Hospital.

I did not actually witness
the accident as I had withdrawn
from the Course with the other
mounted Officers, but I was
on the spot immediately
afterwards and directed Police
action. Dr Lane afterwards
expressed to me his appreciation
of the assistance rendered to
him by the officers mentioned,
I consider that those officers
who attended to the injured
man are also worthy of
commendation, including the
"V" Division officers in charge of
the Ambulance who was
promptly on the spot without
being called and rendered
every assistance to Insp^r Whitebread
and the other Officers with him.

I am unable to give
the name and number of

the "V" Divn P.C. but the whole
of the facts were reported
at Epsom Police Station to which
I beg reference.
                              Geo White Bishop
        Submitted through
Supt Robinson V Division
              Mr Eagle Supt

Davison and the king's horse, Anmer, lie sprawled on the ground at Tattenham Corner after she stepped onto the racetrack. A return ticket to Victoria was found in her purse, leading some to speculate that she had not intended to kill herself.

36

The Balfour Declaration

It is less than a hundred words long. Yet seldom has such a short document had an afterlife of such bitterness, division and violence. The Balfour Declaration, by which the British government of 1917 committed itself to "use their best endeavours to facilitate the achievement" of a Jewish national home in Palestine, led inexorably to the creation of the state of Israel. And in doing so it sowed the seeds of nearly seven decades of conflict between Jews and their Arab neighbours in the region.

The Declaration was born out of Britain's fears that in the impending break-up of the Ottoman empire, Britain would lose out to France in a scramble for the Middle East. Britain wanted to preserve what it saw as its vital interests in the area – particularly Egypt and the Suez Canal. The defeat of the Ottoman Turks had to be secured and the British government was not averse to engaging in a game of triple-dealing by which the territory of Palestine was promised several times over.

Firstly, the Arabs had to be rewarded for their rebellion against the Turks with the promise of independence after the war was over. In 1915 Sir Henry McMahon, the British high commissioner in Egypt, wrote to Hussein ibn Ali, the emir of Mecca, apparently promising to give Iraq and much of Syria to the Arabs, but left the status of Palestine ambiguous. Then, in almost direct denial of the McMahon correspondence, a secret agreement between France and Britain was hatched between Sir Mark Sykes and François Georges-Picot in 1916: Sykes–Picot carved up the Middle East into British and French spheres of influence, with Palestine to be left as an internationally administered zone.

Meanwhile a third force was making itself felt. Some British ministers believed that here was a chance to secure the support of world Jewry in dealing with the uncertain Middle East that would emerge from the First World War. They were well aware of the yearning of the Jews for a presence in Palestine, and were inclined to favour encouraging the Zionist movement, even though Jews amounted to less than 10 per cent of its population. The problem was that the Zionists had just one thing in mind – the establishment of a Jewish state. As far back as 1896 they had argued that this was the only solution to growing anti-Semitism in Europe. This had now blossomed into a determined campaign led by Chaim Weizmann in London. And he was rewarded in November 1917 by the news that the British Cabinet was meeting to discuss some kind of Jewish presence in Palestine. Weizmann and his team were waiting outside the room in the fervent hope that the Cabinet would meet their demands. Suddenly the meeting was over and out came an official with a huge smile on his face: "Mr Weizmann," he exclaimed, "it's a boy!".

If it wasn't everything the Zionists wanted, the declaration of Foreign Secretary Arthur Balfour was for them a massive step in the right direction, even though Britain's rather woolly concept of a "National Home" wasn't the formal promise of a state. The Arabs, on

OPPOSITE Attacks and reprisals between Jews and Arabs mounted in the dying days of Britain's Mandate over Palestine. This is the aftermath of the detonation by Arab militia of three hijacked British army trucks on Jerusalem's Ben Yehuda Street on 22 February 1948. Fifty-eight Jewish civilians were killed.

ABOVE Arthur Balfour was Conservative Prime Minister of Britain in 1902–05. During the First World War he joined Liberal Prime Minister David Lloyd George's coalition government in 1916 as Foreign Secretary. His declaration was to plunge the Middle East into a century – and more – of bitter struggle.

RIGHT The Balfour Declaration was not a government document, but a letter from Foreign Secretary Arthur Balfour to Lord Rothschild, a leading British Jew. Several drafts had been exchanged between the government and the Zionist movement, each vaguer than the last about what the British were guaranteeing.

Foreign Office,
November 2nd, 1917.

Dear Lord Rothschild,

I have much pleasure in conveying to you, on behalf of His Majesty's Government, the following declaration of sympathy with Jewish Zionist aspirations which has been submitted to, and approved by, the Cabinet.

"His Majesty's Government view with favour the establishment in Palestine of a national home for the Jewish people, and will use their best endeavours to facilitate the achievement of this object, it being clearly understood that nothing shall be done which may prejudice the civil and religious rights of existing non-Jewish communities in Palestine, or the rights and political status enjoyed by Jews in any other country".

I should be grateful if you would bring this declaration to the knowledge of the Zionist Federation.

the other hand, felt that Britain had broken its promises to them and that aggressive Jewish immigration into the new "National Home" would soon lead to land grabs in territory they had inhabited for centuries. Balfour did pledge that "nothing shall be done which may prejudice the civil and religious rights" of the non-Jewish population of Palestine, which was after all the vast majority. But the Arabs believed his words were not worth the paper they were written on.

Successive attempts at finding a political solution in Palestine, which would satisfy both Jewish and Arab communities, failed.

When the British acquired a League of Nations Mandate over Palestine from 1920, they had already lost the trust of both sides. Increased Jewish immigration in the 1920s and 1930s, which the British only half-heartedly tried to stem, meant that, ultimately, partition came to be seen as the only solution. When the Peel Commission in 1937 recommended this, the battleground shifted to establishing a map of who should own what.

The British were never able to resolve this and, in the dying days of their Palestine mandate, beset by violence from both sides

and a brutally effective campaign by the Zionists to oust them, they simply washed their hands of the issue. A United Nations partition plan, agreed by all except the Arabs in November 1947, failed to prevent the outbreak of war between them and the newly proclaimed state of Israel in May 1948. Since then, despite occasional false dawns, a lasting peace between Palestinian Arabs and Israeli Jews has been impossible to achieve. Almost the only thing that both sides agree on is that the Balfour Declaration played a key role in the slide to disaster.

37

Haig's "Backs to the Wall" Order

Field Marshal Sir Douglas Haig was not a man given to melodrama or rhetorical flourishes. But his special order of 11 April 1918 was as close as he came to both. It came at a desperate time for the British army in France, of which he was commander-in-chief. Three weeks earlier the Germans had begun a series of major offensives which made rapid progress (by First World War standards) and which threatened to cut the British off from their supply bases at the Channel Ports. Haig tells his men they have their "backs to the wall" and that "believing in the justice of our cause each one of us must fight on to the end." It is an extraordinarily direct and emotional appeal and, equally extraordinarily, it seems to have worked.

The early part of 1918 was a difficult period for the countries allied against Germany. There was little expectation of an early end to the War. The appalling attritional battles of 1916 and 1917, such as the Somme and Passchendaele, had resulted in mass casualties for almost no discernible gain. New weapons had been introduced as the fighting wore on, such as the tank and poison gas, while aircraft development moved at a terrific pace. But nothing had emerged as a breakthrough weapon, capable of more than localized successes. The two sides still faced each other in trench lines protected by barbed-wire, machine-gun nests and artillery, with bloody stalemate the seemingly inevitable outcome of any offensive.

The Germans, though, had a window of opportunity. The October 1917 Revolution in Russia had led to chaos in the Russian army and on 3 March 1918 the new Bolshevik government signed the Treaty of Brest-Litovsk. This took Russia out of the war and allowed the Germans to redeploy divisions to the Western Front. The gain would be only temporary as the United States had entered the war in April 1917. Before long the flow of fresh American troops would nullify the Germans' advantage.

The Allies had sensed a new German offensive might come, but they had done little to prepare for it. The British Expeditionary Force was experiencing a manpower shortage by early 1918, and a recent reorganization had led to a cut of around 10 per cent in its fighting strength. When Erich Ludendorff, the Deputy Chief of the German General Staff, launched his strike on 21 March, he had concentrated 76 German divisions in contrast to the 26 that Haig could command.

Ludendorff hoped the German Spring Offensive would be a decisive blow that would shatter the Allies' morale and knock them out of the war. Its first phase, Operation Michael, gained 3 miles (4.8 kilometres) in the first day, and then pushed ominously towards Amiens. Then, the offensive stalled as the British lines solidified. Nonetheless, there was near panic in the British and French high commands. Haig offered to resign, but was turned down.

Worse followed after the second major German offensive (Georgette) was launched on 9 April. It swept through Passchendaele and almost reached Ypres, seizing with ease territory which had seen months of fruitless fighting and tens of thousands of deaths the year before. By 11 April the British were down to 13 divisions facing three times that in the German spearhead.

This was when Haig issued his order. He needed his men's morale not to crack and he understood that if the German hammer-blows could be absorbed, then "victory will belong to the side which holds out the longest".

Haig's men held. Although the BEF had suffered 300,000 casualties, Ludendorff called a halt on 30 April. Two offensives over the summer directed against the French lines around the Chemin des Dames and Rheims similarly failed to break through. The Spring Offensive had cost the Germans nearly three-quarters of a million casualties and the ground they had captured simply left them exposed in a series of almost indefensible salients.

Through the summer the Allies rebuilt their units and planned an offensive of their own. When they struck on 8 August at Amiens, they achieved the longest single-day advance yet on the Western Front. Eight miles (13 kilometres) seems little enough, but in First World War terms it was enormous. Ludendorff called it the "black day of the German army" and neither his nor the army's morale ever recovered. By late October the Allies' "Hundred Days Offensive" had breached the Hindenburg Line, the system of defences that the Germans had deemed impregnable, but which they had also never expected to be tested. With the armed forces wracked by mutinies and strikes and political demonstrations reaching dangerous levels at home, Germany sued for an armistice which ended the war on 11 November.

Seven months before, this would have seemed an unlikely outcome. Haig has been criticized for the failures of the offensives he launched at such great cost in 1916 and 1917. But his appeal to his men to stand firm with their "Backs to the Wall" and the defensive success he masterminded against the German Spring Offensive saved Britain from defeat. This order was an important milestone on the road to victory.

OPPOSITE Australian troops walk along duckboards near Passchendaele in October 1917. The hard-fought gains of that battle were swept away by the German advances that prompted Haig to issue his "Backs to the Wall" order.

ABOVE In his Special Order of the Day for 11 April 1918, Haig tries to inspire his men to a last-ditch defence. "Every position must be held to the last man ...," he writes. "With our backs to the wall and believing in the justice of our cause each one of us must fight to the end."

RIGHT Douglas Haig in his Field Marshal's uniform (a rank to which he had been promoted in 1916). Unpopular with Prime Minister Lloyd George because of the massive losses the British suffered in the dreadful battles of 1916–17, Haig proved his worth in the Allied counteroffensive of summer 1918 that finally brought victory.

38

First edition of the *Radio Times*

It begins with a rather clumsy stab at a joke by the BBC's Director of Programmes. He harps back to another "power station at Westminster" whose "directors had lofty ambitions". He says he's alluding to Guy Fawkes, his "predecessor in the broadcasting business". But he failed "to make oscillations, owing to Government intervention" and ended up losing his head.

Far from losing its head, the infant British Broadcasting Corporation went from strength to strength after the publication of this, its first magazine, on 28 September 1923. By the 1930s, The Radio Times was selling three million copies and the BBC had established itself at the heart of British life. From the start it provided its listeners with a universal service – from the gravest news to light-hearted domestic comedies. It offered a whole panoply of programmes that were soon very popular.

The excitement began when the Italian inventor Guglielmo Marconi received his first patent for wireless telegraphy in June 1896. Within 20 years, radio stations had sprung up throughout the United States, where more than 400 stations were licensed to transmit by 1913. In Britain, opposition from the Post Office, the body tasked with regulating the new technology, meant that broadcasting was confined to radio amateurs.

A slight relaxation of the regime began in 1920, when Marconi's 2LO station was permitted to broadcast from its Chelmsford offices. Its early programmes included a medley by the renowned opera singer Nellie Melba, and her fame helped increase the clamour for proper British radio stations. By August 1927 there were 127 stations transmitting, many run by lone amateur enthusiasts. In late 1922, to bring order to the increasingly chaotic radio scene, the government sanctioned the formation of the British Broadcasting Corporation. The BBC was to be the sole legal radio broadcaster, a right it enjoyed until 1973.

On only its second day of operation, the BBC helped establish its enduring reputation for news reporting by broadcasting the results of the November 1922 General Election. It was funded in part by a royalty of 10 shillings on all radio sets sold – a levy that would turn into an annual licence fee. From this modest beginning the BBC was re-established in 1927 as a publicly funded but

independent corporation with John Reith as its first Director General.

The *Radio Times* was born because the newspapers began to demand a fee for printing the schedule of radio programmes and Reith preferred to set up a rival publication rather than pay up. Its first edition contained advice on buying and operating radio sets and on the BBC's technology. The rest was a mixture not unlike that of today: reader's letters, jokes, competitions, and features including Major Ratclyffe Dugmore's advice on how to avoid a charging rhino and Hayter Preston's piece on the Ming dynasty poet Ling Po. The programmes that first week consisted largely of music, with a few slots for the weather, a children's hour, daily programmes directed at the Boys Brigade and the forerunner of *Woman's Hour*. News was broadcast only before 7 p.m., at the insistence of the newspaper proprietors who feared the competition.

This became even more the case with the introduction of regular television programmes from 1936, although at first there were probably only 100 sets capable of receiving the transmissions from Muswell Hill. The first television broadcast on 2 November included Chinese jugglers and a musical comedy artiste named Adele Dixon singing a specially composed song entitled "Television". The new medium's power was immediately apparent: television captured Neville Chamberlain waving his "piece of paper" as he landed at Heston airport after his meeting with Adolf Hitler in September 1938. But it was on radio that the country heard Chamberlain solemnly pronounce on 3 September 1939 that Britain and Germany were at war.

The past 75 years have seen a massive diversification of telecommunications. In 1955 the BBC lost its monopoly in television broadcasting. Eighteen years later independent radio stations were allowed. The *Radio Times* was landed with a rival in the 1950s when Independent TV launched the *TV Times*: the BBC had not registered the title, as managers there had thought that television would not catch on. By the twenty-first century, the snowballing number of television and radio channels, including those delivered by the Internet, meant that no one outlet had a dominant position in the way the BBC did in 1923. Yet, just as it did when the first *Radio Times* came out that year, the corporation today retains its quintessentially British character and still proudly proclaims its role as a public service broadcaster.

OPPOSITE Scottish engineer John Reith confessed after his interview in 1922 for a job at the new British Broadcasting Company that "I hadn't the remotest idea what broadcasting was". But he proved an effective leader, creating the blueprint for public service broadcasting copied around the world.

ABOVE Volume 1, number 1 of the *Radio Times* was issued on 28 September 1923. Much of the front page consists of an editorial by Arthur Burrows, the BBC's Director of Programming, in which he proudly explains that since November of the preceding year the BBC has transmitted 8,000 hours of programmes.

39

The Abdication of Edward VIII

The document is terse and formal, as befits a royal proclamation. Yet in fewer than a hundred words it marks the resolution of the worst crisis to hit the British monarchy since the execution of Charles I. Edward VIII's Instrument of Abdication renounced his throne to be with the woman he loved. The British Establishment closed ranks against a man they viewed as utterly unsuitable to be king and the outsider, a foreigner – and, worse than that, a divorcée – who sought to be queen.

Edward had a quarter-century apprenticeship as Prince of Wales. During this time, he acquired a reputation as a playboy, engaging in a series of relationships with married women. Many of them were conducted under the nose of his father, George V, at Fort Belvedere in Windsor Great Park, his official residence from 1930. In 1931 he was introduced to Wallis Simpson, an American socialite who was divorced from her first husband, and estranged from her second.

By 1934, the couple had become romantically involved and the establishment began to take notice. Divorcées were not allowed to remarry in the Church of England, and Edward as its future head would be setting, in its view, an appalling example. Whatever the royal family might do in private, such a public flouting of the generally accepted moral code could undermine the very foundations of monarchy. Short though of instructing Special Branch to gather information on the couple, no real attempts were made to persuade Edward to give her up.

On 20 January 1936 George V died of the chronic lung disease that had plagued his later years. Edward was now king and the question of his attachment to Simpson became more pressing. The whispers against her grew, aggravated by a general upper-class anti-American snobbery. Over the summer Edward went on a Mediterranean cruise aboard the yacht *Nahlin*, accompanied by his lover. While the British press observed a self-imposed vow of silence, the American newspapers gleefully reproduced photos of their scantily clad countrywoman in the entourage of a British king. This was front page news. Back at home British churchmen and politicians, most notably Prime Minister Stanley Baldwin, fumed and plotted.

In October, Simpson's latest divorce petition reached its final stages, making a marriage to the king look like a real possibility. In mid-November Edward's private secretary Alec Hardinge was induced to pen a letter warning his master that "the silence in the British Press on the subject of Your Majesty's friendship with Mrs Simpson is not going to be maintained". But the king did not take the hint. Stubborn and desperately in love with Mrs Simpson, he continued his affair. On 1 December the dam broke, when the Bishop of Bradford made a thinly veiled speech warning the king that he was in need of "God's grace", which the press took as the starting gun for a frenzy of speculation.

Baldwin threatened that the government might resign en masse, and though the idea of a morganatic marriage was floated, by which Edward might marry Simpson but she would not be queen, few politicians supported it. Baldwin blocked Edward's attempt to make a direct appeal by radio to his subjects and a deputation was sent to Simpson – who had gone to France to escape the pressure – which persuaded her to announce that she was prepared to give up her relationship with the king.

Edward ignored it. His mind was now made up and he told Baldwin he "might go" rather than renounce Mrs Simpson. The prime minister needed no prompting and an instrument of abdication was drawn up on 5 December. Five days later, Edward signed it at Fort Belvedere, in the presence of his three brothers Albert (who subsequently became king as George VI) and the Dukes of

Gloucester and Kent. Edward thus became the first English king, since the time of the Anglo-Saxon monarch Sigeric of Essex in the eighth century, to renounce his throne voluntarily.

Edward made an impassioned broadcast explaining that he had given up the crown because he could not fulfil his duties without the support of "the woman I love". He then left for Austria and married Mrs Simpson the next year. After a brief flirtation with the Nazi regime in Germany – he visited Hitler in October 1937 – he was despatched to a safe distance as Governor of the Bahamas and then lived the rest of his life in comparative obscurity in France. Edward had learnt the terrible lesson that, though a king might expect loyalty from his subjects, those subjects expected in return loyalty to their idea of what a king should be. For the Royal Family the abdication left a terrible scar, which even in the twenty-first century has barely healed, making further such renunciations unlikely.

INSTRUMENT OF ABDICATION

I, Edward the Eighth, of Great Britain, Ireland, and the British Dominions beyond the Seas, King, Emperor of India, do hereby declare My irrevocable determination to renounce the Throne for Myself and for My descendants, and My desire that effect should be given to this Instrument of Abdication immediately.

In token whereof I have hereunto set My hand this tenth day of December, nineteen hundred and thirty six, in the presence of the witnesses whose signatures are subscribed.

SIGNED AT
FORT BELVEDERE
IN THE PRESENCE
OF

OPPOSITE Edward, then still Prince of Wales, poses with his brother the Duke of York (to the right) and the Princesses Elizabeth and Margaret. The Duke, who had a severe stammer, never expected to be king, but rose to the challenge magnificently after Edward's abdication.

ABOVE LEFT Edward stands beside Mrs Simpson on their wedding day, 3 June 1937. Although she was granted the title Duchess of Windsor, Mrs Simpson was pointedly denied the title "Her Royal Highness".

ABOVE Edward VIII's instrument of abdication is a simple document, but it came after months of intense and mounting pressure on the king to abandon his relationship with Mrs Simpson. Edward still signs himself as king ("R" for rex). The other three signatories are his next oldest brother Albert, who then became king, and his two other brothers, the Dukes of Gloucester and Kent.

40

The Munich Agreement

It is the most notorious "piece of paper" in modern British history. As British Prime Minister Neville Chamberlain descended the steps of his plane at Heston Aerodrome on 30 September 1938, he was in exultant mood. He believed he had prevented a European war by brokering an agreement with Germany's leader, Adolf Hitler, over the future of ethnic Germans in Czechoslovakia. He theatrically waved the paper containing the terms of a further accord signed between Britain and Germany which, as Chamberlain read out, proclaimed "the symbolic desire of our two peoples never to go to war with one another again".

Later that evening, on the steps of Downing Street, Chamberlain basked in self-praise, declaring that he had achieved "peace for our time", an interpretation born more of relief than foresight. For Europe had genuinely come close to war, but Chamberlain's actions had only postponed the conflict, not prevented it.

The fate of the German ethnic minority in western Czechoslovakia (or Sudetenland) had long attracted the attention of Hitler, who was bent on uniting German-speakers within the boundaries of an enlarged German Reich. The successful Anschluss (or annexation) of Austria by Germany in March 1938 had proven that France and Britain had little appetite for military confrontation. Instead they continued with the diplomatic approach which had failed to deflect Hitler either from re-armament in defiance of the terms of the Treaty of Versailles that ended the First World War, or from open attacks on his neighbours.

Redrawing the map of Europe in 1918 had left some 3 million German speakers in the newly formed state of Czechoslovakia, around a quarter of the total population. The effects of the Great Depression in the 1920s and the rise of the Nazi Party in Germany led to an increase in nationalist sentiment among these so-called "Sudeten" Germans, given focus by the anti-government agitation of Konrad Henlein's Sudeten German Party (SdP). The SdP accused the Czech government of Eduard Beneš of

discriminating against the Sudeten Germans and demanded widespread concessions, including autonomy for ethnic Germans.

Hitler saw it as a golden opportunity to repeat the Anschluss in Sudetenland. His position was strengthened by French and British reluctance to confront Germany; Chamberlain put pressure on Beneš to bow to Sudeten German wishes. Isolated, Beneš buckled and agreed to almost all the SdP's demands.

The more Hitler sensed French and British weakness in defending Czechoslovakia, the less inclined he became to settle for mere autonomy for the Sudeten Germans and, through the agency of Henlein, he provoked demonstrations against the agreement in Sudetenland. The British government finally requested a meeting with Hitler on 15 September, offering him the outright annexation of those areas of the Sudetenland where German speakers constituted more than half the population in exchange for a guarantee he would take no more.

A week later, Chamberlain was offering annexation of the whole of Sudetenland as long as the integrity of the rest of Czechoslovakia was assured, but Hitler still pushed for more, insisting that Czechoslovakia must now be wholly dissolved. On 24 September he issued an ultimatum that the Czech government must evacuate the Sudetenland within four days. Beneš could see that no foreign power would come to Czechoslovakia's defence and at the

four-power Munich conference (between German, Mussolini's Italy, France and Britain) the fate of his country was sealed. The final deal laid down that the whole of the Sudetenland would be evacuated by Czechoslovakia, beginning on 1 October, and that German troops would progressively occupy the territory. International bodies were supposed to administer the Sudetenland pending the results of plebiscites to determine the population's wishes, but these were never carried out.

Hitler had gained international approval for the annexation he always intended to achieve. Chamberlain saw it very differently; the "peace for our time" might not be ideal, nor particularly honourable, but it had staved off a general European war and given Britain a breathing space in which to rearm. With cynicism, mixed with realpolitik and a deep-seated fear of the repetition of the First World War's carnage, Chamberlain had earlier characterized the Sudeten problem as "a quarrel in a faraway country of which we know nothing".

Many, though, accused the Prime Minister of appeasement, of encouraging Hitler's ambitions by showing weakness. Their argument was strengthened by the rapid dismemberment of the rest of Czechoslovakia. Only weeks later in early November the Germans forced the Czechs to cede a third of the province of Slovakia to Hungary and a smaller area (Teschen) to Poland. On 14 March 1939, the remnants of Slovakia seceded to form a pro-German rump state, while the next day German troops marched on Prague and extinguished Czech independence.

We, the German Führer and Chancellor and the British Prime Minister, have had a further meeting today and are agreed in recognising that the question of Anglo-German relations is of the first importance for the two countries and for Europe.

We regard the agreement signed last night and the Anglo-German Naval Agreement as symbolic of the desire of our two peoples never to go to war with one another again.

We are resolved that the method of consultation shall be the method adopted to deal with any other questions that may concern our two countries, and we are determined to continue our efforts to remove possible sources of difference and thus to contribute to assure the peace of Europe.

[signature: Adolf Hitler]

[signature: Neville Chamberlain]

September 30, 1938.

OPPOSITE Prime Minister Neville Chamberlain walks past an SS guard of honour at Oberwiesenfeld airport on his way to the Munich conference on 29 September 1938 surrounded by National Socialist Party leaders.

ABOVE LEFT Chamberlain addresses the crowd at Heston Airport after his arrival back from meeting Hitler on 30 September 1938. Clutching the "piece of paper", he assured his listeners that the agreement he had made with the Führer was "the prelude to a larger settlement in which all Europe may find peace".

ABOVE Of all the documents we've studied this has to be ranked the most infamous. The signature of Adolf Hitler, Germany's Nazi Führer, sits above that of the British Prime Minister on this short transcript that Neville Chamberlain thought had brought peace. It must have seemed bitterly ironic just a year later.

41

Churchill's "Finest Hour" speech

It seemed to be the nation's darkest day, but with a rhetorical flourish in his speech to Parliament on 18 June 1940, Winston Churchill turned it into Britain's finest hour. It was inevitable now that France would fall to Hitler's Nazi offensive. It was also clear that Britain herself faced the grave peril of invasion. Churchill grimly warned that "the whole fury and might of the enemy must soon be turned upon us" and called upon the British people to "brace ourselves to our duties". His resolve played a vital role in stiffening that of fellow politicians and the British people generally, allowing the war machine to recover, rebuild and ultimately play a key role in the defeat of Germany in 1945.

Before the war Churchill s prophesies had had little impact. The 1930s were his "wilderness years", when his warnings of the growing menace posed by Adolf Hitler's resurgent Germany and his calls for Britain to rearm were almost universally ignored. Yet gradually the more politically fashionable policy of appeasement championed by Conservative Prime Minister Neville Chamberlain was seen as bankrupt. Hitler absorbed Austria, annexed Czechoslovakia and dismembered Poland.

Chamberlain had lost the confidence of even his most ardent supporters. Churchill, having previously resumed his First World War role as First Lord of the Admiralty, was appointed Prime Minister on 10 May 1940 with the task of salvaging what he could from the ruins. On that very day Hitler sent his panzer divisions smashing across the Belgian, Dutch and French frontiers. From then on Churchill's premiership was punctuated by speeches which would be remembered for generations. On 13 May, as the German offensive gathered momentum,

he offered those who stood with him "nothing but blood, toil, tears and sweat".

There was little hope in the early days. Having learnt the lesson from the First World War that a strongly defended position was next to impossible to capture, the French relied on the heavily fortified Maginot Line. But the Germans disobligingly attacked elsewhere, through the Ardennes, and by late May the French were in full retreat to the south. The British pulled back to the French Channel ports, hoping to be evacuated. A combination of Hitler's two-day pause in the offensive on 26 May, the assembly of a flotilla of small boats to cross the Channel to Dunkirk, and sheer bloody-minded determination achieved the near impossible. Around 338,000 Allied troops were plucked from the beaches of Dunkirk. But a German invasion of Britain seemed a near certainty. On 4 June, Churchill memorably told the House of Commons that the British would not submit and that "we shall fight on the beaches ... in the fields and in the streets ... we shall never surrender."

France had not quite fallen, but Churchill's desperate attempts to prevent its utter collapse failed. By 16 June, Churchill knew that France would seek an armistice with Germany. With a heavy heart he composed a new speech. As was his custom he made hand-written amendments to the prepared typescript right to the last moment. As he addressed the Commons at 3.49 p.m. that day, he frankly admitted that Dunkirk had been a retreat. But he called upon his listeners to look beyond the immediate recriminations and arguments about tactics and to remind themselves of the higher reasons for which they fought. It was, he told them in sombre tones, for the "survival of Christian civilization", and to defend "our own British life, and the long continuity of our institutions, and our Empire".

Churchill invited the assembled MPs to imagine a future where people would praise Britain's resistance with the words: "This was their finest hour", but he must have had his doubts. He still had to steer the nation through the knife-edge struggle between the Royal Air Force and the Luftwaffe which he called the Battle of Britain (a term first used in the "Finest Hour" speech), as well as through the trauma of the Blitz and the highs and lows of the North African desert campaign. Vindication came only in the final two years of the war. Publicly, though, he never wavered in his resolve, and his set-piece speeches could always be counted upon to calm fears and steady morale.

At the end of war, the nation Churchill had served so well rejected him in the 1945 General Election. He made his first speech as leader of the Opposition. "When we look back on all the perils through which we have passed," he told the Commons, "and at the mighty foe we have laid low and all the dark and deadly designs we have frustrated, why should we fear for our future? We have come safely through the worst." His speech of 18 June 1940 had come at the worst of times, and its inspirational call to fight on had played an invaluable role in making ultimate victory possible.

OPPOSITE Winston Churchill prepares to broadcast a speech announcing the surrender of Germany on 8 May 1945.

BELOW Drinkers at a London pub listen to one of Churchill's speeches on the radio in August 1941. Although the county had endured dark times since his "Finest Hour" speech, the Blitz had ended in May.

FOLLOWING PAGES Winston Churchill's "Finest Hour" speech is typeset almost as blank verse, with the five-line paragraphs each indented. Churchill wanted to be reminded of a psalm or epic poem as he delivered his oratorical tour de force. He made adjustments to the wording right up until the last minute, here in red pen.

The House will hv read the historic
 declaration in which at the desire
  of many Frenchmen,
        and of our own hearts,
          we hv proclaimed our willingness
           to conclude at the darkest
            hour in French history,
          a Union of common
            citizenship in their
                          struggle.

However matters may go in France,
 or with the French Govt.
    we in this Island and in the
      British Empire,
          will never lose our sense of
           comradeship with the French
                          people.

If we are now called upon to endure
 what they hv suffered,
    we shall emulate their courage,
     and if final victory rewards our
                          toils,
        they shall share the gain,____
          aye, and freedom shall be
                  restored to all.

We abate nothing of our just demands.

Czechs, Poles, Norwegians, Dutch and
   Belgians, who have joined their
          causes with our own.
        All shall be restored,
What General Weygand calls 'the battle
 of France' is over.

The battle of Britain is about to
                    begin.

Upon this battle depends the
    survival of Christian civilization.

Upon it depends our own British life
 and the long continuity of our
    institutions, and our Empire.

The whole fury and might of the enemy
 must very soon be turned on us.

Hitler knows that we will hv to break
 us in this Island, or lose the war.

If we can stand up to him,
    all Europe may be freed,
        and the life of the world
            may move forward into the
                broad and sunlit uplands.

But if we fail,
    then the whole world,
        including the United States,
            and all that we have known and
                                cared for,
                will sink into the abyss of a
                    new Dark Age
                        made more sinister and
                            perhaps more prolonged by
                                the lights of perverted
                                    Science.

Let us therefore brace ourselves to
    our duty, and so bear ourselves that
        if the British Empire and
            Commonwealth lasts for a
                thousand years, men will still
                    say,

'This was their finest hour'.

42

Guy Gibson's log of the Dambusters Raid

Wing Commander Guy Gibson's log-book is meticulous and professional. The equal weight given to each day's events, neatly and methodically entered, almost masks the significance of 16 May 1943.

There's just this one brief note: "Led attack on Möhne and Eder dams. Successful." This is Gibson's modest description of the operation he commanded which breached the Möhne and Eder dams. The mission owed its success to his leadership and the revolutionary "bouncing bombs" designed by Barnes Wallis. The only flourish Gibson allows himself is in writing across several columns to record the Victoria Cross he was awarded for his part in one of the most famous air exploits of the Second World War.

By the middle stages of the war, Britain's bombing efforts were concentrated on targets of strategic – and particularly industrial – importance in Germany and the Axis-occupied areas of Europe. The Air Ministry had long identified the Ruhr Valley dams as possible targets. They provided hydro-electric power and water for Germany's vital steelworks. Knocking them out would deal a body blow to the Nazi war effort.

The problem was that Allied bombs were hopelessly inaccurate. Achieving the precision needed to breach the 36 metres (118 feet) of concrete at the base of the Möhne dam would be hard enough. The

Germans had made it even more difficult by installing anti-torpedo nets.

The solution was presented by Barnes Wallis, the Assistant Chief Designer at the Vickers aircraft company. A brilliant designer – although highly intolerant of those who did not fall in with his ideas – Wallis had worked on the design of the Wellington bomber and was aware of the power of strategic bombing. Early in 1941 he wrote *A Note on the Method of Attacking the Axis Powers*, proposing the use of large penetration bombs to cripple Germany's war effort.

Wallis's persistence got him results. He first pursued an unsuccessful attempt to develop an "earthquake bomb" whose shockwaves would literally tear apart the Ruhr dams. Then, in 1942 he hit on the idea of a bomb that would bounce over water, pushed forward by reverse spin. This would enable it to evade the German nets and then, when it hit the dam wall, the spin would push it down towards the base, making any breach much more serious.

Wallis's tenacity made him as many enemies as it won him admirers. When his final recommendation hit the desk of the head of the RAF's Bomber Command, Air Marshal Arthur "Bomber" Harris described it as "tripe of the wildest description". Nonetheless, Harris was overruled by his superior Air Chief Marshal Charles Portal and the attack was given the go-ahead on 26 February 1943.

A wild scramble ensued to put together a squadron of modified Lancasters for the operation. They were to be commanded by Guy Gibson, a veteran of more than 170 sorties, who handpicked the crews for the new 617 squadron. As Wallis rushed to bring his "bouncing bomb" into production, Gibson led practice runs against the Nant-y-Gro dam in Wales and on Chesil Beach. The final bombs, code-named "Upkeep" were delivered to the squadron only on 11 May, just five days ahead of the final attack.

On the night of 16/17 May, 19 Lancasters took off from RAF Scampton, flying in an arc over the Dutch coast to avoid German flak. Gibson's formation – the squadron was divided into three – reached their target, the Möhne dam, relatively unscathed. The first three aircraft released their bombs, but one skipped over the dam, one exploded short and one missed altogether. It looked as though Wallis had been wrong. Then, the fourth bomb hit the target and the fifth,

released by Squadron Leader David Maltby, opened a large breach in the dam wall. Gibson then led his squadron against the secondary target, the Eder dam, which was breached on the ninth attempt. The third target, the Sorpe dam, which was attacked by the second and third formations, was hit three times, but its wall held.

At the Möhne and Eder, more than 250 million cubic metres (nearly 9 billion cubic feet) of water crashed through the breaches within three hours. A wave 10 metres (30 feet) high surged down the valley, destroying 11 factories and 25 road and rail bridges and drowning around 1,600 civilians, many of them foreign forced labourers. Gibson's squadron lost eight planes shot down or ditched, with 54 of the 133 crew killed.

The RAF paid a high cost for the raid, and by September the Germans had repaired the breaches. German steel production did slow down, but the effect of the raid on morale was more lasting. The Dambusters' spectacular feat made the British public believe that their air force could achieve the impossible. It also gave Guy Gibson, who died on his return from a raid on Bremen in

September 1944, and Barnes Wallis, who continued to work on air defence projects until he retired in 1971, a very special place in the pantheon of British heroes.

OPPOSITE Gibson with other members of 617 Squadron, photographed at Scampton in July 1943. From left to right Gibson, Fred Spafford, Robert Hutchison, George Deering, Terry Taerum. Spafford's was the first plane aircraft to attack the Möhne Dam, but his bomb fell short.

BELOW A reconnaissance photograph of the Eder dam taken two months after the Dambusters Raid, shows a 96-foot breach in the dam

FOLLOWING PAGES Guy Gibson's log-book records the final preparations for the Dambusters raid. The "bouncing bombs" were finally delivered on 11 May, less than a week before the raid. The same day Gibson carried out a low-level test, dropping them at 60 feet (18.25 metres). Gibson writes that the final dress rehearsals for the raid on 14 May were "completely successful".

| YEAR 1943 | | AIRCRAFT | | PILOT, OR | 2ND PILOT, PUPIL | DUTY |
MONTH	DATE	Type	No.	1ST PILOT	OR PASSENGER	(INCLUDING RESULTS AND REMARKS)
—	—	—	—	—	—	— TOTALS BROUGHT FORWARD
APRIL	1	LANCASTER	B	SELF	CREW	LOCAL.
						CREW. P/O TEAROW.
						P/O SPAFFORD
						F/LT TREVOR. ROPER
						F/LT HUTCHISON
						P/O DEERING
						SGT PULFORD.
"	4	"	B	"	"	To Lake Nr Sheffield
"	5	"	D	"	"	SCOTTISH X COUNTRY. LAKES.
"	9	"	D	"	"	BASE – DERWENT RESERVE
"	11	MAGGIE	—	"		– UPPINGHAM RES. – BASE.
				SELF	F/LT MAY.	LOCAL MANSTON.
						CRASHED IN FIELD. OK.
"	15	OXFORD	—	SELF	TWO CREW	BASE – READING. FAIROAKS – BASE
"	15	MOSQUITO	4098	S/L LONGBOTTOM (SHORTY)	SELF	FAIROAKS – WEYBRIDGE –
"	16	LANCASTER	Y	SELF	CREW	CORNISH X COUNTRY AT LOW LEVEL WITH DUMMY ATTACKS ON LAKES
"	20	LANCASTER	J	SELF	FAY + CREW	NIGHT X COUNTRY TO MANY RESEVOIRS WITH DUMMY ATTACKS

GRAND TOTAL [Cols. (1) to (10)]

.................Hrs.................Mins.

TOTALS CARRIED FORWARD

SINGLE-ENGINE AIRCRAFT				MULTI-ENGINE AIRCRAFT						PASS-ENGER	INSTR/CLOUD FLYING [Incl. in cols. (1) to (10)]	
DAY		NIGHT		DAY			NIGHT					
DUAL	PILOT	DUAL	PILOT	DUAL	1ST PILOT	2ND PILOT	DUAL	1ST PILOT	2ND PILOT		DUAL	PILOT
(1)	(2)	(3)	(4)	(5)	(6)	(7)	(8)	(9)	(10)	(11)	(12)	(13)
					1.00							
					1.20							
					4.05							
					1.20							
	.15.				5.00							
					.30.							
					5.10							
												4.00
					4.30			4.30				3.00
(1)	(2)	(3)	(4)	(5)	(6)	(7)	(8)	(9)	(10)	(11)	(12)	(13)

163

| YEAR 1943 | | AIRCRAFT | | PILOT, OR | 2ND PILOT, PUPIL | DUTY |
MONTH	DATE	Type	No.	1ST PILOT	OR PASSENGER	(INCLUDING RESULTS AND REMARKS)
—	—	—	—	—	—	— TOTALS BROUGHT FORWARD
APRIL.	21.	LANCASTER	D.	SELF	CREW.	LOCAL. TEST OF SYNTHETIC
						NIGHT FLYING EQUIPMENT.
,,	25	,,	D	,,	,,	LONG LOW LEVEL X COUNTRY
						WITH SYNTHETIC N/F GEAR
						DUMMY ATTACK ON WELSH
						DAMS.
,,	2Y	,,	,,	,,	,,	BASE - MANSTON - BASE.
MAY	1	—,,—	H	,,	,,	TO MANSTON — BASE.
				S/L YOUNG.		
—,,—	2	—,,—	B	,,	,,	Low Level Recco.
,,	3	—,,—	B	,,	,,	Low Level Bombing.
						Special Attack. 10 bombs
,,	4	—,,—	B	,,	,,	MANSTON - LOW LEVEL BASE.
,,	5	—,,—	D	,,	(PINDLY.)..	BASE - GRANTHAM - BASE.
,,	5	—,,—	G	,,	,,	SPECIAL NIGHT ATTACK.
,,	6	,,	G	,,	,,	SPOTLIGHT FLYING
						AT 60 FT AT NIGHT.
					GRAND TOTAL [Cols. (1) to (10)]	TOTALS CARRIED FORWARD
					.................Hrs.................Mins.	

164

SINGLE-ENGINE AIRCRAFT				MULTI-ENGINE AIRCRAFT						PASS-ENGER	INSTR/CLOUD FLYING [Incl. in cols. (1) to (10)]	
DAY		NIGHT		DAY			NIGHT				DUAL	PILOT
DUAL	PILOT	DUAL	PILOT	DUAL	1ST PILOT	2ND PILOT	DUAL	1ST PILOT	2ND PILOT			
(1)	(2)	(3)	(4)	(5)	(6)	(7)	(8)	(9)	(10)	(11)	(12)	(13)
50·25												
					1·05							·40
					5·40							4·00
					2·15							
50·25	480·50	3·10	8·50	4·20	560·40	16·00	–	630·10		NAV. 87·45	10·55	478·30
					2·00							
					1·25							
					1·55							
					1·50							
					·30							
								3·00				
								1·30				
(1)	(2)	(3)	(4)	(5)	(6)	(7)	(8)	(9)	(10)	(11)	(12)	(13)

| YEAR 1943 | | AIRCRAFT | | PILOT, OR | 2ND PILOT, PUPIL | DUTY |
MONTH	DATE	Type	No.	1ST PILOT	OR PASSENGER	(INCLUDING RESULTS AND REMARKS)
—	—	—	—	—	—	— TOTALS BROUGHT FORWARD
MAY	7	LANCASTER	V.	SELF	USUAL CREW	TO MANSTON - BASE.
MAY	8	OXFORD	U	SELF	S/L SMITH	TO HENDON.
"	"	VEGA	?	SELF	F/LT COX	HENDON - MANSTON.
"	"	OXFORD	U	S/L SMITH	SELF	MANSTON - BASE.
"	11	LANCASTER	P.	SELF	USUAL CREW	LOW LEVEL. UPKEEP DROPPED AT 60 FT. GOOD RUN OF 600 YRDS
"	14	"	P.	SELF	" "	BOMBING LOW LEVEL AND V.H.F. TEST.
"	14	"	P.	"	" "	
				P/C WHITWORTH. D.S.O. D.F.C.		FULL DRESS REHEARSAL ON UPPINGHAM LAKE AND COLCHESTER RES. COMPLETELY SUCCESSFULL.
"	16	LANCASTER	G.	SELF	SGT PULFORD P/O DEERING F/LT TREVOR ROPER F/LT HUTCHISON P/O SPAFFORD P/O TAERUM.	LED ATTACK ON MÖHNE AN EDER DAMS. SUCCESSFUL.

GRAND TOTAL [Cols. (1) to (10)]

1924 Hrs. 20 Mins.

TOTALS CARRIED FORWARD

SINGLE-ENGINE AIRCRAFT				MULTI-ENGINE AIRCRAFT						PASS-ENGER	INSTR/CLOUD FLYING [Incl. in cols. (1) to (10)]	
DAY		NIGHT		DAY			NIGHT					
DUAL	PILOT	DUAL	PILOT	DUAL	1ST PILOT	2ND PILOT	DUAL	1ST PILOT	2ND PILOT		DUAL	PILOT
(1)	(2)	(3)	(4)	(5)	(6)	(7)	(8)	(9)	(10)	(11)	(12)	(13)
					1.50							
					1.30							
	1.00											
					1.00							
					3.00							
					1.15							
					3.05			3.05				
								6.40				
50.25	431.50	3.10	8.50	4.20	577.40	16.00	—	644.25	—	NAV. 87.45	10.55	478.30

AWARDED   V.C.   23 : 5 : 43.

| (1) | (2) | (3) | (4) | (5) | (6) | (7) | (8) | (9) | (10) | (11) | (12) | (13) |

43

D-Day map

The map shows the plan for the Allied landings in Normandy on D-Day, 6 June 1944. It was the largest amphibious assault in history, a breathtakingly daring enterprise that played a critical role in the defeat of Germany. Britain's Soviet ally Joseph Stalin had been vigorously lobbying for the opening of a "Second Front" in the West to provide relief for his hard-pressed Red Army. Even after the Allied invasion of Sicily in July 1943 he continued to push for a large-scale attack on Nazi-occupied France.

It may have been late for Stalin, but when D-Day did come, it hastened the end of the Second World War. The following year, 1945, saw the last and greatest of Britain's victories in European wars.

The map indicates the division of the Normandy beaches into sectors – Omaha and Utah for the Americans, Gold, Juno and Sword for the Canadians and British – and then sub-sectors running eastwards alphabetically from Able on Omaha Beach to Roger on Sword Beach, with a separate series on Utah, the westernmost beach, from Peter to William. It was only one part of the careful preparation for D-Day.

A dress-rehearsal at Dieppe in August 1942 went disastrously wrong when Canadian and British troops met unexpectedly strong resistance and suffered 4,000 casualties. But Allied planners learnt from this that a direct assault on a strongly held port was unlikely to succeed and they looked elsewhere for targets. The most obvious place to launch an invasion was in the Pas de Calais; the Channel was only 21 miles (33 kilometres) wide at that point, making the crossing much easier for troop transports andfar easier to protect with fighter escorts. But the Germans were aware of this too, and the area was heavily defended.

Allied planning went into high gear with the appointment of General Dwight D. Eisenhower. As Supreme Commander of the invasion force in December 1943, he focused instead on Normandy. The flat terrain and lack of large natural obstacles, together with the fact that it was – so far – more lightly garrisoned made it an ideal target for Operation Overlord, the code name of the invasion. An urgent programme of mapping was set up, combining pre-war cartography with information from aerial photography (and even postcards and holiday snaps), to create as accurate as possible a picture of the topography of the Normandy coastline.

There was an urgent need to conceal the preparations for Operation Neptune, the initial assault phase of the landings, from the Germans. Operation Fortitude, a massive deception exercise, was devised. This conjured up phantom armies in Scotland which appeared poised to invade Norway and a "First United States Army Group" in Kent, commanded by General George S. Patton. His dummy tanks and infantry manoeuvres kept the Axis high command's eyes firmly turned towards the Pas de Calais.

Hitler's commander in Northern France, Erwin Rommel, was suspicious and reinforced the area with pill-boxes and mines, but

OPPOSITE British troops from the 48th Royal Marines land at Saint-Aubin-sur-Mer on Juno Beach during the D-Day landings on 6 June 1944. Their objective was to close the gap between Sword and Juno beach to prevent German tanks driving a wedge between them.

LEFT US landing craft disembark men and vehicles, as barrage balloons fly overhead to guard against any German aerial counter-attack. US forces suffered around 7,000 casualties on D-Day, the largest number in the heavy fighting on Omaha Beach.

Normandy was still undermanned. On the Allied side there were jitters when the planned invasion date had to be put off for 24 hours owing to bad weather. But the 7,000 vessels which crossed the Channel on the night of 5/6 June carrying almost 130,000 troops, had the advantage of almost total surprise.

More than 20,000 US and British airborne troops spearheaded the invasion. They descended by parachute and glider to secure vital bridges, knock out artillery defences and generally spread confusion in the German ranks. By the time the troop transport ships approached the shore at H-Hour (0630 at Omaha and Utah beaches, around an hour later in the British and Canadian sectors), German communications were in chaos, their commanders struggling to react to the

onslaught. Allied air superiority, provided by 7,000 fighters and 2,500 bombers pounding airfields and artillery positions, made it even harder for the Germans to mount a co-ordinated response.

At Utah Beach the US 7th Corps faced only light resistance and advanced across marshy fields to link up with the airborne divisions. Similarly, at Gold, Juno and Sword the British and Canadians exceeded their first day's objectives, penetrating around 5 miles (8 kilometres) inland. At Omaha it was very different. The defence force had recently been doubled to eight battalions and the amphibious DD Sherman tanks, which had made such an impression elsewhere, were almost all swamped as they struggled ashore. Only after hours pinned down on the beach

by German guns, and amid the corpses of the first men ashore, did the Americans finally break out.

By the end of D-Day there was still much to do, and there would be many missteps before the Battle for Normandy and for France would be won. The failure to capture Caen in the first 48 hours cost the land force commander General Bernard Montgomery dear. The city only finally fell on 9 July. The German inability to repel the D-Day landings, though, meant that Berlin would be inexorably squeezed between the pincers of the Allied push through France and Soviet advances from the East. This map shows the moment that victory lay in the balance, when the Allied gamble might still have resulted in a disaster like Dieppe, but on a far larger scale.

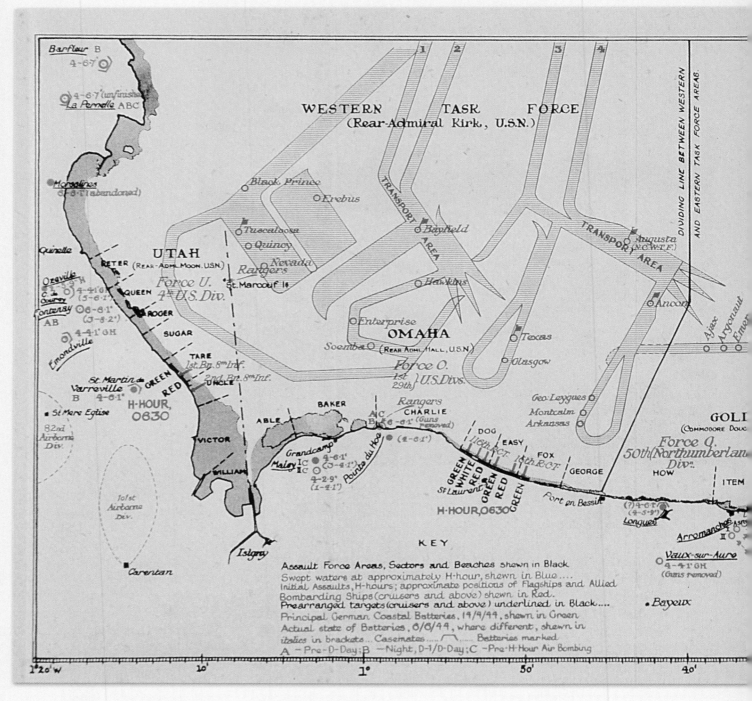

This overall map of the D-Day assault was prepared by the British Geographical Section of the General Staff (GSGS). German coastal batteries are marked in green. Channels swept clear of mines, through which landing craft could pass, are indicated in blue. The units to land on each beach are indicated in red, from the US 4th Division at Utah beach on the west of the landing zone to the British 3rd Infantry Division at Sword Beach to the east.

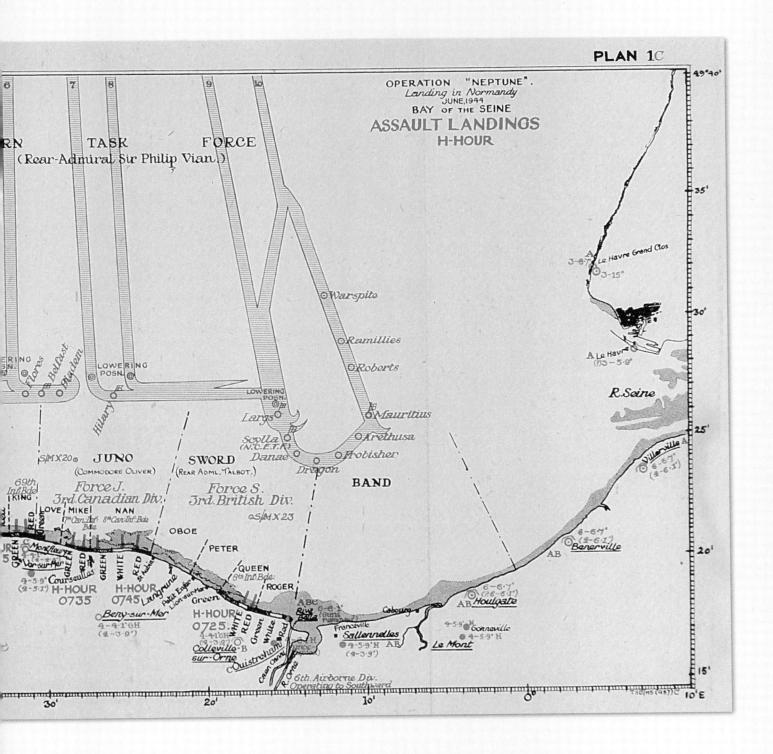

PLAN 1C

OPERATION "NEPTUNE".
Landing in Normandy
JUNE, 1944
BAY OF THE SEINE
ASSAULT LANDINGS
H-HOUR

...RN TASK FORCE
(Rear-Admiral Sir Philip Vian.)

EASTERN TASK FORCE

JUNO
(COMMODORE OLIVER)
Force J.
3rd. Canadian Div.

SWORD
(REAR ADML. TALBOT.)
Force S.
3rd. British Div.

BAND

LOWERING POSN.

LOWERING POSN.

LOWERING POSN.

Largs
Scylla
(N.C.E.T.F.)
Danae
Dragon

Warspite
Ramillies
Roberts
Mauritius
Arethusa
Frobisher

R. Seine

A Le Havre Grand Clos
3-8.7" 3-15"
A Le Havre
(?)-5.9"

Villerville A
6-6.7"
(4-6.1")

Benerville
6-6.7"
(4-6.1")

Houlgate
6-6.7"
(26-6.1")

AB

Connéville
4-5.9" H
4-5.9" H

Le Mont

Cabourg

Sallennelles
4-5.9" H   AB
(4-3.9")

Franceville

ABC 6-6.1"
Riva 7 Guns
Bella (some moved)

Ouistreham
Colleville-B
sur-Orne
Caen Canal
R. Orne
6th. Airborne Div.
Operating to Southward

H-HOUR
0725
4-4.1"GH
(3-3.9")

QUEEN
8th Inf. Bde.
ROGER
Green
White
Red
Green
White
Red
H

8th. Inf. Bde.
OBOE
PETER

St Aubin
Langrune
Petit Enfer
Lion-sur-Mer

H-HOUR
0745
Bény-sur-Mer
4-4.1"GH
(4-3.9")

H-HOUR
0735
NAN
MIKE
LOVE
KING
Courseulles
4-5.9"
(2-5.1")
GREEN
WHITE
RED
RED
WHITE
GREEN
7th Can. Inf.
Bde.
8th Can. Inf. Bde.
69th
Inf. Bde.
Montfleury
Ver-sur-Mer

S/MX20
S/MX 23

Belfast
Flores
Hilary
Diadem

6 7 8 9 10

Ticket to a Beatles concert

This ticket to a horticultural society dance on the Wirral seems ordinary enough. Yet it marks a key stage in the development of Britain's greatest music phenomenon of the 1960s. It is a sign of the emergence of a youth culture which would shape the nation forever. The band playing that night was the Beatles. And the concert was Ringo Starr's first appearance as the group's drummer, completing the line-up that would propel the "Fab Four" to international stardom.

The early 1960s was a time when anything seemed possible. The shadow of the Second World War was growing distant and the nation was more prosperous. New political voices were being heard: the Campaign for Nuclear Disarmament held its first public meeting in 1958, and at the Labour Party's 1963 conference, Prime Minister Harold Wilson proclaimed that a new Britain would be forged "in the white heat" of scientific and technological progress. The country was being rocked by fresh and vigorous cultural movements, centred on fashion and music for the young. Almost lost amid the dizzying clamour of new musical sounds was a Liverpool band established by a group of school friends in 1956. At first calling themselves the Quarrymen, they were inspired by "skiffle", a new genre with its roots in jazz.

The Quarrymen refined their style, increasingly influenced by early rock artists such as Elvis Presley, but at first they attracted little notice. By 1962 they had a new name, the Beatles, and a season at Hamburg's Kaiserkeller behind them. The band had three permanent guitarists— John Lennon, Paul McCartney and George Harrison — but had never found a suitable drummer. They had, though, a gifted manager in Brian Epstein, a Liverpool record-shop owner who met them at the Cavern Club, their regular venue, in November 1961.

Epstein was a vigorous promoter and brought the Beatles to the attention of George Martin, a music producer at EMI. But Martin didn't like the style of the band's drummer, Pete Best. The proposition was simple: if EMI were to sign the Beatles, Best had to go. So John Lennon contacted Ringo Starr, another Liverpool musician they had met in Hamburg, and offered him the job of drummer at £25 a week.

Ringo turned down other offers from rival groups and on 18 August 1962 he became a Beatle. There was a brief practice session and then, at 10 p.m., he played to a capacity crowd at the Hulme Hall, Port Sunlight. It was the local horticultural society's 17th anniversary session. At first Ringo faced hostility from the Beatles long-standing fans, who chanted "Ringo never, Pete Best forever" at his first gigs, but he soon became a key member of the group.

More glamorous shows were to follow. Two weeks later the band recorded their first single 'Love Me Do' at EMI's Abbey Road Studios, and this rose to Number 17 in the charts. Their second, 'Please, Please Me', was also the name of an album that was released in March 1963 and made their reputation. Soaring to

Number 1 in the charts, it stayed there for an astonishing 30 weeks. It was only toppled from the top spot by the group's second album, *With the Beatles*.

By 1964 the Beatles were a global phenomenon. They toured the USA twice and received a telegram of congratulations from Elvis. President Lyndon B. Johnson's daughter even tried – and failed – to get her father to invite the Fab Four to the White House. The clean-cut, vibrant young musicians from Liverpool were now selling millions of records. Ultimately their sales would reach more than a billion albums, making them the best-selling British group of all time. In the United Kingdom alone they had 17 Number 1 hit singles.

Ultimately the pressure of the Beatlemania they had unleashed proved too much. The band broke up in 1970, but it had become the defining sound of a transformational era. The *Evening Standard* declared that 1963 had been the Year of the Beatles. In truth the whole of the 1960s was their decade. A group of working-class Liverpool musicians had become the face of the nation. The country's youth understood that it was no longer the future that belonged to them, but the here and now. The modest crowd who watched Ringo Starr's first performance little realized the piece of history that they had just enjoyed.

OPPOSITE The ticket to the Wirral Horticultural Society's After Show Dance (and their seventeenth anniversary) on 18 August 1962 cost 6 shillings. Although it states that the main act is to be "The Fabulous Beatles Band" it does not mention that this is to be the debut of their new drummer, Ringo Starr.

ABOVE LEFT A very early photograph of the Beatles, just after Ringo Starr joined the band. From left to right: Ringo Starr, John Lennon, Paul McCartney and George Harrison.

ABOVE The Beatles performing at their first concert at New York's Shea Stadium in front of over 55,000 fans. The band played 12 songs, ending with "I'm Down", which John Lennon played on an organ with his elbows. It was the beginning of a triumphant second tour of the United States.

45

Mary Quant miniskirt

The hemlines are short, the shapes simple and the colours bold. Mary Quant, a young designer, was at the forefront of a new wave in fashion that took hold in Sixties London. Hers was one front in a revolution in youth culture that swept away stuffy uncertainties and transformed Britain from a dying imperium into a dynamic emporium.

London-born of Welsh parents, Quant studied art at Goldsmith's College before becoming apprentice to a milliner. She soon began designing her own clothes. Fashion in the mid-1950s was still dominated by conservative haute couturiers whose traditional lines were aimed at an older generation. As disposable incomes rose and postwar austerity receded, the next generation wanted something less staid and cautious.

In 1955 Quant opened a shop on Chelsea's King's Road, financially backed by her future husband Alexander Plunket Greene. Bazaar was the first of a wave of boutiques that defined the London fashion scene of the 1960s; iconoclastic, inventive and aimed squarely at the youth market. Taking her inspiration from the "Chelsea set", a group of young artists and film directors who had gravitated to the King's Road, Quant was prepared to be bold. Her designs incorporated strong colours and simple lines, making it clear that young women no longer had to look like versions of their mothers. There was a certain classlessness about her creations,

a breath of fresh air in a society where stifling etiquette and rigid social divisions had been the norm. As Quant said, "Snobbery has gone out of fashion and in our shops you will find duchesses jostling with typists to buy the same dresses."

Bazaar was a hit and a second branch opened in Knightsbridge in 1957. It spawned a host of imitators, many of them drawing on the "mod" look. This had its roots in the musical movement but quickly moved to the dynamic fashion scene spearheaded by young women such as Cathy McGowan, who rose to fame after winning a contest on the mod music show *Ready Steady Go!* The new fashion wave spread further, with Carnaby Street becoming a centre for inexpensive, trendy merchandise that the young wanted and which they could afford. In 1964 Barbara Hulanicki opened her first Biba boutique. It marked the high tide of the new British fashion explosion, which saw clothes and accessories exported worldwide. The USA, primed to look to Britain for fashion trends by the huge success of the Beatles, proved a lucrative market.

Tourists now came to town not for Buckingham Palace or the British Museum, but because it was "Swinging London". A new energy and vibrancy that drew on working-class roots reshaped the image of Britain's capital city. Playwrights such as John Osborne expressed the anger of young people who felt they had too long been denied their share of power; photographers like David Bailey documented a city where pop idols such as the Rolling Stones and The Who rubbed shoulders with their fans along the King's Road; and on television David Frost and other satirists poked fun at a complacent establishment in *That Was The Week That Was*.

By the mid-1960s the miniskirt had arrived, the most daring fashion statement yet, as hemlines above the knees had long been frowned on. Quant produced miniskirts early, though she claimed, "It wasn't me who invented the miniskirt, it was the girls on the street who did it." Young women, she said, had simply hemmed up her dresses to make them shorter, and she had followed their lead, featuring miniskirts in her catalogue by 1965. In October that year the model Jean Shrimpton caused uproar when she appeared in a minidress at Derby Day at Melbourne in Australia and was politely advised that this and her failure to wear gloves were not quite appropriate. But Australian young women disagreed, and the following year hemlines were firmly above the knee.

The 1960s was a decade of sweeping change in Britain, as the shadow of the Second World War drew back and a new generation grew up that did not simply want to be like their parents. They yearned to create something entirely new and Mary Quant's designs are emblematic of that shift. Their freshness, simplicity and sense of fun helped drive youth culture to centre stage and made Sixties Britain the envy of the world. It was the birth of a sexy, extrovert youth culture that still reigns supreme today.

OPPOSITE Mary Quant at work on a set of new designs in November 1965. By then, she had opened a second branch of Bazaar in Knightsbridge and had sold designs to the US chain store JC Penney. She named the miniskirt after her favourite car – the Mini.

ABOVE Jean Shrimpton attending Derby Day at Melbourne's Flemington Racecourse on 30 October 1965. Her minidress caused a furore in the Australian press. Shrimpton wore the outfit only because too little fabric was sent to make the dress that had been planned for her.

jersey wool bonded
+ glacé kid leather
+ eyelets brass
+ thong boot lace. leathe
shape Bodice front

top stitch
darker soft

1 ³/₄

MQ.

OPPOSITE One of the striking designs by Mary Quant for her 1965 catalogue. This is the first entry of the miniskirt into the iconic designer's repertoire. She said it was a trend forced on her by young women; but she created an ample range of innovative and fashionable dresses to satisfy their demands.

ABOVE Mary Quant's sketch for a very short grey minidress with yellow trimming has a liberty bodice with a front vertical zip, small baby collar and long narrow sleeves. It is annotated with design notes and signed M.Q.

46

Falkland Islands Surrender Document

These words, punched out on a Falklands typewriter, mark the end of one of the shortest and most bizarre wars in British history. Just two-and-a-half months after invading the islands, the Argentine military commander Brigadier-General Mario Menéndez is surrendering to Britain's General Jeremy Moore. He has been allowed to cross out the word "unconditionally" before "surrender" as a small concession to his country's military honour.

The document was actually signed at a quarter past midnight Greenwich Mean Time on 15 June, but that was still 14 June in the Falklands, and to avoid the awkwardness of having two different surrender dates in the same document there was a tacit agreement to falsify the clocks. Within minutes of countersigning this piece of paper, General Moore walked off to speak to Falkland islanders sheltering in a building in Port Stanley: "Hello. I'm Jeremy Moore. I'm sorry it's taken a rather long time to get here."

This British victory reinvigorated Margaret Thatcher's deeply unpopular Conservative government and a year later propelled it to success at an election she might well have lost. For Britain's armed forces it was a massive morale boost – a superbly executed and very risky operation 8,000 miles (12,875 kilometres) from home, straining Britain's declining military power almost to breaking point. It was a feat that many thought impossible. When we woke up to the news of Argentina's invasion and occupation of the islands on 2 April 1982, most of us felt there was nothing Britain could do but accept a fait accompli. But we weren't bargaining for Margaret Thatcher. The Falklands, she

insisted, had been British for two centuries and their 1,700 inhabitants plainly wanted them to stay that way. The military junta that ruled Argentina must be taught a lesson – that aggression did not pay. A task force would be despatched immediately.

Britain achieved early diplomatic success in persuading the UN to order Argentina to leave the Falklands, and in getting the European Community to impose economic sanctions. But efforts to reach a negotiated settlement faltered, as neither side could make the crucial concessions on sovereignty that the other demanded. Both sides preferred to fight.

The initial skirmishes took place at sea. British submarines sank the Argentine warship *General Belgrano* on 2 May, with the loss of 323 lives. Two days later Argentine Mirage jets inflicted critical damage on HMS *Sheffield*. On 21 May, the British carried out a large-scale amphibious landing at San Carlos Bay on the west coast of the main island of East Falkland and, having established a bridgehead there, pushed eastwards towards Port Stanley. Caught by surprise, a large garrison of 950 Argentine troops at Goose Green surrendered on 28 May to the 2nd Parachute Battalion, whose commander Colonel H. Jones received a posthumous Victoria Cross for his part in the attack. From then on, the Argentines were gradually penned into a range of hills which overlooked Port Stanley. The British suffered severe supply difficulties and six ships destroyed by Argentine air attacks, but the Argentine position was even worse: they were unable to reinforce their occupation in the face of the British naval blockade.

In bitter fighting, mainly at night, the Argentines were pushed out of their mountain defences until on 13 June Mount Tumbledown, the last natural barrier protecting Port Stanley, fell. The next day, seeing that further resistance was hopeless, Argentina's Brigadier-General Menéndez began surrender negotiations. The terms may have made a gesture towards Argentina's "honour", but his country's defeat was total. The Argentine military had lost 650 killed and more than 11,000 were taken

prisoner (as against 255 British combat deaths). And Britain's resolve to hold onto this tiny relic of empire, which had looked wobbly before the war, was now immovable.

The surrender was an utter humiliation for the Argentine military junta and had much to do with its early collapse. The civilian governments that have followed continue to spar diplomatically with Britain over Argentina's claim to the islands they called the Malvinas (some, like that of President Cristina de Kirchner from 2007 to 2015 quite aggressively so). But Britain cemented its position in the Falklands, strengthening the garrison, building an airbase and granting the Falkland Islanders unconditional British citizenship. This document celebrates an inspiring military victory, but the cost of entrenching it will last a very long time.

OPPOSITE ABOVE The aircraft carrier HMS *Hermes* is accompanied by a flotilla of small vessels as she returns to Portsmouth after the Falklands War. Sea Harriers operating from carriers played a key role in the British victory, claiming to have destroyed 23 Argentine aircraft.

OPPOSITE BELOW British ships lie offshore at San Carlos Bay, the site of the British landings to retake the Falklands on 21 May 1982.

ABOVE The surrender document signed by Brigadier-General Mario Menéndez for the Argentines and Major-General Jeremy Moore for the British. Although the Argentines are promised that they will be "treated with honour", the surrender is in reality total. All Argentine personnel are to give themselves up together with all their "arms, ammunition, and all other weapons and warlike equipment".

Headquarters, Land Forces
Falkland Islands

INSTRUMENT OF SURRENDER

I, the undersigned, Commander of all the Argentine land, sea and air forces in the Falkland Islands unconditionally surrender to Major General J. J. MOORE CB OBE MC* as representative of Her Brittanic Majesty's Government.

Under the terms of this surrender all Argentinian personnel in the Falkland Islands are to muster at assembly points which will be nominated by General Moore and hand over their arms, ammunition, and all other weapons and warlike equipment as directed by General Moore or appropriate British officers acting on his behalf.

Following the surrender all personnel of the Argentinian Forces will be treated with honour in accordance with the conditions set out in the Geneva Convention of 1949. They will obey any directions concerning movement and in connection with accommodation.

This surrender is to be effective from 2359 hours ZULU on 14 June (2059 hours local) and includes those Argentine Forces presently deployed in and around Port Stanley, those others on East Falkland, West Falkland and all the outlying islands.

.... Commander Argentine Forces
.... J. J. MOORE
Major General
.... Witness
2359 hours 14 June 1982

47

Queen's Speech in the event of Nuclear War

It is the speech the Queen hoped she would never have to make. It was drafted as part of a 1983 NATO exercise which simulated a slide into nuclear war. She would deliver it if war actually broke out.Its calm, clear and compassionate tones are self-consciously resonant of the message her father, George VI, delivered at the outbreak of the Second World War.

In this draft the Queen makes reference to the "deadly powers of abused technology", avoiding direct mention of the nuclear conflagration which would almost certainly have engulfed Europe in the event of direct conflict between NATO and the Soviet-led Warsaw Pact. She also reminds her fearful subjects that "the dangers facing us today are greater by far than at any time in our long history".

What the Queen could not have known – and most of her subjects never knew – was that just six months later she was almost called on to deliver a version of this speech. The dangers facing the world were indeed great. Under Ronald Reagan, US president since 1981, relations between the United States and the USSR reached almost their most frigid point of the entire Cold War. American testing of Soviet radar capabilities by infringing the USSR's airspace, and large-scale wargames such as CIMEX/ WINTEX (for which the Queen's speech was written), further heightened the paranoia of the Soviet military and political elite.

In March 1983, Reagan announced the Strategic Defense Initiative (better known as "Star Wars"), which would give the United States the capability of shooting down Soviet nuclear ballistic missiles in flight. He also, in terms likely to confirm the worst Soviet fears, referred to the USSR as an "evil empire" and warned against its "aggressive impulses". The same year saw the announcement that Pershing II, a new generation of tactical nuclear missiles intended to counter Soviet SS-20s, would be deployed in Europe. The Soviet military saw these moves as an attempt to deprive the USSR of the option of a first nuclear strike, and a dangerous escalation of the nuclear arms race between the two alliances.

In 1981, the then KGB chief Yuri Andropov had already stated his belief that the United States might launch its own first nuclear strike on the USSR. As a result, he set in motion Operation Raketno-Yadernoye Napadenie ("Nuclear Attack") or RYAN, by which KGB agents in NATO capitals were instructed

to monitor signs of an impending attack. Worryingly, these included reporting back to Moscow if a higher than usual number of lights were left on in NATO Defence Ministries at the end of a working day.

Soviet paranoia was at a dangerously high level, its intelligence systems primed to detect the slightest hint of a NATO nuclear strike. And then NATO obliged by simulating just such a move. Operation Able Archer, which began on 7 November 1983, was a routine exercise, but one conducted at a greater intensity than ever before. It simulated the rapid escalation from an alert state of DEFCON 5 to DEFCON 1, which indicated nuclear war was imminent.

The increased use of codes that the Soviet cryptographers could not crack set alarm bells ringing in Moscow and a flurry of warning lights in the Operation Ryan network. Warsaw Pact air units and nuclear forces were put on alert, a move which in turn NATO detected. On 8/9 November KGB residencies were sent a flash telegram asking for information on unusual activities at American air bases.

For two days the Soviet side watched, and the world stood on the brink of nuclear war. The slightest misstep could have led to catastrophe. But NATO did not respond to the state of alert on the Warsaw Pact side, which had been triggered by its own exercise. On 11 November Able Archer ended on schedule, NATO activity reduced, and the Warsaw Pact units were stood down.

Leading politicians in the West knew how close the world had come to war. Those naturally most hostile to the Soviet Union learnt a surprising lesson. Margaret Thatcher, the British prime minister, and President Reagan realized that Soviet fears of a NATO attack were so deeply rooted that closer engagement was needed to avoid another crisis. In his memoirs, Reagan wrote that it made him "even more anxious to get

a top Soviet leader in a room alone and try to convince him we had no designs on the Soviet Union and Russians had nothing to fear from us". The new determination to ease tensions eventually resulted in a series of summits between Reagan and the new Soviet leader Mikhail Gorbachev, from 1985. The beginnings of a thaw in the Cold War were one paradoxical result of its near explosion into a real war.

The Queen never did make the speech, and as the Cold War ended with the collapse of the USSR in 1991 the chances of her having to do so became remote. For 48 hours in November 1983, though, the prospect of her having to pick up these pages and make the most fateful speech of her life seemed very real.

OPPOSITE The Queen is presented with a posy of flowers by a young Canadian girl during a visit to Victoria, British Columbia in March 1983. The Queen continued her royal duties unabated as US-Soviet relations spiralled downwards that spring and summer.

ABOVE US President Ronald Reagan meets Soviet President Mikhail Gorbachev during their summit in Geneva on 19–21 November 1985. It was the first meeting between Soviet and American leaders for eight years and began a thaw in relations that led to important arms control agreements in 1987.

FOLLOWING PAGES Written for her in 1983 by civil servants, this is the text of the speech the Queen would have been expected to make in the case of a nuclear attack against Britain. She calls the threat that hangs over Britain "the deadly power of abused technology". In a Churchillian touch, she is made to say "our country's will to survive cannot be broken".

SECRET

THIS DOCUMENT IS THE PROPERTY OF HER BRITANNIC MAJESTY'S GOVERNMENT

MISC 93(83) 31 COPY NO

4 March 1983

CABINET

WINTEX-CIMEX(83) COMMITTEE

EXERCISE EXERCISE EXERCISE

Text of a Message to the Nation broadcast by Her Majesty The Queen at Noon on Friday 4 March 1983

****

When I spoke to you less than three months ago we were all enjoying the warmth and fellowship of a family Christmas. Our thoughts were concentrated on the strong links that bind each generation to the ones that came before and those that will follow. The horrors of war could not have seemed more remote as my family and I shared our Christmas joy with the growing family of the Commonwealth.

Now this madness of war is once more spreading through the world and our brave country must again prepare itself to survive against great odds.

I have never forgotten the sorrow and pride I felt as my sister and I huddled around the nursery wireless set listening to my father's inspiring words on that fateful day in 1939. Not for a single moment did I imagine that this solemn and awful duty would one day fall to me.

We all know that the dangers facing us today are greater by far than at any time in our long history. The enemy is not the soldier with his rifle nor even the airman prowling the skies above our cities and towns but the deadly power of abused technology.

But whatever terrors lie in wait for us all the qualities that have helped to keep our freedom intact twice already during this sad century will once more be our strength.

My husband and I share with families up and down the land the fear we feel for sons and daughters, husbands and brothers who have left our side to serve their country. My beloved son Andrew is at this moment in action with his unit and we pray continually for his safety and for the safety of all servicemen and women at home and overseas.

It is this close bond of family life that must be our greatest defence against the unknown. If families remain united and resolute, giving shelter to those living alone and unprotected, our country's will to survive cannot be broken.

My message to you therefore is simple. Help those who cannot help themselves give comfort to the lonely and the homeless and let your family become the focus of hope and life to those who need it.

As we strive together to fight off the new evil let us pray for our country and men of goodwill wherever they may be.

God Bless you all.

****

EXERCISE   EXERCISE   EXERCISE

2

48

World Wide Web memo

It is a memo that revolutionized all our lives. British computer scientist Tim Berners-Lee's report on "Information Management" seems at first glance like a rather disorderly mind map. But it laid the ground-work for what would become the World Wide Web. This is the main system by which documents are linked on the Internet, and makes information digitally accessible to billions of people.

Berners-Lee graduated from Oxford in 1984 and became a software engineer at the CERN laboratory near Geneva, Europe's leading centre for particle physics research. There he found many competing computer systems, and it was difficult to share information efficiently between them. Already in the late 1960s the ARPANET, the forerunner of the Internet, had been developed, connecting several university sites in the United States (including UCLA and Stanford). But this was simply a way of making one network accessible to another. Exchanging information, and in particular documents, was difficult and cumbersome.

Several systems already existed which might help. The Transfer Control Protocol (TCP) enabled secure transmission of data over distributed networks by breaking data up into small pieces. Hypertext had been developed at a conceptual level by Ted Nelson in 1965 as a means to create links between one document and another. Berners-Lee saw that creating a computer language that used hypertexts and a system of unique identifiers for each server on the internet could create a vast virtual web. This would make information accessible in a few key clicks that had taken hours (or even days) to access before.

Unfortunately, the memo was not received well by Mike Sendall, Berners-Lee's boss. On its front cover he wrote the comment "Vague, but exciting" and expected matters to rest there. But Berners-Lee was not deterred and he kept lobbying for what he was now calling the "World Wide Web" (he was determined to avoid naming it after a figure from Greek mythology). In 1990 he presented the idea again and this time Sendall gave him the resources to pursue it (notably a NeXT computer, produced by the company Steve Jobs set up when he left Apple).

Within months he had created the three fundamental elements of a web-browser: HTML (Hypertext Markup Language), which would become the language of the web; URI (Uniform Resource Identifier, also known as URL), which uniquely identified the location of documents and other resources; and HTTP (Hypertext Transfer Protocol) to enable smooth retrieval of information across the Web. Berners-Lee combined these to form the first browser. By late in the year he had completed the first web page, which was basically a guide to the principles behind the new World Wide Web.

Early on, Berners-Lee decided the underlying code would be transparent and royalty-free to help his system supplant older information transfer methods which often relied on proprietary code. As the number of websites grew, slowly at first, the Web gained more attention, crucially from software engineers. In May 1992 one at Berkeley University invented a way to include graphics and to use a mouse to point and click.

The Web as we know it today was born, and the number of websites mushroomed. In December 1991 the first web-server outside Europe was connected, at Stanford's Linear Accelerator. In 1993 there were still

only around 100 sites connected to the Web, but by the end of the following year this had grown to nearly 3,000. By the beginning of the twenty-first century this had topped 20 million and today there are around a billion sites. Of the estimated three billion people who have some form of access to the Internet, the overwhelming majority do so via browsers that connect to the World Wide Web.

Berners-Lee's memorandum, and his subsequent development of the tools to create the World Wide Web, transformed many areas of society. Without it, Internet shopping, digital encyclopedias, timetables on the web and interacting with almost any major corporation would be impossible in the form in which we now do it. The hypertext language has grown more sophisticated, the principle of net neutrality (by which no user has access to a "fast lane") has been added, but the basic architecture of the web is still founded on the principles that Berners-Lee sketched out in his 1989 proposal. His original memo may have been "vague": it did not predict the explosive effect it would have, but its results have most certainly been "exciting".

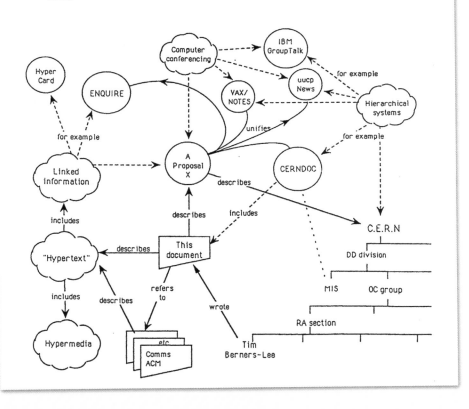

OPPOSITE This NeXTcube workstation was purchased by CERN to allow Tim Berners-Lee to implement the ideas he put forward in his World Wide Web memo. It became the first ever web server and still has the original sticker advising that it should not be powered down.

ABOVE LEFT Tim Berners-Lee founded the World Wide Consortium in 1994 to ensure that web technologies were interoperable and that the web did not fragment into separate spheres. He was knighted for his services to computing in 2004.

ABOVE Tim Berners-Lee's 1989 proposal to reorganize the information storage system at CERN in Geneva seems innocuous, proposing a solution to "the loss of information about complex evolving systems". Yet the combination of hypertext to link information in separate documents with a protocol to allow efficient computer interfacing gave rise to the World Wide Web and sparked an information revolution.

49

The
Good Friday
Agreement

It reads like a Who's Who of the Troubles, the sectarian violence in Northern Ireland which cost more than 3,500 lives between 1968 and 1997. Many of those who signed this front cover of the Good Friday Agreement, which brought an end to the conflict, had been involved in some way: as political leaders, negotiators or even as participants in paramilitary organizations. The signatures – of David Trimble, leader of the Ulster Unionist Party; Gusty Spence, a Protestant paramilitary leader; Tony Blair, the British prime minster; John Hume, leader of the moderate Catholic SDLP; and Martin McGuiness and Gerry Adams, leaders of Sinn Féin, the political wing of the IRA – show former foes setting aside their differences to negotiate a constitutional settlement for Northern Ireland.

It had been a long road. The conflict had roots reaching into the twelfth century, when King Henry II of England first sent knights to conquer Ireland. By 1922 Ireland had secured its independence from the United Kingdom after a bitter struggle culminating in open warfare between 1919 and 1921. Northern Ireland, which had a Protestant majority was given the right to opt out of the new Irish state. In December 1922 it duly did so, leaving 26 largely Catholic counties in the Republic of Ireland and six northern counties in Ulster containing about two-thirds Protestants. That left a Catholic minority of around a third and a Protestant majority who preferred to be called "loyalists".

By the 1960s resentment in the Catholic community over discrimination in jobs, housing and policing was boiling over. A civil rights movement began a series of marches to lobby for fairer treatment for Catholics. Bans and attacks on these marches culminated in serious riots in Londonderry on 13 August 1969. Radicals on both sides turned to armed paramilitary organizations such as the Protestant UDA and UVF and the Catholic IRA to protect their communities and defend their political interests. The IRA fought to drive the British out and unite Northern Ireland with the Irish Republic. Protestant paramilitaries struggled just as vigorously to remain part of the United Kingdom.

The British government responded to the violence by sending in the army. Barricades

were thrown up in parts of Belfast and bombings and shootings became a frequent occurrence, giving the city the air of a war zone. Incidents such as Bloody Sunday, when British troops shot dead 13 unarmed civilians in Londonderry, fuelled support for extremists on both sides. The British government was at a loss as to how to stem the flow of blood and to satisfy the intransigent demands of rival political leaders. It could only replace the autonomous Northern Ireland Parliament with direct rule from London, pour in more security forces and hope for the best.

By the early 1990s it was clear that neither the British government nor the IRA were likely to achieve their objectives in the near future. Tired of the economic, political and human costs of the Troubles, people's attitudes softened. In 1994, informal talks began between Gerry Adams, the Sinn Féin leader, and John Hume of the moderate nationalist SDLP. In late 1995 US Senator George Mitchell was commissioned to write a report on the decommissioning of paramilitary arms, an important obstacle to further progress. Initial talks between Catholic nationalists and Protestant loyalists then stalled after the IRA broke a ceasefire with spectacular bombings in London's Docklands and central Manchester in February and June 1996.

But the will to peace was now strong and the talks resumed in March 1996. Senator Mitchell ably bridged the gap between the

two sides, pushing difficult decisions on decommissioning and reform of the Royal Ulster Constabulary (which was seen as pro-Protestant) into the future. On 10 April 1998, Good Friday, all sides agreed to the 65-page document he had assembled. It set up a new power-sharing assembly in Northern Ireland and devolved power once again from Westminster. It established institutions to handle relations between Northern Ireland and the Irish Republic and between the London and Dublin governments. Crucially, all sides pledged not to use violence to change the status quo and proclaimed that the people of Northern Ireland would have a final say on their future. The deal was achieved only by compromise and concessions on both sides.

The Agreement came into force in 1999. Despite setbacks, including the reimposition of direct rule from London between 2002 and 2007, it has succeeded in bringing Catholics and Protestants together to govern Northern Ireland in the interests of both communities. And crucially it brought an end to the violence. Elements within the IRA refused to accept the deal and continued violence, but they were a small minority and the level of deaths dropped off dramatically after 1998. Symbolically, in 2007 the First Minister of Northern Ireland was Ian Paisley, a loyalist firebrand and long-time nemesis of the IRA, while his deputy was Martin McGuiness, a leading member of Sinn Féin. That the two could work together was a sign of the Good Friday Agreement's success in reconciling former foes.

The Belfast Agreement: An Agreement Reached at the Multi-Party Talks on Northern Ireland

OPPOSITE A civil rights demonstration in Belfast in 1968. The placards read "Reform Now" and "One Man One Vote", a measure of the anger felt by many Catholics about their exclusion from political power and discrimination against them by the police and employers.

ABOVE, LEFT A British soldier strikes a protester during Bloody Sunday in Londonderry on 30 January 1972. The British authorities set up barricades to stop a 10,000-strong civil rights march reaching the city-centre. Skirmishes broke out and British paratroopers shot dead 13 unarmed civilians.

ABOVE The signatures on the front cover of this copy of the Good Friday Agreement represent a gallery of leading politicians, activists and paramilitaries during Northern Ireland's Troubles. The key signatures of David Trimble, the Ulster Unionist leader, and Sinn Féin's Martin McGuinness are above and below the title.

50

The Scottish Referendum

The ballot paper for the referendum held in Scotland on 18 September 2014 asks a simple question: "Should Scotland be an independent country?". Yet the arguments which raged during the campaign were far from simple: drawing in questions of national identity, the right to self-determination, economic viability and natural justice, all overlaid with emotional arguments about what it meant to be British.

BALLOT PAPER
VOTE (X) ONLY ONCE

Should Scotland be an independent country?

YES ☐

NO ☐

The idea of Britain (or England, or even Scotland) has changed many times over the ages. The Roman province of Britannia encompassed modern England and Wales, much of Scotland, but none of Ireland. It was not an independent country, but a distant colony of Rome. The kingdoms of England and Scotland which emerged from the kaleidoscopic rise and fall of powers in the ninth and tenth centuries fought bitter wars. Scotland fiercely resisted absorption by its southern neighbour and it was an accident of dynastic politics that brought them together in a personal union under James VI of Scotland, who became James I of England, in 1603.

The Kingdom of Great Britain came into being only in 1707 when Scotland was constitutionally wedded to England (and Wales, which had lost its independent status in 1536). Ireland, though English-ruled since the twelfth century, remained a separate entity until it was joined with Great Britain in 1801 to form the United Kingdom.

Scarcely had the United Kingdom reached its greatest extent, than it began to dissolve. Irish agitation for greater freedom was long-standing, but it reached a crescendo in the later nineteenth century. After the first introduction of an Irish Home Rule bill in 1886, it still took a violent campaign to dislodge the British and achieve independence in 1921. Even then the northern part of Ireland remained part of the United Kingdom.

Scottish nationalists saw the success of their Irish counterparts and lobbied for home rule for themselves. A bill to that effect was introduced in 1913, but the First World War caused it to be shelved. Despite the founding of the Scottish Nationalist Party (the SNP) in 1934, the nationalist cause lost momentum.

It was the discovery of oil in the North Sea in 1969–70, holding out the prospect of a rich, independent Scotland, that revived the debate. The feeling that Scotland had been neglected by governments in Westminster also helped fuel nationalist feeling. A referendum was held in 1979 on whether a devolved Scottish assembly should be set up. A majority said "Yes", but their vote was invalidated by a low turnout. When the exercise was repeated in 1997, over 74 per cent voted for a Scottish Parliament with powers less than the SNP wanted.

The devolved assembly created a new sense of politics in Scotland. Politicians could now legislate and make their careers entirely separate from Westminster. Yet it also created tensions with England, as parliamentarians there questioned why Scottish MPs could vote on matters affecting England, but not the other way around.

The election of a majority SNP administration in Scotland in 2011 presented a chance to push for the party's long-cherished goal of complete independence. Convinced the nationalists would fall far short of gaining the necessary support, Prime Minister David

Cameron conceded that Scotland should be allowed to vote on its constitutional future. With deft manoeuvres, the SNP leader Alex Salmond managed to get the referendum scheduled for 2014. This, not coincidentally, was the 700th anniversary of Robert Bruce's decisive defeat of the English at Bannockburn.

The campaign was more bitterly contested and far closer than many at Westminster had complacently assumed. Rows erupted over whether an independent Scotland would automatically gain European Union membership, join NATO or retain the British pound as its currency.

Almost 85 per cent of eligible voters turned out on 11 September: 55 per cent voted "No" and Scotland remained in the United Kingdom. Or for the time being, at least. In the United Kingdom General election of May 2015, the SNP almost swept the board, winning 56 out of Scotland's 59 seats. Some began to mutter that the "once in a generation" referendum of September 2014 should be revisited, and that the nationalists might win a second vote.

The arguments over Scottish independence became caught up with those on British membership of the European Union when a referendum on British withdrawal was called for June 2016. The SNP argued that for English voters to opt to leave the EU was profoundly unfair if the majority of Scottish voters wanted to stay. In that case, they maintained, there should be another referendum on Scottish independence. If a second referendum on Scottish independence were passed, the shape of Britain would change once more. The debates over the nature of Britain will rage on. But, as a look at many of the documents in its history reveals, it was ever so.

OPPOSITE The question to appear on the Scottish independence referendum ballot paper was the subject of prolonged negotiations between Scottish nationalist and the British government.

TOP Pro-independence "Yes" campaigners demonstrate outside the BBC's Scottish headquarters in Glasgow on 14 September 2014. They are protesting against the BBC's coverage of the Scottish referendum campaign which they claimed was biased in favour of the "No" campaign.

ABOVE Anti-independence "No" activists assemble to hear Scottish Labour leader Johann Lamont speak in Govan, in the heart of SNP "Yes" territory. Glasgow, the local government area which includes Govan, was one of the few areas to vote for independence, casting 53.5 per cent "Yes" votes.

Index

Page numbers in **bold** type refer to main entries, which will include pictures; *italic* type refers to other illustrations or their captions.

Credits

The publishers would like to thank the following sources for their kind permission to reproduce the pictures in this book.

Key: t = top, b = bottom, c = centre, l = left and r = right

Bridgeman Images: Ashmolean Museum, University of Oxford, UK: 55; /Blenheim Palace, Oxfordshire, UK: 64–65; /© British Library Board. All Rights Reserved:

147 r; /De Agostini Picture Library: 24, 66–67;/ Hever Castle Ltd, Kent, UK:

35 l; /© Historic England: 98 /Houses of Parliament, Westminster, London, UK: 56–57; /Institute of Mechanical Engineers, London, UK: 97; /Kunsthistorisches Museum, Vienna, Austria: 40; /Lambeth Palace Library, London, UK: 48; /Leeds Museums and Galleries (Leeds Art Gallery) U.K.: 31; /Photo © Philip Mould Ltd, London: 69 b; /Museum of New Zealand Te Papa Tongarewa, Wellington, New Zealand: 70; /National Gallery of Victoria, Melbourne, Australia: 89 b; /© National Library of Australia, Canberra, Australia: 71; /New York Public Library: 28–29; /Noortman Master Paintings, Amsterdam: 50; /Private Collection: 42–43, 95, 118; /Private Collection /Olaf Protze/LightRocket: 68; /Private Collection/Ken Welsh: 119, 120; / Private Collection /© Look and Learn: 122–123, 125; /The Stapleton Collection: 46–47 t; /Royal Collection Trust © Her Majesty Queen Elizabeth II, 2016: 30, 36, 114; /The Stapleton Collection: 12; /Photo © Tallandier: 84; /Trustees of the Bedford Estate, Woburn Abbey, UK: 37; /Universal History Archive/UIG: 15, 79, 107, 134; /© Walker Art Gallery, National Museums Liverpool: 86–87

© The British Library Board: c.34.k.18 F6009186: 51; /Add.37192, f362v-363: 112–113; /Add.45416.f1: 149

© The Trustees of the British Museum: 10–11

CERN: 185 r

The Master and Fellows of Corpus Christi College, Cambridge. MS 383 f.12v: 13

Darwin Online: 99

Getty Images: 7; /AFP. 180, 181; /AFP/Hugo H. Mendelsohn: 146; / AFP/Andy Buchanan: 189 t; /George C. Beresford/Beresford: 147 l; / Bettmann: 35 r, 50, 132, 153 l; /Central Press: 155 l; /John Downing: 178 t; /Fairfax Media: 175; /Dan Farrell/NY Daily News Archive: 173 r; /Fine Art Images/Heritage Images: 136; /Harry Hammond/V&A Images: 173 l; /Frederick Hoare/Central Press: 187 l; /Major Horton/ IWM: 156; /Robert Howlett/Hulton Archive: 106; /Hugo Jaeger/ Timepix/The LIFE Picture Collection: 154; /Hulton Archive: 150, 168; /

Keystone: 174; /David Levenson: 180; /Felix Man/Picture Post: 157; / Jeff J Mitchell: 189 b; /Museum of London/Heritage Images: 139; / National Galleries Of Scotland: 52–53; /Popperfoto:128, 130–131, 133 r, 144–145, 152; /The Print Collector: 124, 133 l; /SSPL: 110t, 110b, 111; /Time Life Pictures/Mansell/The LIFE Picture Collection: 22; / Ullstein Bild: 59l; /Universal History Archive/UIG: 27, 137b, 149b; /View Pictures/UIG: 54

Library of Congress, Washington: 74, 75, 169

The National Archives, Kew: 16–19, 21, 23, 26, 34, 38–39, 41, 48, 60–61, 62, 69, 80–83, 85, 90–93, 96, 100–101, 103t, 103c, 105c, 108–109, 116–117, 121, 126–127, 129, 135, 141–143, 153, 155 r, 158–159, 160, 161, 162–165, 170–171, 179, 182–183

National Army Museum: 119 b

© National Maritime Museum, Greenwich, London. All rights reserved: 42–43, 72–73

National Portrait Gallery, London: 103

Crown copyright © National Records of Scotland. SP6-31: 32–33

Private Collection: 151, 188

REX/Shutterstock: 187

Royal Naval Museum: 170–171, 178 b

Science Photo Library: 184; /Sam Ogden: 185 tl

Shutterstock.com: 20

Topfoto: 104; /Ann Ronan Picture Library/Heritage Images: 105 b; / The Granger Collection: 115, 148; /The Print Collector /HIP. 105 t

Tracks Images: 172

V&A Images: 176, 177

The Vindolanda Trust: 9

Whyte's: 187

Every effort has been made to acknowledge correctly and contact the source and/or copyright holder of each picture and Carlton Books Limited apologises for any unintentional errors or omissions, which will be corrected in future editions of this book.